To Peggy,
with best wishes

Shrunken Heads

BY THE SAME AUTHOR

Power With People

Shrunken Heads

The Insane, the Profane, and the Profound
on the Road to Becoming a Psychologist

by

Gregory W. Lester, Ph.D.

Ashcroft Press

First printing 2005

ISBN 0-9641458-1-2
LCCN 2004096974

ATTENTION CORPORATIONS, UNIVERSITIES, COLLEGES, AND PROFESSIONAL ORGANIZATIONS: Quantity discounts are available on bulk purchases of this book for educational, gift purposes, or as premiums for increasing magazine subscriptions or renewals. Special books or book excerpts can also be created to fit specific needs. For information, please contact Bookworks Distributing, 15110 Benfer Road, Houston, TX 77069.

DEDICATION

TO THOSE WHO MATTER TO ME
BEYOND DESCRIPTION:

To Pam:

Finding you was the luck of a thousand lifetimes. How can I know you so well and still be so happily surprised by how you are, day after day? Thank you for making me proof that one can marry above one's station in life.

To Ann:

My affection for you lives in a place beyond words and time. My sole regret is that I will never be able to repay what you have given me. And for the record—this book is *not* my attempt to get you the whole inheritance.

To Kaboodle:

You were the most wonderful beast who ever lived, my fluffy little litter mate. I cherish every moment of the nineteen years you gave us. Even the hole in my heart feels sweet.

CONTENTS

PART IV: INTERMITTENT REINFORCEMENT

PART V: CONTINUOUS REINFORCEMENT

PREFACE

It has taken me over twenty years to write this book. Well, to be more exact it has taken me over twenty years to get up the guts to write this book.

Every time I tried to write about the things that happened in graduate school, I would read it over and think "Huh? No way. Can't be. It couldn't have been *that* bad." And, filled with loathing and self-doubt, I would stop writing.

Then, a while back, I ran into a man with whom I had gone to graduate school and who I hadn't seen in over twenty years. During our discussion of "what we were up to these days," I casually mentioned that I was considering writing a book about graduate school. I was completely unprepared for his reaction: *panic* crossed his face.

"Oh my God!" he cried. "Do you really think you should do that?"

"Why?" I replied, taken aback.

"Aren't you afraid that if you talk about what happened you'll get into trouble?"

Stunned, I stared at him in silence.

"And do you think anyone will *believe* you?"

Shocked, and not quite sure how to respond, I was quiet for a moment and then changed the subject. But his reaction told me something I needed to know—my memories of what happened were probably pretty accurate after all. So I decided to go ahead and write the book.

Nevertheless, in deference to my classmate's frightened reaction to the very idea that this book might exist, I'd like to preface it with four brief comments:

First, I didn't make any of it up. Really. As weird and as wild as some of the things I've written may seem, I was there. I saw, heard, and did the things I report. They happened. Granted, I do have my own slant on some of the things that went on, I do recount some

ix

things I was told by other people, and I do take a little artistic license here and there. But, in general, I have tried to be as factual about events as my writing abilities and memory would allow.

Second, I have *not* been factual about identities. Because this is supposed to be a book about *my* experience, not other people's lives, I have gone to some length to disguise many of the people involved. I have mixed people together, split people apart, shifted characteristics from one person to another, changed pertinent details, and occasionally made things up so I can recount a real event without referring to a real person.

Third, nothing I have written is generated by ill-will. I'm not mad at anyone. I'm not trying to "get back" at anyone. I'm actually glad to have been involved with most everyone in the book, because they all had a hand in the way I turned out. And while I may be screwed together no more tightly than any other human being—and I suspect there are those who feel that I am somewhat less so—I'm not altogether unhappy with the result. On most days.

Finally, to everyone who appears in the book or who helped me with the book—thank you. If this book is any good at all, it is because of you.

PART I
STIMULUS

THE DECISION

Careers come about in a variety of ways. Sometimes slowly, sometimes by accident, often by default. Mine was created during a seminal moment, a flash of insight so dazzling that it designed my entire future in less time than it takes an electron to pop out of the atomic clock, wave hello, and announce the arrival of the next quantum instant. And as is so often the case with such life-changing incidents, it was not a particularly complicated event: I realized my family was crazy.

Now, my family was not crazy in the way that made the neighbors lock up their children when we were around. Not like that. My family was crazy in a quiet, covert way. In a private, personal way.

For all intents and purposes—and from most perspectives—my family seemed fine, nothing far from ordinary. We were reasonably affluent, lived in the suburbs, and enjoyed country club memberships, private schools, and owning more cars than garage space. The problem was that while everyone acted like, talked like, and insisted that everything was fine, just *fine*, everyone felt bad—often very bad— essentially all the time. But neither on the surface nor in most of our behavior did there seem any *reason* that we should feel bad. There were a few minor exceptions, of course, like the cold war between my siblings and my mother that would occasionally erupt into verbal exchanges of small arms fire, mortar rounds, and threats of emotional air strikes. And, of course, the screaming fights on family trips that transformed a week of vacation into an elongated experience of paralyzing emotional terror. Oh, and let us not forget the icicles hanging from the relationship between my parents as they poked and prodded each other with those ten-foot-poles.

But none of that counted, you see. We were *fine*, by golly—that was our story, and we were sticking to it.

So while we were all secretly consumed with trying to keep our heads above the water of our private, internal pools of despair, we all walked around talking, acting, and looking for all the world like real, live, functioning human beings. The result was that through the majority of my childhood I felt not only miserable, but insane as well. After all, if everything was fine and I felt *this* bad, there must be one large and serious screw loose deep in the bowels of my mental machinery.

So my sudden realization that it was not "just me," but that the whole package was certifiable came as a moment of profound relief on the order of finally finding that bathroom stop on the highway after being sure *an hour ago* that you were gonna pop.

My realization happened in college.

I attended college in the 1970's, during the tail end—perhaps the "mature" period, if one can apply that term to an era of such hideously grotesque excess—of what came to be called the "Human Potential Movement." During the late 1960's and early 1970's psychology suddenly went mainstream and became pop culture. Everywhere you turned, psychological gurus were popping out of cakes into overnight celebrity. Alan Watts stirred the Episcopal ministry, western psychology, eastern mysticism, and a healthy dose of alcoholism into a tasty brew of life philosophy. Fritz Perls invented Gestalt Therapy, took up permanent residence at California's Esalen Institute, gave brilliant workshops, railed against Freudians, screwed every nubile female he could get his body on, and offended the sensibilities of anybody with any sensibilities left to offend. Werner Erhard made millions screaming at people in hotel ballrooms and getting into scrapes with everyone from ex-wives to the IRS to "60 Minutes." B.F. Skinner singlehandedly undermined 1000 years of belief about the nature of human beings, capping his horrifying—or enlightening, depending on your point of view—escapades with the publication of his best-selling book "Beyond Freedom and Dignity," with his claim that human beings have no real "internal" life, no psyche and no soul, and the only thing that really exists is behavior and external control. As far as he was concerned we are simply smart—and maybe not even all *that* smart—rats, who walk on two legs and lack decent fur. His hypothesis frequently seemed born out when, after hearing him talk, people did feel like rats—*really angry* rats.

Smack in the middle of this frenzy of psychological empire-building popped an obscure California psychoanalyst by the name of Eric Berne. Having changed his name from Bernstein due to the pervasive psychiatric anti-Semitism at the time (a similar problem for Freud,

4

by the way), as brilliant as he was quirky, and having been deeply stung by being rejected for training by his revered psychoanalytic institute due to "insufficient orthodoxy," Berne huffed off and extracted delicious revenge by developing perhaps the most brilliant, prominent, and influential popular psychology theory of all time, an approach he called Transactional Analysis.

Eliminating the mind-numbing algebraic jargon characterizing classic psychoanalysis, Berne assembled a comprehensive theory of human functioning that, to the unbridled horror of the psychiatric establishment, used colloquial terms and a personality structure so simple that it was understandable to virtually anyone, not just the psychoanalytically anointed.

In no time at all TA, as Transactional Analysis became known, climbed aboard elephants, crossed the Alps, and conquered the psychological world. Best-selling books, a Broadway play, and a top-40 song all paid homage to the usefulness and accessibility of Berne's work. He was profiled in *Life* magazine. TA workshops, trainings, and therapists fanned across the globe preaching the gospel of this new, understandable, non-psychoanalytic, practical, results-oriented psychology that at times was even—God help us—*fun* for patients. Transactional Analysis became a phenomenon.

The most famous book written on TA, the one that brought it to the masses, appeared late in my college tenure. In a tome entitled "I'm OK—You're OK," one of Berne's disciples, a psychiatrist by the name of Thomas Harris, managed to do the unthinkable: like Ray Kroc and hamburgers, he took a simple, popular dish, and by paring it to its bare essentials made it even more simple and more popular. He wrote a book so readable that even the most primitive of minds could understand it—even a confused kid trying to figure out how to turn college into something sufficiently useful as to justify the tens of thousands of dollars being spent by his parents in a courageous, if potentially hopeless, attempt to turn him into something resembling a worthwhile human being. That was me.

It was Harris's book that produced my seminal moment. Reading it produced the insight that, in an instant, created the rest of my life. And it came just in time, too, because prior to reading his book I had not, to put it bluntly, the tiniest glimmer of the beginning of the start of a vague notion of what I was going to do with the rest of my life. I was clueless.

THE REVELATION

I had not started out that way. I had marched off to college clear-headed and purpose-filled, intent on becoming, of all things, a film-maker. Although I had never had a class in film-making nor set foot on a sound stage, the claim that I could make movies was no idle threat. I had hard evidence to prove my cinematic talent.

During high school three of my friends and I made a movie that won the Cinematic Division of our state's annual Youth Talent Contest. Our film had been written up in the newspaper, featured at the state fair, and was the centerpiece of our high school graduation ceremony. At age 18 we were film-making successes, glorified by our school, our teachers, and our state. To this day the man who sponsored our project feels that our high school shamelessly exploited us by using our film as evidence that the school was some kind of creative powerhouse that it definitely was not.

But in truth, neither were we. In one of those mind-numbing twists of fate that makes you question the mental health of those who constructed the universe, our little film that made such a big splash was the accidental by-product of an adolescent scam.

Really. During our senior year of high school and desperate to escape a class we found to be intolerably beneath us, three of my friends and I wheedled, whined, begged, pleaded, cried, and attempted to blackmail one of our teachers into sponsoring us in an "independent study project" that we could use to replace the dreaded class. Because we didn't care what we had to do—we just wanted to get out of the class—we suggested any number of things, often off the tops of our heads, that we thought he might bite on. This was the early 70's where virtually anything could pass for "education," so one of our suggestions was to make a movie. That would be a creative and worthwhile endeavor fit for a high school independent study project,

6

right? It also just so happened that my father was a photography nut who owned an 8 millimeter movie camera that I knew how to operate. Those were sufficient qualifications, as far as we were concerned, to sanction our dropping the class and replacing it with an independent study project of our own choosing and design. Call us grandiose, call us arrogant, call us presumptuous—understatements bordering on the delusional.

Undaunted by our teacher's entirely appropriate resistance to our self-serving demands, we continued our assault with the relentless persistence uniquely characteristic of the pseudo-human, cloven-hoofed creatures between the ages of 13 and 18. Day after day we bombarded him with grandiose promises of steadfast commitment and great wonders to come. Finally, for reasons I still do not fully understand and which represent on his part either an appalling lack of judgment or a serious psychiatric illness or both, he caved.

But being the standard-issue adolescent males that we were, once he agreed to work with us and we were free of the despised class, we did not experience gratitude. Oh, no. We experienced a need to ensure that for the next semester his life would be a living hell. As compensation for putting himself on the line for us in front of God and everybody, we launched psychological guerilla warfare that made the North Vietnamese look like Tommy the Tank Engine.

Specializing in brain-numbing mind games and emotional fingernails-on-a-blackboard, when we would meet to discuss our project and he would ask how the movie was coming along we would look at each other in mock horror and exclaim "Movie!? Movie!? Oh my God, we knew we forgot something! We're supposed to be making a movie! Surely you don't mean you expect us to actually *do* it?! How can you be so unreasonable? Obviously we don't have enough time left in the semester to do anything worthwhile. Can't we have another week before we have to show you anything? And where *is* that darn movie camera? I'm not sure my father will let us use it. I haven't asked him yet. Do you think I should?"

On and on it went. We went light years beyond awful. For the entire semester not only did we refuse to show him one minute of film, we refused to even discuss with him one *idea* about a film. More than once our teacher stormed out of our meeting, fled to his office and sat alone, silent, in the dark, fondling his plan for our col-

7

lective academic demise with the F's he was planning to tattoo on our Permanent Records.

Unbeknown to our beleaguered teacher, though, beneath our one-tiny-grain-of-sand-short-of-homicide-inducing adolescent male exteriors lurked a work ethic so intense and so consuming that it was hideously shameful to any self-respecting teenager. Entirely unwilling to admit to anyone that we actually *cared*, behind everyone's backs we were working ourselves to death trying to make that damn movie.

Having absolutely no idea what we were doing, we worked in a naive, blind, hysterical frenzy, turning beginner's luck into every form of creative, weird, and novel film-making we could think of. We designed animation, we filmed scenes forward and backward, we experimented with lighting, color, timing, split-screens and multiple exposures. Possessing only bravado and a willingness to try anything and everything no matter how misguided, stupid or dangerous, we found ways to use a crude, spring-driven 8 millimeter movie camera (you had to *wind* it, for God's sake) to create superimposed credits, slow-motion action, and stop-motion scenes with everything from birds to cars to airplanes. Any classmates or girlfriends we could bribe, terrify, or extort into silence were pressed into service as extras. We emptied our parents' houses of anything useful for shooting a movie. Their cars disappeared for days at a time as we tried to make some kind of driving scene work out. We learned to cover our tracks by always—always—refilling gas tanks and denying everything with a typical, pouty adolescent "How in the name of all that is good and right could you ever accuse such an upstanding citizen as *moi* of such a terrible thing?" Weary and bleary-eyed the entire semester, we kept ourselves perpetually exhausted by staying up nights and weekends furtively trying anything and everything we could think of to create a movie. It's a wonder we didn't flunk every *other* class.

But to our teacher we presented an impenetrable veneer of hostile, aggressively passive adolescent males abusing his good will and trying to get away with doing nothing. We showed up to meetings acting (or, truth be told, once or twice actually being) drunk, pretending we were deaf, and claiming illiteracy and memory loss about the movie we were supposed to be making. At times we refused to talk to him at all, making comments only to each other during our meetings with him. Giggly and irreverent far beyond a fault, we raised "pain in the ass" to the level of NASA particle-beam satellite-killer technology.

All good things must end, however, and when the semester drew to a close so did our little song and dance from hell. It came time to put up or shut up and we were faced with having to actually show the movie to our teacher. Nearly drooling down his shirt at the chance to finally nail us for our horrible behavior and failure to do anything worthwhile all semester, our teacher demanded that we show him the film at his house one evening. I assumed this was his way of preventing his long-overdue grand-mal seizure of shrieking, Tourette's-like obscenities from resulting in his dismissal, arrest, or reincarnation as a scum-eating spore.

To his mild surprise we showed up at his house complete with a can of film, a projector, and a soundtrack. But swearing to God himself that we had only managed to meet the night before to throw together a couple of scenes that we were reluctant and embarrassed to show him, four students with a movie and one teacher with Post Traumatic Stress Disorder sat down to decide the fate of the world.

I must tell you that, for four adolescent boys, the final effect was nothing short of breathtaking—the type of satisfaction the iceberg surely felt watching the Titanic go down. Even given all of our nastiness all semester, the man had no idea of the degree of malevolence he had been dealing with. None of our provocations, prevarications, or outlandish behavior could match the worst insult of all—after leaving no doubt in his mind that we were world-class fuck-ups, we had actually done it. We had made a movie. A real movie. A good movie. An *amazing* movie. He discovered that everything he thought about us was wrong. Everything that was real had been an act and that which could not possibly exist had come to pass. As he watched our final product and could identify the literally hundreds of hours it had taken to produce and the seemingly endless number of cinematic bunnies we had managed to pull out of a primitive 8 millimeter movie-camera hat, he not only had no idea how we did the things we did, but was unaware that such things were even possible. He could make no sense of it. You could almost watch his hold on reality drip out his ears. Antimatter ruled the universe.

It was beautiful to behold.

At the end of the showing and unable to formulate a response, he demanded we show it to him again. We did, and it didn't help. He wanted to praise us, and he wanted to kill us. He was in speechless awe at the movie we had created and in trembling rage at the hateful and contrived show we had put on for the entire semester. To have behaved like *that* and then to have created *this* was, well, there were no words. It was unthinkable, unknowable, impossible. It just *wasn't.* He ultimately stood up, marched to the telephone, called a friend of his—the principal of a competing high school—and demanded that he allow us to come over to his house and show *him* the movie, *right then.* So—just like that—we packed up, lock stock and movie projector, traipsed off to the principal's house in the middle of the night, and showed *him* the movie.

By this time my friends and I were not only metaphorically drunk from the ecstasy of having mashed our teacher's psyche into a substance roughly resembling puppy chow, we had also managed to break out large quantities of beer and become—literally—drunk. This made for a good time to be had by all—meaning us—and while we giggled and laughed and shared inside-jokes, our teacher and The Other Principal conducted a whispered, serious debate about the fate of our creation.

What was this adolescent cinematic masterpiece? Our film was a 12 minute essay on the human experience of time. Like amateur Stephen Hawkings—lacking only the qualities that make him a smart, talented, and worthwhile human being—we (to quote from the newspaper article that reviewed our film) "cinematically portrayed the infusion and dominance of the thing we call 'time' through the human condition."

The movie did all measure of things with the topic of time. It traced history with time running forward and backward. Clock hands morphed into real hands and strangled people. People walked fast and slow, forward and backward, appeared and disappeared. Animation became real and real became animation. Split-screens contrasted different time speeds, frames, and eras. This was accompanied by illustrations of everyday life and a soundtrack of songs and sayings about the place and role of time in the human experience. Receiving a standing ovation at our high school graduation, the film (quoting the article again) "offered a dizzying glimpse into the way we live and die in the grip of never-ending, never-stopping time." Everyone loved it. Everyone was impressed by it. Everyone thought it was *cool.*

And cool is what we became.

Fast forward through the previously mentioned accolades and awards and our being dubbed a brilliant little bunch from a brilliant little school, and the point is that I bought the whole package hook, line, and sinker. And I took my self-perceived brilliant little film-making self off to college to make brilliant "real" movies.

Which was when the shit hit the fan. No sooner had I gotten into "real" film-making than I realized it was nothing whatever like our independent study project. It was no fun at all. Instead, it was like, well, *work*. And nasty work at that. Full of unpleasant tasks, hours of boredom, prima donna actors, creative conflicts, failed and embittered former film-maker faculty and an endless parade of wanna-be's, I hated it. Just hated it. No, strike that. I detested it. It made me want to heave. It *sucked*. The people in it sucked, the teachers in it sucked, and the courses in it sucked. But what sucked most of all was the idea of spending the rest of my life doing it. My future became, as old H. Ross was fond of saying, A Giant Sucking Sound.

So, to my chagrin, in short order I found myself feeling not like a college student at all, but like a wanderer in a dark forest filled with unfamiliar and undesirable career options, while a full-grown career crisis hung from my back with its teeth buried firmly into my neck.

I responded by spending the next two years acting like some lunatic lab tech set loose in the cadaver storage frantically dissecting anything and everything that might prove to be a viable alternative career option. And where I got was exactly—nowhere. I tried literature (too boring, esoteric and impractical), music (too much of a long-shot, career-wise), theater (ditto), religion (me? now there's a laugh), engineering (a math genius I am not), and philosophy (too much beer can do amazing things to your judgment). At some point I glanced up at the life clock and noticed that I was running out of time. And options. Not to mention money. My anxiety rose steadily as my parents' vaguely threatening metaphors involving huge sums of money, kitchen sinks, and large drains, escalated in frequency and intensity.

During the time I was looking for a new career by flopping around like some angry carp on wet linoleum, the only thing I consistently enjoyed were my psychology classes. I found them interesting and fun, taught by professors who seemed unpretentious, happy, and excited about the things they were doing. But for some reason—that most likely involves an insufficient quantity of correctly functioning cells in the logic portion of my brain—it never once occurred to me to consider psychology as a career. Because I never imagined *enjoyment* having anything to do with what I should do with my life, I continued to take some psychology classes for fun while I searched for what I "really" wanted to do.

Then came the fateful day when I picked up a copy of "I'm OK—You're OK," had the words jump off the page, burn through my eyes, hijack my brain, take over my future, and settle the issue once and for all.

Reading that book was as close to enlightenment as it gets. Suddenly it was all there—right in front of me—everything I needed, everything I wanted. It was an experience of Understanding It All. I suddenly had answers to questions that I didn't even know I had. The book explained in words I could understand why I had always felt the ways I felt, what had happened to me to make me like I was, where it all came from, and even what I could do about it.

And I did. In what may be the single most dramatic reaction to a "self-help" book ever recorded, I immediately made serious changes in my life. I ended some terribly destructive relationships. I became involved in several areas and activities that I had previously been frightened to participate in. I confronted, head-on, some issues and conflicts that had been causing me grief—and I took care of them. To my surprise and delight I found myself, for the first time, feeling happy.

It was fantastic. Like the feeling of having sex for the first time, I was reduced to knowing only one thing: *I want more.* Suddenly, I cared about nothing but psychology. I wanted to read about it, I wanted to understand it, I wanted to learn about it, hell, I wanted to *do* it. It was at that moment, during that flash of recognition, that I knew I was going to become a psychologist.

Whatever that was. You see, I had no earthly idea what a psychologist was. Or what it took to become one. I was majoring in *film*, for Christ's sake. But all I needed to know was that psychologists did psychology, so that's what I wanted to do. So a psychologist was what I was going to be. End of story.

THE ANNOUNCEMENT

Well, not quite the end of the story. My decision immediately created more problems than it solved. Because it came late in my college career, the finality of my resolution about becoming a psychologist could not change the fact that I could not switch my major away from film-making without substantially extending my undergraduate tenure, which I was unwilling to do—or more precisely, my parents were unwilling to underwrite. Further, having majored in film, I had nothing in my background to give any self-respecting psychology graduate program a reason to give me a first look, a second look, or even a dirty look. Add to that the horrible odds of getting into graduate school at all—at the time there were 300 applicants for every opening in every psychology graduate program in the country—and the upshot was that I was toast before I even started. To live out my plan, it seemed, I would have to do something drastic.

So I did. When in doubt, as they say, fall back on what you know. So I resurrected an old tried-and-true plan, and in the final twist of irony in my short, unhappy film-making career, I ended it the way I started it—with an independent study project scam.

Because I wanted to maximize the time I could get involved in psychology and minimize the time I had to spend finishing my degree, I pulled every string I could find the end of to arrange an independent study project that would allow me to complete my major with minimal time and effort and achieve the exact number of class hours—and not one more—than I needed. I figured that would be the best way to be able to spend most of my time focusing on psychology rather than focusing a camera. By calling on my adolescent-honed wheedling abilities, I conned my way into getting class credit for teaching a bunch of fourth graders to make an animated film. The whole experience turned out to be horrible, complete bedlam, and I lost a good friend over it, but it got the job done. I got finished with my major and, as far as being a film-maker was concerned, I could call it a day.

Oh yes, and I did one other thing—I announced to the world that my plan was to become a psychologist.

Which turned out to be the single biggest mistake of my life, a screw-up on the order of shoving one's arm into the mouth of a cranky Great White while simultaneously attempting to remove one's own appendix with a rusty steak knife. To say that my announcement provoked surprise in my friends and family would be like saying Charlie Manson made a boo-boo. It produced Armageddon. The Apocalypse. People were horrified and appalled. I could not have garnered a worse reaction had I announced that I planned a long and prosperous career of raping and murdering children. In a jaw-dropping display of blood-lust, people felt compelled to tell me in no uncertain terms what an idiot I was and how offensive my career choice was. To them. Personally. More than once I expected them to actually spit.

One of my best friends, in perhaps the most determined of all the half-hearted attempts to guise spewing venom as something akin to normal social discourse, noted to me that a "friend" (at least he didn't say a "little bird") had told him that "psychology was definitely *not* the thing to go into." Another said it was a serious mistake that I would live to regret. Still others glared at me in horrified silence, their gaping, cavernous mouths screaming disbelief at my having grown horns and a snout right before their eyes. Some people simply refused to believe me or to take my announcement seriously. Others called me names. More than once I heard that I was being foolish. More than twice I heard that all shrinks are their own first patients.

My parents imploded. Acting like they had sired a gun-runner for some third-world despot, they came frighteningly unglued. My father, a flight surgeon and physician of the old school, felt that all shrinks were crazy (Here's how it goes: "A surgeon knows nothing and does everything, an internist knows everything and does nothing, a pathologist knows everything and does everything—too late, and a psychiatrist knows nothing and does nothing.") and non-medical shrinks were the craziest of all, charlatans of the worst kind. He was too flabbergasted to organize a cohesive response, and settled on acting like the whole thing did not exist and would—if there was a God—go away.

My mother took the news worse. Much worse. A died-in-the-wool medical professional for whom power, position, and prestige were everything, she experienced my choice of psychology—and rejection of medical school—as both a personal affront and a deliberate attempt to wound her by entering a field that embraced the idea that the mother is primarily responsible for the despicability of certain offspring—such as myself, obviously. Unable to either contain her disgust or admit it, she settled for making hostile, sarcastic digs at me whenever the topic came up. Not that *she* thought badly of my choice, you understand, but my uncle, her brother the-neurologist-turned-psychiatrist, said that studying psychology would be "beating my head against a wall." And my interest in Transactional Analysis? Well, not that *she* thought badly of it, of course, but Her Brother The Real Doctor said that you had to be careful, you know, because "those kinds of groups are pretty much cults." One evening she capped off a particularly snotty period by responding to my challenge of one of her reasonably frequent outlandish claims about some kind of human behavior by hissing "Well, Mister Smarty Pants, why don't you go look it up in one of your *psychology* books." I turned on my heel, walked out, and spent the next thirty minutes trying to choose the best available wall against which to bang my head. Hard.

But even more astonishing to those who knew me than my choice of a crime-spree masquerading as a career was my entirely out-of-character behavior in response to their criticisms: I didn't seem to care.

You must understand that this was not like Greg at all. Generally one to be cowed by and to acquiesce to the demands and opinions of others, (Once, when I was a child, one of my older sisters was angry at me for doing something my father told me to do and that she, in her infinite wisdom, decided I should not have done. In response to my telling her that he had told me to do this particular thing that she found so offensive, she haughtily asked whether I "always did everything everyone told me to do." In a moment of candor so shocking as to render her speechless for the first and perhaps only time in her life, I replied, "Yes, I do.") this time I was damning the torpedoes and proceeding full-speed ahead. Without shame or guilt and right under everyone's collective nose I was proceeding along my misguided, self-destructive course, seeming to lack even a nanosecond of what anyone considered to be normal hesitation or remorse. I even typed my graduate school applications on my long-suffering parents' typewriter. How was one to figure that?

This way: Without telling anyone, I had come to an internal resolution that entirely neutralized their criticisms and freed me from all career-related internal distress. Here's what happened:

I realized that all of the negative reactions to my decision could be summed up in the sentence "All shrinks are crazy." When the tidal wave of criticism first hit me I was taken so off-guard by its virulence that this accusation did unnerve me. But after some serious soul-searching I assembled the following logic that, for me, put the matter to bed, tucked it in, sang it a lullaby, and turned out the lights:

Point 1: In truth, I had to admit that it was quite possible that everyone was right, that all shrinks were crazy. I mean, I didn't really know, now, did I?

Point 2: Because I wanted to be one so badly, I was obviously the same kind of person as the people who were already in the field.

Point 3: If they were crazy and I was just like them, then most likely I was crazy, too.

Point 4: There was essentially nothing I could do about that.

Point 5: Therefore, I had only two options: 1) I could go into a different career where I would be "sane" but unhappy because I did not want to be there; 2) I could become a psychologist where, however daft we may all be, I would be happy because I would be where I wanted to be and I would be with people who were like me.

And in perhaps the most mature, independent, and best decision of my life, I decided to choose happiness over sanity and public opinion.

Not only did my resolution grant me great inner peace, it had the pleasant side-effect of leaving me entirely immune to career-related insults. I quite simply no longer cared what anyone thought about what I was going to do. *Anyone.* If it was all true and psychologists were a bunch of dangerous, baby-eating lunatics, it mattered not at all. The truth was that I wanted to do whatever they did, even if it involved chanting obscure incantations while swinging dead chickens over my head during full moons. The bottom line was that I figured

I would be with my own kind, so I would be happy. *And to hell with anything else.*

So I smiled and nodded politely while being told how seriously I had gone 'round the bend. Then I went to my room and worked on my graduate school applications.

To my friends and family my lack of concern about their reaction was the straw that broke the camel's back, the needle on the gauge pointing to the red zone of stark raving mad. It also rang the death knell of any attempt to return me to my senses. With little effort to conceal it, family and friends alike stopped arguing with me or even commenting on my conversion to the Dark Side, and turned instead to method acting. They grimaced, sighed, rolled their eyes, and gossiped among themselves about how Mr. Pleasant and Mr. Adaptable had popped his mental cork, fizzed over the side of his mental bottle, and become Mr. Unreasonable and Mr. I Don't Care What You Think. It just all seemed so completely *impossible.* Here I didn't care what they thought, and I was under the delusion that I was happy while I was obviously insane, sliding head-long into a pit of snakes, slathered with rodent-scented body lotion. They were beside themselves.

But even *that* wasn't the worst part for them. There was one last thing. What really got people's goats, what milked their mental cows completely dry, was that I seemed so goddam *determined.* Talk about impossible—determination is entirely foreign to my bloodline, so no one could fathom how I had developed it, and such a bad case of it at that. What, on earth, they cried, was *this?* Unbelievable, unthinkable, yet undeniable, there it was—raw, sweaty, throbbing and vein-filled, ugly as sin—determination. Grab Grandma and cover Junior's eyes, this was not fit for public consumption.

In truth, they had no idea. Determination was not even close to what I had. In yet another secret decision I had resolved that, if necessary, I would spend the rest of my life doing whatever it took to gain admittance to psychology graduate school. Whatever was required to beat out those 299 other people for an opening, I would do it. If it took moving to Outer Mongolia, I'd pack a bag. If it took until I was 80, I'd bring my walker. If I had to worship Satan and sacrifice virgins, I could be flexible. I considered anything short of murder (and even then I was willing to consider special circumstances) to be fair game. I was going to get into graduate school, I was going to go to graduate school, I was going to graduate from graduate school, I was going to become a psychologist, I was going to do psychology, and nothing and no one was going to stop me. Period.

In short, my decision to become a psychologist made me happy, immunized me from criticism, gave me unimaginable resolve, and scared the bejesus out of every single person I knew.

PART II
RESPONSE

GETTING IN: ROUND I

It doesn't sound all that complicated, right? To get into graduate school, apply to graduate school. Not rocket science. So I got a list of psychology graduate schools, ordered application materials, and sat down to fill them out and send them in.

Which was when I experienced a fresh round of emotional vertigo. I discovered that one does not apply to "psychology graduate school" at all. One applies to a *division* of psychology graduate school. I had no idea that there were divisions *within* psychology graduate school that are so different from each other that they are for all practical purposes entirely different departments. And they turn out very different kinds of psychologists. So before you applied to graduate school you had to know what "kind" of psychologist you wanted to be so you could apply to, and hopefully end up in, the right group.

Say what? "Right group?" What "kind" of psychologist? I didn't even know what a psychologist really was, much less anything about the "types" of psychologists that existed. I just wanted to "do psychology." Most people had called that "clinical psychology," but I didn't know that term from a hole in the ground. And now I was seeing all kinds of alien adjectives crammed in front of the word "psychologist." I knew what none of them meant. So I took a deep breath and retired to the library to study up on what psychology "divisions" were in order to figure out which division I should apply to. Here's what I found out:

One division, called "experimental" psychology, is the "basic research" arm of the behavioral sciences. This is where you study the general psychological and behavioral functioning of living creatures in order to try to understand what makes us all tick. The work is often done on small animals like white rats, what with their behavior being a bit easier to control when doing something like conflict research than are two 300 pound, inebriated antisocial bar bouncers. The work essentially involves doing things to these creatures and watching how they respond. You might want to find out, for example, if when you insert into a rat's brain an electrode large enough to make room to park your SUV, the rat continues to try to groom itself after you've also glued its tail to its butt.

I liked that. Experimental psychology seemed like pretty cool work.

Another division was called "social" psychology. Social psychology involves the study of attitudes, group behavior, and other aspects of everyday social human functioning. In this area you do things to creatures one level above that of white rats, generally called the "college sophomore," to see how they respond. Here, for example, you might study whether a group of people working on a crossword puzzle can find a seven letter word for "declaudication" while from the next room come frantic screams of "No, not the meat hook! Please, not the meat hook!"

Not bad, not bad at all. Social psychology seemed real fine, too.

Then there is "clinical" psychology. In this division you do things to yet another species, called "patients," to see how they respond. Here, for example, you might try to figure out what you would need to say to someone to stop some kind of self-destructive behavior, such as screwing the neighbor's chickens (A real case of mine, by the way.).

OK, no contest. I knew immediately that I *really* liked clinical psychology.

Not only did each division make you a different kind of psychologist, each division also prepared you for a different type of job. Experimental psychology, for example, prepared you for a job in academia. In this job you join a college faculty, do whatever is required in order to prevent ever being fired by obtaining something called "tenure," and then spend the rest of your life being something called "boring" so you can gleefully watch college students try to hang themselves rather than listen to your ridiculously outdated and dry classroom lectures.

I liked the idea of academia. That sounded pretty good.

Social psychology also prepared you for a career in academics, but in addition you could work with research organizations or join something like an advertising agency. In this job you would either find the best ways to get grants so you could continue to be employed and avoid starving to death, or you could look for ways to enable the people you worked for to sell things with such increasing efficiency that they could get rich and sell the company to someone who would summarily fire you.

Working as a social psychologist sounded like fun.

Then, of course, there was clinical psychology. Clinical psychology also prepared you to work in academics, but you could also work directly with actual patients in a hospital, clinic, or psychology "practice." This was where people came to you for help and you tried to do something that helped them more often than it hurt them.

No contest. When I said I wanted to "do psychology," I meant I wanted to apply it, to use it to mess with real, live human beings who do real, live, stupid things that they'd be better off not doing. I wanted to work with patients. So that meant I needed to apply to "clinical psychology."

Which was when I discovered that, to my horror, so did everyone else on the planet. Apparently I was not the only person who felt enlightened by The Human Potential Movement, because remember that 300-to-1 ratio of applicants to positions in psychology graduate school I mentioned previously? It was true *only* for clinical psychology. The other divisions were not so sought-after and as a result were much, much easier to get into. Clinical psychology, on the other hand, was the second-most-difficult graduate program to get into in the country, not far behind the legendary horrors of trying to gain admittance to veterinary school. (A friend of mine gave up trying to get into veterinary school after simply reading the requirements for *interviewing* for admission.) Trying to get into medical school, by contrast, was a picnic. The father of one of my classmates was an OB/GYN who told me that he had never seen anything like it. He said that given his grades and credentials, his son—my classmate—could have gotten into any medical school in the country. But he had a *terrible* time gaining admittance to a clinical psychology doctoral program.

Nevertheless, being young, idealistic, and breathtakingly stupid, I proceeded completely undaunted by the numbers. I applied to a half-dozen of the top clinical psychology graduate programs in the country.

And I promptly got a half-dozen rejection letters. I learned that "Sorry, but you just aren't right for us" was code for "You, my friend,

23

have got no qualifications at all and we're sitting here staring at applications from Nobel prize nominees and people who have been submitted to the Vatican for sainthood. What were you *thinking?* That we'd want *you?* We don't want you. We'd take a *dead person* over you. Have you considered a career as—say—a film-maker?"

In my effusive, immature naivete, I had managed to ignore the clearly impossible odds and erroneously conclude that drive, desire, and full-bodied sincerity would somehow produce a miracle, open the skies, elicit manna from heaven, and allow me to gain admittance to a clinical psychology doctoral program. Meanwhile, on this side of the galaxy, reality still ruled and it was not to be.

Despite the blatant predictability of my unanimous rejection by anyone with even the smallest respect for the laws of nature, I felt so blind-sided by my failure to begin pursuing my dream that I became depressed to the point where my girlfriend at the time began to worry about me. We spent a very long winter with me in a very dark mood. Had I not still been so determined to become a psychologist, I could probably have been suicidal. I was *very* upset.

But as it was, the rejection did have the positive effect of making me far more realistic about what I was up against. The game was not over, not by a long shot. The entrance ticket was just a bit more expensive than I had figured. Apparently it was going to cost me some time and energy to get the credentials that would enable me to get into clinical psychology graduate school. So credentials are what I set out to get.

Because I was already out of college and had worn out my parents' admittedly generous financial welcome, it seemed unrealistic to seek more course work in the area (as it was I had graduated with relatively little course work in psychology, one very small part of the very big problem that I was a very lousy applicant). But what I *could* get that I could offer to graduate programs was *experience.* So I decided that I would go out and get so much of any and every kind of experience that graduate schools wanted that before long they would like me and want me and cry and wail and threaten to commit mass ritual suicide if I didn't agree to enter their program. So I got information from every school that would speak to me or write to me and found three interests they all seemed to have in common:

Interest Number 1: The Graduate Records Examination, or GRE's. The graduate school version of the SAT, programs cared about scores on this test far more than college grade point average. "Worship" might be too strong a word for how they felt, but not *too* terribly strong a word. Several programs actually took all applications with GRE scores below a certain number and threw them out without even looking at them. Ouch.

Interest Number 2: Research. These were academic institutions, after all, and big-time research meant big-time money and big-time stature. So they loved research experience. I didn't, but they did, so that settled *that*.

Interest Number 3: Clinical work. Programs were interested in two questions: 1) Have you worked with patients? 2) Do you have any idea what you're doing? For me the answer was "no" and "no," but by going out and getting some experience I figured I could turn the answers to "yes" and "yes" and prevent my next round of applications from becoming the source of laughter on admissions committees and being discarded with the morning's egg shells, coffee grounds, and empty Southern Comfort bottles. (I sat on the admissions committee when I was in graduate school, and I know—they really do laugh. Out loud.)

So the first thing I did was to take the GRE's. Twice. Despite the awfulness of taking that test (think "SAT's on steroids"), I figured I had a reasonably good chance of improving my score by taking it a second time. And, in fact, I did increase my score respectably, or at least enough to get the Post Office to agree to deliver my next round of applications. First mission accomplished.

Second, I used my relationship with a couple of my college faculty to get myself introduced to some psychologists doing research at a local Child Behavior and Research Center. If I got my name on some research publications, or at least had letters from a couple of psychologists who were sufficiently facile liars to be able to convince programs that I had a serious obsession with research, I figured I would have accomplished a major step in my makeover from idiot-applicant to must-have applicant.

There were no job openings at the place, so I volunteered my time for free. Disbelieving their good fortune but being anything but stupid, like pigs at a trough the staff at the Center gobbled up every speck of my time they could wangle. Treating me like the slave labor I was, they used me for everything and anything they could think of. Ultimately, I ended up in the unique position of being essential and influential while fitting nowhere in the system—I wasn't staff, I wasn't faculty, I wasn't a student. I wasn't paid. But I even had *keys* to the place, for crying out loud, and for the next year I became a fixture there, a required member of the team even though I was no known species of legitimate participant. (It was at this time that I began to refer to myself as a "mutant," because while fitting no definable category I still ended up being the necessary, must-have, go-to guy. For some reason that role has followed me throughout my career.)

I considered my second mission to be accomplished.

The third thing I did was apply for a job at the county psychiatric hospital. Given that I was 22 years old with a maximum of fervor and a minimum of experience, all I qualified for was to work as a psychiatric aide (wonderfully titled to sound important and credible as a "Mental Health Specialist," or MHS). Given the high stress, high turnover, high risk, and low wage of being an aide at a county psychiatric hospital, I landed the job with little effort or fanfare. A slightly comatose monkey could have gotten it.

No matter. I was thrilled. My missions were accomplished. I had my GRE's and I was going to get a year of research experience and a year of clinical experience. One short year, I figured, and I would have the credentials that would get me into graduate school. I rented an attic apartment for very little money (and very little heat, as it turned out) and got to work getting the year under my belt.

There was just one hitch. In all of my wonderful resolve about spending the rest of my life doing whatever was required to gain admittance to graduate school, I failed to take into account the one thing, perhaps the only thing, that could successfully derail my plans—having too short a life span to finish doing what was necessary to get in. And I almost did, because during my year of experience I came very close to dying—or, more precisely, to being killed.

A YEAR AT THE
PSYCHIATRIC HOSPITAL

The morning I began work at the psychiatric hospital was like having to wake up to be in a dream. No, I was not yet a psychologist. No, I did not possess a doctorate or a psychology license. I hadn't even been admitted to graduate school. I had no title, training, or maturity (well, not much). But despite all that I was still going to get to *work with patients*—up close and personal, face-to-face, as part of a "treatment team." I was going to find out what this clinical psychology stuff was all about. I was going to get to be involved in front-line psychology. Praise God and pass the ammunition, let's *do* this.

In reality the first thing I did on my first day within two minutes of walking onto the county's psychiatric unit was to find myself smack-dab in the middle of what for all the world looked like a back-alley brawl. Four staff members had surrounded a very large, very angry, and very surly-looking male adolescent patient. They were saying something to him that I could not quite make out, but it was clear that they were not offering to drive him to the mall. He sat stock still, arms crossed, jaw clenched, shaking his head no, looking for all the world like some awful animatronics caricature of an impossible teen-age boy out of a "Families From Hell" exhibit you might find at a deranged Disney World.

Suddenly, one of the staff members said "OK then, let's go," and they set on him with the fervor of football players on a fumble where the one who came up with the ball would win not only the game, but also the opportunity to perform hideously obscene acts with the cheerleading squad. The patient yelled and screamed and fought as they wrestled him to the ground, piling on top of him in a squirming, writhing mass of indistinguishable bodies, arms, legs, and swear words. Furniture was knocked over, lamps shook and rattled. A staff member yelled at me to grab a leg. Assuming he meant a leg belonging to the patient, I broke my paralysis long enough to yank on what looked to be the youngest ankle sticking out of the mass of flesh writhing on the floor before me. With what felt like great effort and violence we bundled the kid up, lifted him off the ground, carried him to a small, bare, windowless room, held him face-down, and sprinted out the door, one-by-one, before he could follow, locking it behind us as we slammed it in his snarling face.

As the scene concluded, whatever neurons were active in my brain stopped firing all at once. The blood drained from my face and any other still-living tissue and I entered a never-never land of wondering what in God's name I had gotten myself into. This bore precious little resemblance to the TA therapy groups I'd read about where people dispassionately analyzed the things they were doing and made rational plans to improve. That was civilized. This was something else. It was war, or kidnaping, or children running with scissors, or something equally horrible. But whatever it was, it did not seem like *psychology*. Not the psychology I was expecting, anyway.

I must have looked awful. A staff member approached me, put his arm around me, and said "Here, go outside and talk to Jake. He'll explain all this to you." So, feeling like something out of Night of the Living Dead that had gone way too long without eating a living being and was functioning poorly even for someone who had been in a grave for an undetermined period of time, I slowly shuffled outside behind Jake to have it all explained to me.

Unfortunately Jake, as I found out later and everyone else knew already, was a cretin of the first order, a self-important imbecile who could not have explained poop to a fly. Widely and frequently mocked behind his back, he took this time with me as his moment in the sun, his opportunity to wax eloquent to the new kid, the unknowing one, The Little Guy Who Couldn't. "Explaining all this to me" consisted of his serving up some ridiculous, moldy, day-old verbal concoction that sandwiched a chunky smear of Freudian theory between slices of self-righteous smugness. He mumbled something about how sometimes "people want to be held and can't admit it," and then "things happen, and compassion demands we respond," and blah, blah, blah.

He could have been telling me that a pigeon had nested in my pants and set fire to my butt for all the sense it made to me. I could hear nothing but random screams emanating from whatever brain cells could still cough up a response inside my aching head. As far as

28

I was concerned there was no "wanting to be held" in that episode of violence. There was nothing positive at all. It was simply raw and upsetting, more like government goons from a grimy third world country dragging off a political dissident never to be heard from again than therapists caring for patients. I don't think it was the worst experience I could have had by that point in my life, but having never been slowly tortured to the brink of death by blood-sucking fiends, I guess I'll never really know.

Paying far more attention to the skipping beats of my heart and the possibility of suffering a fatal heart attack or debilitating stroke at my tender age than to Jake's imitation of a post-lobotomy Freud, I managed to feed enough blood to my volitional muscles to go back inside and spend the rest of the shift getting oriented to the unit and its procedures. But that night I lay awake in bed wondering why there was no God and whether I might be better off crawling up the side of and flopping back into the frying pan of life as a film-maker.

True to my resolution, however, I proved to myself that I really was willing to do anything to get into graduate school—I went back to that hospital the very next day. And the next, and the next, and the next after that.

All told, I worked at that hospital for nearly a year. And during my time there I learned a great deal of very useful things that serve me to this day. I learned about the mental health industry, psychiatric illnesses, psychology, psychotherapy, and psychoactive drugs. I learned that psychiatric nurses know God and rule the world. I learned about group therapy and individual therapy. I learned about treatment plans and case consultation. I even got comfortable with the idea that it was, in fact, sometimes helpful to tackle patients and drag them off to seclusion rooms.

I also learned about fear and terror and the rapid pace at which one can develop an eye-popping anxiety disorder. While I found that I did, indeed, love psychology, I also discovered that working at that hospital frequently necessitated self-medication with whatever mood-altering liquid, powder, or pills were most readily available. It turned out to be a scary place, that hospital, and sooner or later it got to us all. The staff, ever eager to champion the underprivileged, made fine imported automobiles well within the financial means of even the lowliest of our local drug dealers.

Worse yet, about a week after starting work at the hospital I suffered another shock, this one personal. And physical. One morning I noticed a sizeable protrusion in the area where the front of my right leg attaches to my body. It didn't seem like it should be there, given that: a) I didn't remember it being there; b) the other side didn't have one; c) it was as big as a large marble; and d) the damn thing *hurt*. It hurt like hell. I had some trouble walking, it hurt so much.

I had no idea what it was. Remember—I was 22 years old at the time, and while I may have come from a medical family, we were a classic example of "the cobbler's children have no shoes." I was for all practical purposes a complete ignoramus regarding all things biological. So for the life of me I could not figure out what on earth this big bump was that was chafing the elastic in my underwear and making it hard to walk. All I knew was that it didn't seem like it should be there, I couldn't find another one like it anywhere else on my body, and it *hurt*.

So I took myself off to the doctor who, I must say, listened with the patience of Job and avoided snickering even once as I described not only my puzzling and painful marble-sized protrusion, but also the various naive theories I had concocted about what it might be— like maybe a hernia, or maybe a muscle tear from too much kicking and being kicked while practicing the martial art that I had become enamored with. After smiling politely while letting me run out of steam, my doctor cleared his throat and said the following, which I swear I am not making up:

"Not really. What you have is called a lymph node, or in this case a *swollen* lymph node. Lymph nodes swell in response to events in the body such as infections and tumors. So you have something going on that is causing that lymph node to swell. My guess is that you have some kind of infection. I'm not sure exactly what kind of infection it is, but the *worst* thing you might have is bubonic plague. The plague attacks the lymph system directly."

And then the son-of-a-bitch laughed.

I couldn't tell if he was being funny, or ironic, or if he was merely uncomfortable. What I can tell you is that *I* didn't laugh. *I* broke out in a cold sweat and tried to remember if I'd been recently cavorting with any strangely behaving, foaming-at-the-mouth rodents.

Then he started doing tests. First, the test for plague. Dodged that bullet. Then a test for gonorrhea. Huh? Very surprising. And

30

unpleasant. Not to mention embarrassing. But he was the doctor, so I went along. No gonorrhea. Next, a vial of blood to check for a handful of common infections. Nope. A second vial to check for less-common infections. Still no go. Finally, he said "You know, there is one other thing that it could be and that we haven't tested for. So let's do that." OK, let's. A third vial of blood.

Bingo. He called me, *totally* excited. Wouldn't you know, he said, it darn sure was that last thing. Not much to be done about it, though—so sorry—but I should prepare myself for what was about to happen to me because I had—ta da!—mononucleosis. And since there was no treatment for it, I would have to just let it run its course. Take care, now. Bye, bye.

Oh, no, wait, he said—one more thing—don't kiss anybody. And oh, no, wait—one *more* thing—expect to be flat on my back for at least a month. Maybe more.

OK, so I may have been a biological moron, but this sounded like bad news even to me. Further, even *I* had heard of mono, and even at my primitive, slightly post-adolescent layman's level of medical knowledge, I knew that the diagnosis was trouble.

During my high school and college era, herpes and AIDS were hardly blips on the radar screen, and it was "mono" that was *the* "romance and relationship" disease. People talked about it all the time. Colloquially called "the kissing disease" because it is so often spread that way, in high school and in college I had heard story after story of people being completely disabled by it, often for months at a time. It was said that they'd had to drop out of school, forego all physical activity, and have other people take over everything in their life. It was said to be very bad stuff, that mono, very bad indeed.

Even so, I decided that before I actually whipped myself into the debilitating state of panic that by this point I was busily planning, I should probably get more complete information about the illness than the eighteenth-hand adolescent gossip I was currently relying on. So following my conversation with my doctor I went to the library to do some research. I gathered every book, journal, and article I could find on mono, lugged it to a table and dumped it into a pile. I began picking my way through it.

I needn't have bothered. My informal knowledge, it turned out, was pretty darn accurate. One member of a family of diseases that messes rather seriously with one's liver, mono is caused by a virus called Epstein-Barr, and is often only slightly less debilitating than its more famous cousin, hepatitis. I read case study after case study of people who were completely disabled by it for one month, for two months, for three months. Experiences of overwhelming and intractable fatigue. Nausea, fever, chills. Unable to get out of bed. Abject debilitation. A long, slow, protracted period of recovery.

I closed my eyes, laid my head down on the stack of books, and tried to decide what in hell I could have done in a past life that was so awful as to give me *this* much bad karma. Not only was I risking life and limb working at a psych hospital, not only was I working twenty and thirty hours a week *for free* at the Child Behavior and Research Center, and not only had I just begun the year where I was betting the farm that I could get sufficient credentials to gain admittance to graduate school, but now I was going to be in the grips of a disease that was not life-threatening, but that was darn near everything but? I'd have to lie in bed for months? With debilitating fever and chills? And overwhelming fatigue? Just how, exactly, was this going to work?

As I sat there in the library, my head on the journals, my eyes closed, I realized the simple truth: it was *not* going to work. I was facing two completely incompatible options. If I did what I was supposed to do to recover from the illness and stopped doing anything that required more exertion than blinking my eyes *really* hard, I would fail to get into graduate school the next year and would have to start over from scratch. But if I *didn't* stop all the stuff I was doing, my disease might worsen to the point where I would become gravely ill and then it could be many, many months before I'd be functional at all. I was caught between the proverbial rock and a hard place, the devil and the deep blue sea, an unstoppable force and an immovable object. I considered my options. One was becoming hysterical. The second was to make a plan.

I decided to make a plan. So as I continued to sit in the library, my head on the journals, I made a decision: to hell with it. Mono or no mono, I was not stopping. I was not going to waste an entire year and have to start over. I might not be able to do *everything* I had planned to do, but maybe I could do *enough*. Maybe I could drag myself around long enough to enough places to get the minimum amount of experience that would get me admitted to graduate school while also not doing so much that I'd get so sick I'd never recover. I decided that the way I'd proceed was to do as much as I could do, to act as though I were not sick for as long as possible (while refraining from kissing anyone in order to keep from spreading the thing), and to cut out as many expendable areas of activity as needed in order to conserve my energy. I thought about ways I could minimize my energy expenditure in other areas so I could devote nearly every ounce of strength I might have left to shuffling myself between the hospital and the Child Behavior and Research Center.

Now, I am well aware that this strains credulity, but I swear on a stack of Bibles it's true. What happened next is that I got up from where I sat in the library, went home, and proceeded to act as though I wasn't sick. I went to work at the psych hospital or the Child Behavior and Research Center for every day of every week for the next year. And through it all I acted as though I'd never even heard of mononucleosis, much less been diagnosed with it. I missed not one single day of work at either place. Like the Energizer Bunny, I just kept going. And I didn't even give up too many other things, either. I just cut back on some of my sports activities for a while. In short, mine is still the only case I've ever heard of where someone continued to function normally during a full-fledged case of mono.

Think about *that* the next time you pooh-pooh mind over matter.

But there is one other thing. Keeping going at the psych hospital turned out to be even more difficult than I'd anticipated, because there was an extra added attraction that I have, as of yet, failed to mention. After being hired I discovered that I had agreed to work what is euphemistically called "rotating shifts." Perhaps you've seen the TV ads for working rotating shifts. They start out by showing a brain, and a voice says "This is your brain." Then the voice says "This is your brain on rotating shifts." Then a hammer mashes the brain into a substance resembling beef stroganoff. Then a flame thrower melts the mush into oblivion. Then angry mobs dance in the street with glee.

A hospital has three shifts: day shift runs from 7 AM to 3 PM, evening shift is from 3 PM to 11 PM, and night shift is from 11 PM to 7 AM. Working "rotating shifts" means you work all three—which I did. It was not unusual, in fact, for me to work all three shifts *during the same week.* So on Monday I might work the day shift, getting to work at 6:30 AM and getting off at 3 PM. On Tuesday I might work a night shift, arriving at work at 10:30 PM and getting off at 7 AM.

Then I might work again that very evening, going back to the hospital at 3 PM and leaving at 11 PM. And remember, I was also going to the Child Behavior and Research Center to work between those times.

Working rotating shifts is an experience everyone ought to have—unless, of course, you have already lived for an extended period inside a paint shaker. When you work at—literally—all hours of the day and night, you lose track of small things. Like when the sun is going to come up. Or how to judge whether or not it is appropriate to telephone a friend ("Oh, it's 3 AM? Sorry, I thought it was noon."). Or whether you're supposed to be ordering breakfast, lunch, or dinner.

Sleeping is fun, too. I remember one Christmas where I had worked rotating shifts for the five days prior, and by Christmas Day I had been awake for a full 36 hours. I remember that I would think I was pretty much OK, when suddenly my visual field would begin to shake like I was drunk. Then I would have mild visual hallucinations. By the time we had dinner I wouldn't have been surprised if I'd seen the turkey suddenly stand up from its platter, strut across the table, and break into a chorus of "Don't Cry for Me Argentina." I finally built blackout shutters for the inside of my bedroom windows so that no matter what time I went to bed I could make the room completely dark. That seemed to help. A little.

One positive thing about that year is that the level of stress we experienced at the hospital made for an *extremely* cohesive staff. Like soldiers in combat, we bonded with each other in every way possible. And the parties we threw? They were amazing. As were our forays out. One night about twelve of us were at a bar drinking after a particularly harrowing day. We were telling mental health war stories and entertaining ourselves wonderfully. During a pause in the conversation I looked around and noticed that several tables of people around us had completely stopped talking, were in rapt attention to our conversation, and looked *horrified*. In a drunken stagger I rose, turned toward them, and pronounced—loudly and to all present—"Don't worry, we have the mental health of your community well in hand!" My colleagues jumped on me, dragged me out of the bar, and we beat a hasty retreat.

Hey—at least I didn't get into a game of pool with some bikers who threatened to turn it into a life-threatening brawl like a couple of my coworkers did when we were out drinking one night. I do have *some* standards.

A YEAR AT THE CHILD BEHAVIOR
AND RESEARCH CENTER

Working at the Child Behavior and Research Center provided me with a rational, intellectual yin to the hospital's wild-eyed yang. Where at the hospital I was often an upset body dragging other upset bodies around, at the Center I was a brain figuring things out with other brains. Exactly the opposite of the hospital, the Center worked on reason, conversation, and planning. It was calm, cool, and collected, with nowhere near the level of drama available at the hospital. It was satisfying, level-headed, calm, fascinating, and often nowhere near as fun.

At the Center I worked with staff psychologists and psychology graduate students (who I circled like an envious predator, pondering whether, if they were to mysteriously disappear, I could take their spot in school) to create studies, operationalize research protocols, implement procedures, analyze results, and get articles published. It was phenomenally intellectually rewarding.

The stark contrast between the world of the hospital and the world of the Child Behavior and Research Center gave my life a somewhat fragmented tone, a multiple-personality flavor. I lived in two entirely different worlds—one wild, one calm, one emotional, one rational, one chaotic, one ordered, one clinical, one research. I decided early on that combining the two worlds was a bad idea, possibly even dangerous, so I carefully kept them separate. I could not envision inviting people from both places to the same party, for example, for fear of setting off some kind of disastrous matter-antimatter chain reaction, rending the space-time continuum, and producing some bizarre scene where Joan of Ark finds herself alone in the Oval Office during Bill Clinton's tenure with him locking the door and making goo-goo eyes at her. No, thank you.

My two worlds managed to collide only once, and it wasn't pretty. The hospital sent me to a local conference on the effects of childhood trauma, and unbeknown to me the psychologist running the Child Behavior and Research Center was also attending. Walking down the center aisle of the meeting, as he passed my chair he held out his hand and slapped me a "high five." A head nurse from our unit, sitting next to me and not knowing me very well at the time, was taken aback at this unexpected street-style, wordless greeting. And here, I had seemed like such a *nice* fellow (She told me later she had seriously considered the idea that it was some kind of drug-greeting. *Excuse* me?) and this threw her conclusion into question. But then, this also happened before lunch, where a hospital administrator who was also attending the meeting even managed to criticize the way I poured her coffee. Geez.

The other significant aspect of my work at the Child Behavior and Research Center, of course, was that it was on a volunteer basis, so it made a significant contribution to my ongoing, and at times perilous, state of poverty. After all, I was only working part-time at the psychiatric hospital, and for minimum wage at that. So the Center staff, ever alert to the possibility of losing their resident slave to something that prevented rather than propagated malnutrition, struggled to do whatever they could to keep me. Usually this involved feeding my ego, occasionally swelling it to the point of needing its own area code. I was fond of sitting on tables at the time, partly to irritate the psyche of a psychologist who felt compelled to interpret every behavior of every person and partly for no reason I can identify, and I would be sitting on a table in a conference room with five or six Ph.D.'s and Ph.D. candidates (all sitting in chairs), brainstorming some research issue or other. I might make a comment and the project director would say something like "Stop, wait—did everyone hear what Greg said? Let's think about this for a minute. What if he's right, and we..." Well, I tell you—my head would swell, my pride would jump, my heart would race, and I would mentally rush onstage, grab the Oscar and scream "You like me! You really, really like me!"

Of *course* they liked me—I was trustworthy, I was zealous, I was willing to do just about anything for anyone at any time, and I was *free*. So the staff fed me the praise that, they hoped, would avert my attention from the fact that they were trying their very best to work me to death for free. Being the sucker that I am, they succeeded nicely and all was well.

MY NEAR-DEATH EXPERIENCE

Ah, the county psych hospital. It was often an amazing place, and the people we dealt with were often amazing people suffering from amazing conditions.

One evening I was in the Day Room talking to a newly admitted young woman when she became what might be called "alarmingly" friendly. She began to bat her eyes far more often than required to moisten one's cornea, her voice became increasingly breathy, and she demonstrated an amazing ability to walk with her butt as she slowly inched closer and closer to me on the couch. The whole thing had the surreal feel of being slowly swallowed by a large doe-eyed python.

I became increasingly uncomfortable and anxious, all the while trying to carry on a casual conversation as if nothing were wrong. Just as I was ready to break into a full flop-sweat and the patient was about to make actual physical contact with me, one of the psychiatric nurses appeared over my shoulder and said to me in a tone that would have stopped the satanic head mistress of a sadistic girls' reform school in a B-grade horror movie dead in her tracks: "Greg, come into the nurses' station, I want to talk to you"—although words more consistent with her tone would have been "Greg, come into the nurses' station, I want to disembowel you." I didn't care, because by then my conversation with the patient had become so strange and unnerving that I was willing to partake of any alternate activity no matter how critical, humbling, or damaging to crucial body parts.

Like Mary's Little Lamb I obediently followed the nurse into the nurse's station and proceeded to lie down—I am not kidding—on the desk. I felt exhausted and exasperated. Bending over and staring at me from three inches away, eyes glowing like The Terminator, she screamed "When it starts getting weird, get up and walk away! Just leave! Don't sit there and let it get crazy! Leave, for God's sake! Leave!"

I nodded in acknowledgment of final confirmation that I was a world-class idiot, and did what the nurses always demanded the aides do when we displeased them—I went out to get food for the staff. By the time I returned, feeling better and bearing burgers, fries, and shakes for all, there was a huge commotion on the unit. And an ambulance. Why? Well, it seems that when I left, the patient to whom I had been talking had slipped into the bathroom of her room and slit her wrists *"over the trauma of my having so suddenly abandoned her."*

Now *that* was one serious eye-opener. It was also my first introduction to a phenomenon called "Borderline Personality Disorder," a topic with which I would later become so familiar that I would actually give trainings to mental health professionals on how to deal with it. God knows they couldn't do worse than I did on that night.

Another time a male patient was being admitted to our unit from a local Community Mental Health Center, and I was working up the admission. We had finished most of the paperwork when I was asked to walk him over to the cafeteria to get something to eat. Simple enough, right? You so overestimate me.

We left the unit and began walking toward the next building. The patient smiled at me. Then, suddenly and without warning, he transformed into Carl Lewis and, turning on his heel, sprinted away from me and toward the parking lot, pulling out his car keys as he went.

Stunned, I stumbled after him. He reached his car, jumped in, locked the doors, started it, threw it into reverse, and floored it to back out of the parking space. At that point, like the fool that God clearly intended me to be, just as the car lurched backward I grabbed the handle of the door and tried to open it. I don't know what I would have done had the door actually opened, but it didn't, so all I had to worry about was half-running and being half-dragged across the asphalt as the patient sped backward out of the parking space, threw the car into drive, lurched forward, and slammed into another car. That jerked me forward and threw me, head-first, somersaulting over and over, to the pavement—which, by the way, hurts one hell of a lot more than movies would have you believe, where the hero is thrown from the hood of a car and immediately stands up, smiles, pats his perfect hair, and throws the gorgeous female lead to the ground and makes love to her in the left-turn lane.

The patient backed up again to clear the car he had hit, and sped off toward the street. It became quiet and I lay, slightly dazed and moderately seriously injured, in the parking lot. I rose to my feet in time to notice that we had drawn a sizable little crowd of onlookers, including the psychologist who had admitted the patient. I rubbed my sore shoulder, bleeding head, and bruised ego, and tried to explain what had just happened.

Well, it seems that the whole thing was my own fault. During the admissions process I had broken a cardinal rule of admissions—I hadn't taken away the patient's car keys. Hell, I'd forgotten to ask if he *had* car keys. I felt horrible. To their credit, the hospital let me live and was sufficiently forgiving as to let me keep my job. I'm not sure they should have.

In the final irony, that very same patient was picked up and readmitted the very next day—and I again did the admit. But that time I *did* get his car keys, by golly. There is a formal name for this phenomenon: "one-trial learning."

Another time a delivery arrived at our unit and as the delivery person unlocked the door one of our more violent and unpredictable patients shoved it open, pushed the delivery person down, and sprinted out of the unit. Being the closest staff member to him, I ran out after him. Several other staff members ran after me.

The patient dashed across the hospital grounds and into a street in an adjoining neighborhood. I ran after him as the staff behind me returned to the hospital to fetch a van to use to corral the patient or recover my body, whichever they found first. In desperation, halfway down the second street I yelled out his name and told him to stop. In response—just like that—he stopped. He stopped and stood, stock still, in his tracks. Then he turned and slowly walked toward me. Despite feeling a sudden need to receive the last rites, like an actor auditioning for Broadway I created a character who was most definitely not me and who was able to bark in a commanding tone: "We have to go back to the hospital now." The patient said "Okay," and together we walked back toward the unit. At that point the van arrived, we got in, and we went back as if nothing had happened.

Now *that* was weird.

But nowhere near as weird as the fateful evening where I stared into the executive board room where awaits one's Maker. *It* was awful.

I was working an evening shift at the hospital. Now, you must understand that evenings were the most difficult of all shifts. At their best they were strange, and at their worst they were terrifying to behold. Imagine the combination of a moonless night, a seance, and the ever-present possibility of radioactive mutants suddenly shoving flesh-dripping hands through the windows of your house and you get the idea of how they felt.

During day shifts patients were busy with activities, appointments with therapists, meals, and excursions. They were occupied and their time was structured. On night shifts, with the exception of the occasional shrieking psychotic episode, which was surprisingly easy to handle, they were generally asleep. But during the evenings they were not only awake with nothing much to do, but the demands of the day had drained whatever energy they had available for self-control or rational thinking. The result was that the setting sun transformed our generally well-run little unit into a hotbed of bedeviled brains and buggy behavior. Even if nothing bad actually *happened* on an evening shift, that was completely beside the point—every moment still felt like something awful was *about* to happen. "Oh, this week you're working *evenings*" was a statement on the order of "Oh, the interrogators from the Spanish Inquisition want to ask you a few *questions.*" Everybody knew what it meant, as did every body part, which wanted to flee in a different direction.

In truth, though, just like the appearance of the Four Horsemen is said to foretell the end of the world, if you were paying attention you could usually see it coming—an increasingly heated conversation between patients, a solitary patient sitting in a corner talking to themselves in escalating tones, the teenagers suddenly disappearing or becoming unexplainably quiet—all were signs that it was time to become more vigilant, to increase staff visibility around the unit and to put in a call to your loved ones to tell them how very sorry you were for being such a creep for all these years and how you hope they will find a way to forgive you and remember you fondly.

One of the patients on our unit at the time was a very large, bearded man who, although I was never sure whether he actually owned a motorcycle, knew how to ride one, or could pronounce a word with that many syllables, could nevertheless have posed for the cover of a Hell's Angels greeting card designed to illustrate raw, unrestrained impulse and unfamiliarity with any form of civilized behavior no matter how ordinary, insignificant, or hinted at in the Ten Commandments. Given to wearing leather everything and black fingernail polish, he could have been the prototype for "Raising Arizona's" "Lone Biker of the Apocalypse." He had come to us from some faraway place in Europe, and it was rumored that his family was politically prominent, had a great deal of money, and had shipped him off to America to be kept in cold storage at our hospital due to his wart-like effect on the nose of the respectable part of the genealogy. Apparently they had no idea what to do with him.

Neither did we. But no matter. For whatever reason—probably having to do with some kind of karmic retribution for bad behavior on the part of the staff's ancestors as they wriggled out of the primordial ooze—he was big, he was bad, and he was ours.

He was also medicated to the hilt. In an ongoing war among staff and physicians about its appropriateness, the man was receiving copious quantities of addictive, mood-altering, pain-killing narcotics under the name of "treatment." A unit consultant reading the man's chart noted that he had never seen codeine, morphine, and the like used for "psychotherapeutic" purposes. Once he caught sight of the patient he realized he had never seen anything like *that*, either. Except maybe for the one he saw eat Tokyo in that movie that time.

In any case, the patient was usually drunk on narcotics and somewhat—how do I say this—*insistent*—about receiving more when he felt them wearing off or experienced the distant drums of impending withdrawal. The problem was that his psychiatrist was so ambivalent about the whole thing that while he would agree to prescribe the drugs, he would never prescribe *enough* of them to make it easy on anyone. As a result, we made regular calls to the shrink to get him to order more meds for the patient. To his credit the guy was usually pretty good-natured about giving in to our requests once they took on the tone of frantic screams and desperate pleas that the elimination of life as we knew it was imminent if he didn't get us that prescription *right now.*

Usually, but not always. On this particular evening, his unavailability combined with a particularly nasty little evening-shift petri dish fermenting bad patient behavior made for a mix that none of us saw coming until it was nearly too late. At least for me.

The evening shift began at three o'clock. It had been a difficult day already, and on this particular night the evening shift had started badly and continued badly. By seven o'clock we had already filled our three seclusion rooms with out-of-control patients, and the rest of our patients were teetering on the brink of being out-of-control themselves. Two of the seclusions had required staff from other units to dash to ours to assist in controlling the outbreaks. Then we'd had to switch the seclusion rooms two patients were in, meaning we had to have enough people to hold two patients and carry them past each other. The process had taken over an hour, we had essentially neglected all of our other edgy and potentially dangerous patients, and had the whole thing not been horrible it would have made a slapstick psychiatric Keystone Cops movie that no one would have taken seriously. We were all exhausted and several of us were nursing cuts and bruises from the evening's festivities. I still bear a scar on the back of my right hand from that night where a patient managed to pry a hand loose and use a fingernail to scratch the daylights out of me.

At about nine o'clock I was sitting in the Day Room, watching TV with the patients, trying to be a Calming Presence given the earlier traumatic events that had so upset everyone, when the aforementioned Biker Patient, agitated and angry over his lack of drugs to stem the unpleasant feelings beginning to poke through his narcotic-induced haze, screamed at me in his accented English that someone had fallen to the floor behind my chair. I turned around to see that, sure enough, one of our female patients was sprawled out on the carpet. You must understand that this was not an altogether unusual occurrence for this particular patient, who would fairly commonly collapse into one form of heap or other, sometimes right in the middle of group therapy, which was a bizarre experience given that everyone had basically learned to ignore the whole thing and act like it wasn't happening.

Nevertheless, I got up to assist the patient and make sure she was OK, and as I did I could hear Biker Boy mumbling about how awful it had been that I hadn't see the patient fall, who did I think I was anyway, that I was an idiot who didn't know what I was doing and couldn't even understand an introductory psychology textbook.

I ignored the ravings as best I could, figuring they would pass. I would shortly find out how wrong I was. I also found out later, and which I did not know at the time, that Mr. Biker had a "thing" for the patient-in-a-heap, so he felt aggressively protective of her. Apparently my failing to see her fall, being slow to respond, breathing too loudly, or some such fault added up to a sin of mortal proportions in his eyes and a serious crime against his imaginary paramour.

But given that I knew none of that at the time, after being assured that the heap on the floor was in fact our patient, and was in fact OK, I turned my attention to the others in the room. They did not look good. They were agitated, upset, argumentative, and edgy. I was taking stock of the place when, just like that, one of them came at me. I managed to dodge the lunge and simultaneously let out a scream that I needed help. The patient came at me again and I grabbed hold and we rolled onto the floor with me attempting to get the upper hand in the ensuing struggle. Two staff members joined me and we wrestled with the patient while calls went out to the other units that we needed help and we needed it *now*.

Finally reinforced with five out-of-breath staff members from other units, we managed to drag the patient off toward a seclusion room before we remembered there was no room at the seclusion inn. We had already stuffed a patient into each confinement room. Trouble.

Now, making decisions while clinging to a squirming, writhing, screaming, psychotic psychiatric patient is not the easiest thing ever designed for a human being to do. Nevertheless, we had to reach some conclusion lest we spend the rest of our rapidly shortening lives sitting on top of this very vocal, very unhappy patient. We voted to release the least troublesome of the previous inhabitants of the seclusion rooms and to replace them with our current prey.

A decision of questionable quality, as it turned out. The other patient was as agitated as ever and whipped the other patients into an increasingly angry and aggressive frenzy just by walking around them. Everyone was already upset by all the commotion earlier in the shift, and the matter was helped not at all by the inflammatory behavior of our newly sprung patient.

The staff members involved in the situation were gathered, as was the usual custom, in the nurse's station to talk about the seclusion that had just occurred, when Biker Guy started yelling threats at the staff in general and at me in particular. Things were getting ugly.

His rants became the least of our worries, though, because at the very same moment the recently released patient went berserk. Screaming and yelling and cursing, she flung some unidentified object across the Day Room and stormed down the hall toward the recreation room. The other staff members and I looked at each other, they headed one way and I headed the other, and we emerged in the recreation room on either side of the patient. She took a swing at one of the other staff members and we jumped on her. More writhing mass. More decisions about what to do. Finally it was decided we would take her to another unit and seclude her there. That would get her completely off our unit and hopefully de-escalate things. It took all but two of us, a psychiatric nurse and myself, to handle the patient, so they left and we stayed.

I remember clearly, as if it were yesterday, what happened next. I was in the recreation room sitting on the pool table (remember—I was into sitting on tables in those days) while the nurse, who had by then become a good friend of mine (it was widely rumored that we were sleeping together, which we were not) was sitting in a chair close by. We were catching our breath and looking at each other with a traumatized "What on earth is going on here, what should we do next, and do you have any mood-altering substances if we ever make it through this shift" expression, when around the corner into the rec room charged Biker Dude, his demeanor having changed to End Game, Out of Control, Mass Murder Biker Dude. He stormed into his room— which opened onto the recreation room—and we heard the sound the staff most dreaded, the psychiatric equivalent of a pilot hearing a wing fall off the plane: he ripped the towel bar off the wall of his bathroom.

The very few times in the history of the hospital that things had gotten bad—really, really bad—patients had ripped towel bars off bathroom walls to use as weapons. They were generally effective as such, too, what with being metal and about the length and weight of a billy club. In past cases they had been wielded only against inanimate objects including glass shower doors and coffee tables that had apparently been sufficiently offensive as to deserve destruction, but from that time forward every staff member was acutely aware of their potential to cause real physical harm to real physical people. In the dark recesses of our minds we all harbored the knowledge that some day one of us might face the threat personally. We lived in unspoken terror of that day. Well, this looked to be the day. And I looked to be the one.

Without saying a word, the nurse and I both knew what was about to happen—this patient was going to attack—and try to kill— *me*. He seemed to focus his blame for everything that had gone wrong

44

that evening on me. Given that the staff from the other units were busy hauling our other patient to a seclusion room in another building, we were on our own.

The problem was that this patient was bigger than both of us combined. We shared a moment of existential paralysis during which we both experienced the unspeakable—this guy was big enough, mean enough, strong enough, and crazed enough that he just might succeed. (Some months later we did have several life-threatening injuries in similar situations, including a staff member being hit over the head with a pool cue, knocked unconscious, and put into the hospital for several weeks, and another being slugged in the eye by a patient, landing in the hospital, and having the patient's own psychiatrist suggest that the staff member file assault charges against the patient.)

I don't know exactly how to describe the sensation of realizing someone is about to try to kill you and has a better-than-slim chance of succeeding, but I can tell you it is nothing like what you'd think. It was neither panicky nor even particularly fearful. It was remarkably calm and slow, almost detached. I recall thinking, quite clear-headedly, "Oh, so this is what it's like to die," as I mused about my chances upon being confronted by the equivalent of King Kong wielding the top fifteen floors of the Empire State Building. Have no doubt—I did not feel good about my chances. While I had attained a fairly advanced belt rank in the martial arts and could probably have held my own against the guy in a street brawl, when I signed on with the hospital they made it *very* clear that I was to use *none* of "that stuff" with their patients at any time under any circumstance, lest I find myself in a *world* of hurt.

Even so, I felt little choice but to face the situation. I was one of just two staff members available, and I had to deal with it. There simply was no justification for running and no justifiable place to run to. It would be the equivalent of abandoning one's post in war time. So, feeling as though my emotions had been sucked out of my body, I sat where I was, contemplating the idea that I would be killed on this night, in this room, by that patient, with that towel bar, with the detachment and clinical interest of watching a documentary. It was one big "Hmm."

That existential moment, lasting probably three seconds while seeming like an hour, was broken when we heard the patient head toward the door of his room. For one brief instant, through the door-

45

way, the patient's face was visible and our eyes met. I felt a stark, chilling shudder at seeing in his expression a clear intention to annihilate me. It was an experience extraordinarily difficult to describe, well beyond horror, and innately contradictory—something akin to looking into a mirror and being able to see with your very own eyes that you have no head. A chill ran through me and I suddenly felt like I might throw up—which I don't imagine would have helped things much.

Then, in an occurrence that defies believability and that I would have scoffed at as being completely ridiculous had it been used as a turn of events in fiction, at that very same instant, out of nowhere, as if beamed in from the Starship Enterprise, around the corner into the rec room, right smack dab in front of the patient's room, walked our unit's recreational therapist. None of us knew she was on the unit, as it was virtually unheard of for her to be there in the evening, particularly this late. In fact, she had just stopped by to pick up something from her office after being out on a date, and she was completely unaware of the current goings-on.

The nurse sitting with me called out to the rec therapist in a loud, desperate whisper to close and lock the door to the patient's room. Looking bewildered, the rec therapist nevertheless complied, shutting his door and locking it with her key that was—conveniently and luckily—dangling from a cord around her wrist. Had she not been standing in precisely that location with her key in precisely that position of immediate access, the whole thing might have ended very differently and you just might be reading a Tom Clancy novel instead of this book.

As it was, just as the recreational therapist pulled her key out of his door (don't ask me why the doors locked from the outside) the knob turned as the patient tried to open the door from the inside. He couldn't.

There was a God.

And then it started: The War Against the Door. But like a successfully contained nuclear meltdown, it stayed inside the room. The patient proceeded to break every piece of furniture he could lift against that door, and because he was very strong just about every object in the room made it there. Chairs crashed, tables broke, lamps shattered, and footstools met their ignoble end as he struggled to batter it down in order to get to me. Lord help us, he even used the bed frame.

In yet another turn of good fortune, the doors on that unit turned out to be made of solid wood rather than being hollow. And in a display of the greatest love an inanimate object has ever shown a human being, despite the terrible onslaught it endured, that door held. It didn't budge an inch. As far as I'm concerned it saved my life.

The nurse, the rec therapist, and I cringed and winced at each ear-splitting crash against the inside of the door. For possibly the only time in the history of that hospital, staff members actually stood around with no intention of intervening in a patient's behavior even if it resulted in the patient's death. Truth be told, at that point we didn't much care what happened to him—we were far too involved in the issue of our own survival. At least I know I was.

I made a mental note to make a sizable donation to the Door Manufacturer's Benevolent Fund as we considered what to do next. The truth was that none of us knew. We had not been trained in handling so many things going so terribly wrong to such a terrible degree in such a short period of time. I felt overwhelmed and confused, and I think they did, too. As I recall we did a lot of staring at each other. There was, however, one thing of which I was very, *very* sure: hell would have to freeze over, crack into pieces, and be served in mixed drinks before I was going into that patient's room or being in *any* room with him for the foreseeable future.

We spent a long time considering options and checking on our other patients, who seemed remarkably calm now that things had gotten really serious, and the consensus of the staff—meaning one psychiatric nurse, one recreational therapist, and myself—was that the best thing to do was for me to get the hell out of there while the others, not targeted for assassination by Biker Boy, would stay around, pick up the pieces, and document what was by then the closest thing to a riot the place had ever experienced.

At that point it was about 3 AM. With my shift supposedly having ended at 11, in less than a heartbeat I gathered my belongings, my exhausted body and my battered psyche, and I fled that unit.

As I drove away from the hospital, alone in my car, I began to fall apart. Really. Seriously. I don't mind telling you that even describing it from a detached historical perspective, I was in *very* bad shape. I felt traumatized, disoriented, dizzy, and had no idea what to do with myself or even what appropriate behavior under the circumstances might be. I decided I could not tolerate being alone with the technicolor "what if" fantasies playing in my head, so I drove to a friend's house, banged desperately on her door, and when she answered collapsed into her arms in an incoherent mass, transforming into a sobbing, blubbering invertebrate right before her eyes.

Horrified by the specter of this limp, uninvited, and vaguely humanoid-like mess she found herself hanging onto, she dragged me into her apartment, into her kitchen, and began an infusion of peppermint tea and kindness. I struggled to explain what had happened and why my internal organs now resembled one amorphous, gelatinous mass.

Great will be the reward in heaven for my friend who, rudely awakened in the middle of the night by something resembling a large, sniveling jellyfish, was willing to spend nearly two hours soothing my psyche and patching me back together with empathy and understanding. She was wonderful, an angel from heaven. But just as I was coming to my senses and thinking I might be able to leave and take some semblance of emotional stability with me, I managed to garner one final humiliation: I noticed a strange parka hanging on the back of a dining room chair. A man's parka.

It was then that I realized that I had unceremoniously barged in on her when her new boyfriend (and future husband) was over, spending one of their first nights together. Feeling a rush of embarrassment and guilt about everything from my out-of-control crying and terrible timing to the hole in the ozone layer, I dissolved one final time, apologized profusely for my intrusion and in the face of her repeated kind reassurances that it was really OK, and sniffled off to my attic apartment to huddle alone in the dark and wish for everything and everyone to simply go away.

Life is often not so cooperative, however, and as luck would have it I was scheduled to work at the hospital the very next day. I remember lying in bed wondering how I could possibly do it and, if I could, how I should behave.

At this point I must tell you that the answer to that question is that I have no idea. You may have heard of a phenomenon called "repressed memories" where traumas are supposedly forgotten, deeply buried in the psyche, and are only dragged out through hypnosis, past-life regression, or some other dramatic tool that manages to conjure up "forgotten" tales of satanic ritual abuse and assorted ghastly tortures. I can tell you right now that I am a died-in-the-wool skeptic about such things as repressed memories of satanic ritual abuse, past-life regression or any of that other stuff. But I can personally attest to the reality of a superficially similar phenomenon that is well-documented in valid studies. Often called "anteriograde amnesia," it is, believe me, as real as a mosquito in a swamp looking for a vein to snack on.

Anteriograde amnesia is a phenomenon whereby one's memory is impaired by a trauma in a manner that results in an inability to code the events *after* the trauma into long-term memory. The trauma itself remains clear (even at times to the extent of producing the vivid, terrifying flashbacks that are part of another very real phenomenon called Post Traumatic Stress Disorder), but what happened immediately afterward is lost, probably due to the somewhat scrambled condition of one's cognitions at that time.

Even now, many years after that night at the hospital, and despite my doggedly reliable, steel-trap, photographic memory (the accuracy of which has gotten me into trouble more than once) I have absolutely no recollection of what happened as a result of that night or how my work at the hospital went for several weeks afterwards. After my night of lying in bed wondering how to behave when I returned to work, I have no recollection of what happened at the place for several weeks. Did we talk about it as a staff? Did we try to put it behind us by ignoring it? Did we process it with the patient? Without the patient? Did the administration talk to me about it? Was the patient confined? Reprimanded? Transferred?

I have no idea. I know I went back, (Remember that resolve about doing anything it took to get into grad school? Intact.) but I can't tell you one single thing about how it was all handled or what happened as a result. It simply never made it into my long-term memory, and for all practical purposes it isn't there. So I can tell you nothing about the resolution of the situation other than I managed to survive it. That will have to be enough.

GETTING IN: ROUND II

Although I can't tell you what happened after the riot at the psychiatric hospital, what I can tell you is that shortly thereafter I started receiving responses from my second round of grad school applications. While I had been working at the hospital I had been reapplying to graduate school, and this time, I can assure you, I moved heaven and earth in an attempt to make no assumptions and leave nothing to chance to ensure I'd get in.

Where the first time I had applied only to the top six or so clinical psychology graduate programs, this time I applied to no fewer than 22 programs, ranging from the best to the strangest. I figured my task was to get in and I'd worry about where I ended up later. I applied to clinical psychology doctoral programs, general psychology masters' programs, social psychology doctoral programs, and a few hybrid programs that fit no precise description. I was shooting for at least going somewhere for something close to what I wanted and worrying later about how to get exactly where I wanted to be.

I drove the faculty who agreed to provide recommendations for me insane by delivering gigantic piles of forms for them to fill out for my applications. They spent hours completing recommendation forms and writing letters to programs from sea to shining sea saying that they really, really, thought the program should take me (probably so they'd never have to write me another recommendation letter). One professor told me he had "never gotten so sick of checking boxes and filling in blanks" in his entire life. But he did it and was congenial about it, so I was appreciative and told him so. (Bizarrely, two of the three faculty members who wrote my letters of recommendation died within a year of my starting grad school—one in a car wreck and the other by suicide. Stranger still, although it happened in an entirely remote part of the state, my girlfriend-at-the-time's sister was the nurse who tried to save the life of the one who died in the car wreck. Heart breakingly sad, and just too weird.)

In sum, I spent several hundred hours completing the applications and several thousand dollars in application fees.

And I was much more intelligent in my approach. For example, as part of their application process, most programs required essays and statements about career goals and the like. In my first round of applications, apparently suffering from the delusion that graduate programs cared about what *I* wanted, I told the truth that I wanted to go into practice. In this round I wised up and understood that they didn't care about what *I* wanted, they cared about what *they* wanted. So I took each application, studied the program's faculty and course structure, figured out what they probably wanted to hear, and wrote essays and career goals consistent with that. If a program seemed to emphasize clinical work, I talked about my love of clinical work. If a program liked research, I inundated them with pleas to let me do more research than any human being in recorded history. A couple of programs had religious bents, and to them I trotted out my college religion classes and the joy that made my soul glad when I could combine the spiritual and the psychological. I wrote and rewrote my essays until they were impeccable in grammar, tone, style, and content. I had psychologists at the Child Behavior and Research Center review, edit, and critique each and every one until they were perfect.

In short, these weren't applications, they were market-researched advertising campaigns. They were painted like a Picasso, carefully designed to look casual and natural, yet perfect. They contained scripted ad-libs and practiced nonchalance, a full-fledged, full-court press in any and all ways that were possible to portray on paper that I was not just the perfect candidate, I was the perfect candidate for *them*.

If you think this was disingenuous or manipulative, let me be clear—I learned shortly after I started graduate school that this was the way the game was played, that virtually no one got in unless they figured out how to do this—I was just a slow learner. I think in some perverse way it is actually appropriate to the profession, given that having the savvy to talk to programs in the way that gets them to listen probably translates reasonably well into having the savvy to talk to patients in a way that gets them to listen.

But never mind all that, because once I started getting replies it was deja vu all over again. Rejection letters, smarmy and sleazy, slithered into my mailbox and slimed my magazines, telephone bill, and weary psyche. I still have one of them that now, twenty-seven years later, I keep as kind of a pet—"My Favorite Rejection Letter," I call it. It is a full-page letter from a fairly good program (the program from which one of my future professors had graduated some years prior, in fact) brimming with enthusiasm, empathy, and optimism while essentially saying "Please proceed directly to hell." It finished rejecting me with the sentence "And we still believe that a psychologist is a good thing to be."

What? First off, I cared less about what *they* believed about being a psychologist than I cared about peasant farmers in the middle ages. *I* considered a psychologist a good thing to be, and that's all that mattered to me. Second, that's one hell of a thing to say to someone who you've just informed you are not going to help become one. I think out of all of the blood-sucking rejection letters I got, that was the only one that offered some comic relief. I figured the letter's irony was either unintentional or unfathomably cruel, so I gave them the benefit of the doubt and had a good laugh. (The very worst rejection letter I got was from a school with a religious bent that, shortly after rebuffing me, began sending me letters soliciting financial donations. I fired off a *very* nasty letter decrying their shamelessness and demanding removal from their mailing list, which happened—until I got another solicitation letter from them about a year later. In a blind rage I wrote a hysterical, ranting, and certified-delivery letter threatening all manner of legal murder and mayhem if they didn't take me off their goddam list *again* and *forever*. Sufficiently chastened, I must say that they wrote me perhaps the most apologetic letter I have ever received, confirming that they were indeed incompetent dog poop for somehow getting me back on their mailing list, and promising that I'd never hear from them again. I didn't.)

In the midst of this new storm of rejection I did get one mildly hopeful letter. I received a short note from a mid-quality clinical psychology doctoral program indicating that I was on their list of alternates, so I should hang on until they saw how their "real"choices responded.

Hang on? Honey, they didn't know the meaning of "hang on." If the last appendage left on my body was a nostril hair, I could hang on. Oh, I hung on all right. And I got a followup letter a week or so later that said I should start the rinse cycle, I had been washed out. So much for mild hope.

I also did get some other positive responses which made me feel better, but not as much better as you might imagine. Because they were all from my "backup" programs that were compromises to my real goal and were programs I had applied to in case I didn't get into a doctoral clinical psychology program, none of them were wonderful. Some weren't even very nice. For example, I got a telephone call from a social psychology doctoral program on the east coast that said they wanted me. They even wanted me pretty badly. As fate would have it they called when I was working a shift at the hospital, they got me when I was extremely busy with patients in the occupational therapy unit, and they demanded that I give them an answer to their offer this-very-instant-no-questions-asked-why-would-you-have-any-reason-to-hesitate-and-do-you-really-think-anyone-else-will-have-you?

Stuttering and stammering, alternating between the joy of knowing I could at least go to grad school *somewhere* in *something* and reluctance to accept a social psychology position before hearing from all of my clinical programs, I begged for 24 hours to think about it. After a good deal of guilt-inducing hemming and hawing they finally decided that they could be oh-so-gracious and grant me permission for what they clearly considered to be a meaningless exercise of thinking it over, given their full certainty that by the next day I would have seen the error of my ways, come to my senses, say how wonderful it was they wanted me, and offer to self-immolate in gratitude.

Instead, the next day I got a most puzzling letter, and I mean "puzzling" in the best possible sense—it was *not* a letter of rejection. Instead, it was a very short note from that same mid-range clinical program that had made me an alternate and then flushed me down the toilet, to say that the rejection letter had been a mistake, to disregard it, that they were keeping me on their list. I still remember the last line: "You will be hearing from us again."

OK, now that was *real* news. For the first time in recorded history a real, honest-to-goodness clinical psychology doctoral program, approved by The American Psychological Association, located on a college campus with Ph.D.'s and students and classes and textbooks and everything, said they actually *wanted* to talk to me, that I was not a totally worthless piece of slime. Or at least I was a totally worthless piece of slime they might want to take the time to reject *on the phone*. Wow. My breathing quickened and my pulse raced for the next twenty-four hours. And in a fit of dramatic risk-taking, the next morning I turned down the social psychology program, who sounded genuinely shocked and made it abundantly clear that they were *far* less than pleased with me.

And then it happened. The unthinkable, the unimaginable. I arrived home from work at the hospital the following day and my girlfriend, who also worked at the hospital and who had begun living at my apartment in order for us to save on our bills and investigate the post-mortem consequences of that sinful state called "cohabitation," said that I'd gotten a phone call from "some guy at some university." She was vague and uncertain about the message. In truth she seemed strangely detached from the whole matter, and quite frankly didn't make much sense in telling me about it, which initially seemed bizarre given that she knew what I was going through and the stakes involved. I was nevertheless able to discern from her ramblings the possibility that this could be news I might care about. Resisting my urge to throw up from anticipation or resurrect medieval torture methods to get the information out of her, I followed her around the apartment, pursuing the issue long enough to find out that the call had been from a professor at the very university that had thought I was at least one step above being a leper who was too dangerous to talk to.

She decided she needed to search for where she'd written the phone number. I considered this a good idea, although I struggled with urges to kill her for the anxious state she had put me in and her tardy nonchalance in getting me the whole story. While time slowed to a halt and I watched my fingernails grow long, she looked around the place and finally located the scrap of paper containing the number. The note included the man's name and phone numbers at his office and at home. It was late. I dashed to the phone. I called him at home. I could hardly speak.

A man answered the phone. I identified myself and said that I was returning a call from a professor who had called me earlier. The man responded that he was that person, he was the head of the clinical psychology doctoral program, and he chuckled that I sure called him back quickly.

Quickly? Quickly? Quickly by the standards of a giant redwood, maybe. It had taken me nearly two years to get where I was, to be able to have one conversation with one clinical psychology program that was doing something besides laughing in my face and telling me what a good profession psychology was and what a crying shame it was that I was never going to be a part of it. This was not "quickly," psycho-boy. The guy behind you honking at you after the light turns green? That's quickly. This was long. Long struggle, long pain, long suffering. He had not a clue.

And then he said it. He actually *said* it. No torturous build-up, no explanation of why they had reached the decision that no one else could tolerate. He said they had an opening and wanted to offer it to me. To *me*—the leper of psychology, the Ebola virus of applicants, higher education's largest single recipient of frequent-rejection miles. He *said* it. I felt disembodied, depersonalized, as if watching myself watch myself watch myself. He asked if I would like to think about it. I said: "Sure. I accept." He laughed again and said that I certainly didn't waste any time. At that point I tried to say something light and pleasant, something other than "I want to have your baby," because how could he know what I had gone through, what it had taken for me to get him, someone, anyone, to say that sentence to me? He could not know. I wasn't sure God could know. He said they would send a followup letter, and, just like that—the conversation ended and nearly two years of struggle was over. Simply over.

I hung up the phone and, unable to speak, feared I might wet my pants. I didn't really care if I did, as I felt as though I had died and gone to a heaven I had dreamed of yet never really believed existed. For all my struggle to get into a program, once I had been told I'd been accepted I could not for the life of me fathom that it had really happened. I vacillated between fear they would claim it was a mistake ("But you can't take it back, you can't take it back!" I practiced saying in my head over and over, compulsively reviewing my worst-case scenario.) and feeling that I had accomplished the impossible, achieved the unimaginable, and need fear nothing but Kryptonite. God help me, it looked like I really and truly was going to have the opportunity to become a psychologist.

And then, in yet another perverse example of history repeating itself, when I shared my news with others I felt like I would have done just as well to have checked myself directly into the gas chamber. My girlfriend's frontal lobes went south and appeared to have been scrambled and deep-fat fried with onions and peppers at the realization that what I had told her she needed to know about me at the beginning of our relationship was actually true—I was going to go to graduate school no matter what the cost, even if it meant leaving town, leaving friends, and even leaving her. I had seen in her eyes that she had proceeded into our relationship with the secret, smug conclusion that I was either full of hot air or was sufficiently stupid to realize that I would never, *ever* be able to get into a clinical psychology program, and as a result would be staying with her for the foreseeable future. Apparently she figured she had nothing to worry about.

She was wrong. The realization that I had been telling the truth all along and had indeed done what it took to get in and was in fact going to leave her and everything else hit her like the pavement against a motorcyclist's head in a high-speed lay-down. In the most honest-to-goodness behavioral replica of a closed-head injury I have ever seen, after getting the news I had been accepted into school she never seemed quite the same. But she did manage to express her feelings about the whole matter after a fashion. She began systematically, and "accidentally," destroying my belongings, including my prized, custom, expensive stereo speakers. She topped off the tank of her apparently very deep reservoir of anger by initiating a torrid affair with the man who had been my favorite supervisor at the hospital. I don't know if she ever realized that *I got the message already* that she thought I was a creep, but I can still vividly recall several of my more serious crying jags over the whole affair thing. And the guy was *married*, too, which I'm sure ended up doing wonders for *his* relationship. All in all one of the more painful episodes in my personal life.

My coworkers at the hospital, most of whom were also applying to graduate school and were also getting rejected from program after program, managed to be a bit more polite to my face and to urp up a few acidic and smelly, but nevertheless reasonable facsimiles, of congratulations when I told them I'd gotten in. But by the look in their eyes I knew that I should never again walk down a dark alley without first looking over my shoulder.

And my parents? Well, my parents took on the demeanor of people who had learned that the game was over and the sun was going to super-nova after all, so they might as well relax because their long episode of worry and anxious hope was finally finished. The end was at hand, there was no need for struggle, and they were free to relax, say their goodbyes, and sit down with a stiff drink in front of their favorite TV show to wait out the tragic, and no longer avoidable, catastrophe: their son was going to run off and become a psychologist. I have a fantasy that they reminded each other it was best to focus on the good memories.

PART III
BEHAVIORAL
CONTINGENCIES

STARTING GRADUATE SCHOOL

So off to graduate school I went.

Now, it is said that above the gates of hell lies the inscription "Abandon All Hope, Ye Who Enter Here." Clearly Dante, fun little drug-abusing, nightmare-ridden fellow though he may have been, never attended graduate school. If he had, the sign would have read "Hey—It Could Be Worse," because graduate school was. My graduate program picked the term "dysfunctional" out of the gutter of common vernacular, took it home, fattened it up, and bred it to a level of elegance and sophistication never before seen by mortal Man. From professors who did their dead-level best to come across as raving lunatics (one professor said—and I swear this is the God's honest truth—that he "used to be a 100% son-of-a-bitch," but now was "about a 50% son-of-a-bitch, and that was about right") to students who were academically brilliant but whose mental dogs—so to speak— were not all barking, the place was 500 pounds per square inch of human oddity.

Further, my program had a second-class paranoia that wouldn't quit. Excruciatingly aware that they were not shepherding a big-name, big-research-money doctoral program, the faculty compensated by wildly overdoing everything at all times. Students were required to carry course loads that were far higher than required by the rest of the university—probably the rest of the universe. The workload required just for classes went so far beyond daunting that it lapsed into paralyzing. It was not uncommon that just in order to keep up you would feel that you needed to read something on the order of four textbooks a *day*. Then, of course, you had term papers (and there were no computer searches in those days—all research was done by hand, in the stacks of the library, carrying bound journals around), midterms and finals, not to mention whatever other various projects a professor might feel like assigning along the way.

And that was just the *beginning*. In order to graduate, four, four-hour long exams were required, in addition to everything else, on topic areas that may—or may not—have been covered by courses. Students were required to carry a clinical caseload of patients, to write and complete a formal research project, to pass 12 *additional* hours of written exams that covered everything that was—or wasn't—covered in their program of study, to have two faculty test them on their treatment of a patient, and to have another two test them on a full diagnostic work-up of a patient.

All that was bad enough, of course, but the really fun part was the rule that if you failed any portion of any of the above mentioned exams twice, you were out. Just like that. You did not pass go, you did not collect a Ph.D., you did not become a psychologist—even if you were a straight "A" student. It didn't matter. OK, kids, can you say "terrified of flunking out 24 hours a day, seven days a week?" I knew you could.

But the very worst part, the thing that kept us all on 24-hour suicide watch, was a dark, ever-present, ominous presence lurking in the storm clouds on the horizon called a "dissertation."

A dissertation is a research project that is the last step in obtaining a Ph.D. It is supposed to be a "major" piece of research that will produce a "major" contribution to your field of study. In truth, it is a "major" pain in the ass. In a convoluted, torturous process, you "invited" faculty to join a committee that would oversee your work. Then, after doing the academic equivalent of cutting the switch that would be used on your own intellectual backside, you cooked up a research project, wrote an extensive and formal proposal that you revised and re-revised at the whim of your committee, and presented it to them so they could tell you what a bad job you did on it and how you'd better revise it some more if you didn't want them to laugh you out of school. Finally, after you rewrote the project so many times you wanted to vomit when you entered a room where the document was or when someone spoke a sentence with a word from your proposal in it, they graced you with their oh-so-generous permission to proceed. You then had to perform the study, analyze the data (while analyzing my study I once stood, feeding computer cards into a computer terminal for—no exaggeration—8 straight hours), write the whole thing up in book form (mine was 165 pages long and it was just average in length) and then attempt to prove to the very same faculty who gave you permission to do the study that your results were sufficiently valid and worthwhile as to justify their giving you that damn Ph.D. This was done in something called a dissertation "defense" meeting.

Do understand that in this context the term "defense" is a bit misleading in the same way that a bullfight is mislabeled by being called a "fight." "Slaughter" is not quite right either, but lacking an unabridged Oxford dictionary to find a better word, it will have to do. Given that this was the faculty's last chance to use you for target practice before you could slink out of range of their ability to hold the rest of your life over your head, they considered dissertation defense meetings a type of sport. Committee members often vied to see who could dissolve the candidate into tears, trigger a panic attack, make them soil their pants, renounce their citizenship, question their gender, or doubt their bloodline. A week before my dissertation defense a member of my committee told me—in private, of course—that were I to fail to provide him with chocolate donuts during the meeting that I should begin practicing for my new career by repeating "Paper or plastic?" (I am absolutely not making this up. I mean, ask yourself—*could* I make that up?) During the actual meeting, a faculty member blamed the lack of positive results in one section of my study on—I am not making this up, either—a popular 1960's television show. That's right, a TV show. (More about that later.) At another point I tried to answer a question from one of my committee members and another member basically told me to "shut the fuck up" so that he could argue with the other committee members about the question.

And compared to many others, my defense meeting was downright *civilized*.

The whole dissertation thing was such a fearsome proposition that students commonly avoided doing it, sometimes for years after they had finished everything else. I think the record in my department for failing to complete a dissertation was 12 years. I would not be surprised to hear that there are still classmates of mine who have not completed their dissertation some twenty-five years later. If so, I completely understand. In the process of writing mine I completely destroyed a typewriter—essentially wore it out—and had to borrow one from someone else to finish the document. (More on that later, too.)

The result of all this was that we all felt perpetually and precariously balanced on the precipice of flunking out at every waking moment of every day. Our normal, accepted emotional state was terror. Somewhat disgusted by this, toward the end of my first year in school I complained to one of my professors about the chronic state of terror the program induced. He chuckled and said "If you just stay that way for four years, you'll probably graduate." Real nice.

Oh, yeah—one more thing. All of this excess resulted in our receiving the finest and most thorough training imaginable, unmatched by any other clinical psychology program I have ever seen. We got trained like hell.

But I get ahead of myself. Let's start with the beginning.

GRADUATE SCHOOL, PART I: THE TOWN

I am somewhat torn about what to call the populated area inhabited by the university with my graduate program in it. It was not quite large enough to be called a "city," but it was somewhat too large to call a "college town." It was sufficiently rural to be called "the country," but because it contained the most significant population density for a six-hour drive in any direction it was "the big city" as far as the immediate region was concerned. Given its contrasts, we'll just settle for what we graduate students tended to call it: *There.* (As in "Oh, I see—you're in graduate school. *There.*") What did we mean by "*There?*" We meant a place that had certain, shall we say, quirks.

First, there was the landscape—or, when described in common terms, "nothing." This was the plains, mind you, so the most notable geographic feature was the fire ant mounds that dotted the place. Otherwise, it was flat. Really, really flat. And it was extremely dry country, so for all practical purposes there appeared to be no indigenous vegetation. Well, that's not really true. The Sand Spur, I determined, was indeed native to the area, which you would find out quickly if you demonstrated sufficiently poor judgment as to walk outside in socks or try to ride a bicycle.

I found this one out the hard way. Before I moved to graduate school I had been *very* into bicycling, and I owned what at the time was a really cool, lightweight, high-tech, expensive racing bicycle that when not in use I proudly hung on my wall like Jerry's apartment in "Seinfeld." The problem was that it had tires where the tubes were actually sewn inside the outer layer of rubber. Called, for obvious reasons, "sew-ups," you could inflate those puppies to pressures approaching those at the bottom of the Marianas Trench. This minimized contact with the ground and made for some fast cycling. It also made fixing a flat a *huge* ordeal. It required a tedious and laborious process of finding the leak, tearing off nylon protective tape, cutting the stitches, pulling out the tube, repairing the hole, stuffing the tube back in, sewing the thing back up (while being careful not to put the needle through the tube so you didn't have to immediately repeat the whole process), and gluing the nylon tape back on. A task not undertaken lightly. And the tires were not, by any measure, cheap, so replacing them when you had a flat was not an appealing option.

Well, after my first ride in town where I picked up so many sand spurs that I appeared to possess the world's first and only *studded* bicycle tires, I spent the long walk home—carrying my bike on my shoulder—calculating that at this rate the time required to repair my tires would consume essentially my entire waking life, and the cost of replacing them would require me to set up my own Columbian drug cartel. And so, my beloved bicycle basically hung on my wall until I left for internship.

Second, there was the climate. Because the place was located on many hundreds of miles of completely flat plains, there was nothing and no one to stop the weather, no matter what it might be. So there was wind. Big wind. Violent wind. "Oh my God" wind. Many times, in a panic, I would struggle to rescue my car door after opening it and having the enormous wind grab it and, like some invisible giant, angry with all manner of modern transportation, try to wrest it from its hinges. And God help you if you were unlucky enough to find yourself in the path of one of the giant, razor-like tumbleweeds that the wind would regularly blast down streets at a hundred million miles an hour. You were finished. As was the paint job on your car.

And there was rain. Virtually without warning the skies would open and unleash a torrent of water not seen since the audience's eyes during the death scene in "Camille." Down it would come not just in buckets, but in double-hulled oil tankers, flooding the completely inadequate storm drains, mowing down shrubs, covering small children, carrying away farm animals, and creeping its way up to—or occasionally into—your front door.

And there was heat. During the summer the place baked like the surface of the sun, but with less shade. My last summer *There* I simply gave up on sane methods for staying cool and spent nearly every afternoon at the university pool—a new and very nice facility, I might add. I got a wonderful tan, which the faculty viewed as conclusive evidence of my arrogant sloth, and was able to soak in the water as often as need be to prevent heat stroke or my face melting like the Nazis in the final scene of "Raiders of the Lost Ark."

And there was cold. As hot as the summers may have been, the winters were positively brutal. Combine freezing temperatures with the strong, unrelenting winds, and by comparison the dark side of the moon looked positively habitable.

Which meant there was snow. The year I moved *There* to go to graduate school, the place had more snow than the northern city I had moved from. I personally thought the town looked better covered in snow, but given that it was not a northern town and was in all ways inadequate to handle such things, during and after snowfalls movement of any sort became exceptionally treacherous. One day, after a substantial snowfall, I was walking from my duplex to a nearby grocery store. A car sped by, hit the pool of snow and slush backed up in one of the (previously mentioned) inadequate storm drains, and covered me—head to toe, just like you'd see in some comedy sketch—in water, ice, and snow. After being showered, and again just like in that comedy sketch, I stood stock-still and deadpan, staring straight ahead, completely drenched, with ice sliding off my nose and water and snow making their way down all parts of my body. To their credit, the people in the car slowed down, and when I got close to them as I resumed walking, expressed their embarrassed regret. I nodded forgiveness and shuffled along the sidewalk, dripping ice and spewing snow from my hands and feet like the Abominable Snowman.

But mostly, there was dust. God, was there dust. That, in fact, is what the place was most known for—dust. When the wind would blow (always) and the ground was dry (almost always), the dirt would swirl, rise, and cloud the air like an honest-to-goodness blizzard. Not infrequently it would become so thick that visibility was reduced to half a block, the sun would glow like a pale round disk at which you could safely and directly stare, and people walked around with wet bandanas and handkerchiefs tied around their face lest they ingest a goodly portion of the landscape. And most unbelievable of all, rain never helped—in fact, the rainy season and the dust season *were at the same time.* One day it would rain like the final flood, and the very next day the dust would be so thick you'd be unable to see your hands. It was *bizarre.*

Staying inside didn't help, either. Like The Blob, the dust could find its way into, and onto, virtually anything anywhere. It was not uncommon, after an especially robust dust storm, for me to be able to write my name—with my finger—on my stove top. Cars fared no better. When some years later I sold the car I drove during graduate school, the AC still puffed dust every time you first turned it on.

Third, there was the housing. Now, I lived in a fairly decent, admittedly very inexpensive, duplex for my entire time in graduate school. But it sported a few oddities of its own. Such as the driveway.

My driveway, such as it was, was not paved. It was dirt. It wound around several buildings in my little complex of duplexes until it got to me, and by the time it did it had accomplished several rather astonishing feats, including wading into and out of potholes that looked for all the world like precursors of a Black Hole, and traversing grassy knolls so treacherous that they may *still* contain the second Kennedy shooter.

All seasons held intrigue when it came to braving my driveway. In the hot and dry summer—which was most of the year—driving on it stirred up so much dust that had you left your windows down or the AC on in your car, your lungs ended up looking like something for which the CDC has yet to invent a name. This meant that no matter how hot it was, once you turned into my driveway you rolled up your windows and turned off the AC. It didn't matter if by the time you got to my house your car had been formally christened a Native American Sweat Lodge, the laws of survival dictated that first and foremost you avoid breathing that air.

In the rainy season it was even more fun. Remember, we did not have ordinary rainstorms *There*, we had apocalyptic deluges. So in no time flat, rain would turn my driveway into the single most dangerous body of water in the Continental United States. And never mind just trying to drive it without showing up on the news as swept away never to be heard from again—if you actually *made* it to my house, getting from your car to my back door required a raft, a lifeboat, and a team of Navy SEALS. And forget your shoes—you'd be throwing those damn things away. If first they didn't rot off your feet.

Then, of course, there was the building itself. A wood frame structure covered in siding, the architects and contractors who constructed my duplex had left out one tiny detail, commonly called "shelter from the elements." The place leaked like a sieve. Only it didn't leak in the normal way, with water coming through the roof. Oh, no. It leaked *sideways*, through the walls. So although I avoided being pelted with water during the flood season, I was regularly blasted with whatever environmental elements were currently carried on the winds. That meant dust during dust season, heat during summer, and cold during winter. And the heating and cooling system in the place might have just as well not existed for the little good it did.

The summers weren't too bad. I generally handled them by spending the hottest part of most days in the air conditioned library or psychology department. (Of course, this didn't always work—one night I called "time and temperature," and at exactly 11:45 PM it was 96 degrees outside.) It was the winters that wreaked havoc on me because the night, when I was usually at home, was the coldest part of the day.

It was during this time that I developed a specific algorithm for heating the human body to the precise level that allows for comfortable sleep during life-threatening cold. I would get so chilled just sitting in my house that out of desperation I took to soaking in hot baths to get warm. I discovered that if I soaked until I began sweating (down my forehead, to one side of my eyebrow, in front of my ear) I would have raised my core body temperature sufficiently to allow comfy and cozy sleeping for most of the night. This procedure required between 30 and 35 minutes of soaking, with reheating the water an average of twice. Of course, there could be some variation in both soak time and number of reheats, depending on the severity of the cold and the wind on any particular night. I will include a graph in the next edition of the book.

Speaking of baths, the plumbing in my place was not a paragon of sophisticated modernity, either. One day my toilet plugged unmercifully and I called the manager to have someone attend to it. Out they came. They concluded that a tree in the back yard had grown roots into my sewer and that it was, indeed, a problem. So they dug a hole beside my back door, pried open the sewer line, and fed in an electric rooter to try to ream out the offending roots. No go. The rooter kept blowing the circuit breakers in my duplex. The workman said he would have to come back with some other way to do the job and that I could continue to use my plumbing in the interim.

So I did. Almost a month went by. I noticed that not only had no one returned to work on my plumbing, but the hole dug by the original workman was now overflowing with, well, stuff that quite frankly didn't look like it should be there. So I called the management again, told them of my predicament, and they immediately sent someone out who knocked on my back door and said "Do you realize that you have an open sewer in your back yard?" Uh, *yeah*. That time, probably spurred by fears of disease, pestilence, and having the place condemned as a menace to public health, they found a way to fix it.

Fourth, there was the wildlife. Comprised almost exclusively of creatures possessing an exoskeleton with multiple body sections sprouting various creepy appendages protruding, hanging off, and trailing behind, the place virtually vibrated with scurrying entities at all hours of the day and night. One night I got out of bed and padded out to the kitchen to get a glass of water. Halfway there I felt a crunch beneath my right heel followed by a distinct sensation of "ooze." I hobbled to the corner, turned on a light, and found myself face-to-face with six of the biggest, meanest, baddest looking cockroaches you can imagine. These were not bugs, they were small birds. They were hang-gliders. I looked at them, they looked at me, they looked at their fallen comrade—now a white gooey mess beneath my heel—and casually turned away and sauntered off, as if to say "We do *not* want to talk to *you*," and disappeared into the walls, floor, and ceiling of my house. Repulsed beyond words, after spending a sleepless night I drove straight to the hardware store, bought a gigantic can of bug spray, stuck in a nozzle, and pumped so much poison into the corners and crevices of my house that the site probably still produces serious birth defects.

Outside was no better, because there lurked the fire ants. In case you are unfamiliar with fire ants, let me describe them. They are called "fire" ants because their bite feels like fire—like someone touching a lit match to your skin. That's all you need to know. They are very, very nasty little creatures, highly defensive of their mounds, and jealous guardians of their territory. And they had attitude—they were there first, and they knew it. Given that their territory was essentially every square inch of unpaved ground, trying to stay the hell away from them took some fancy footwork. They were intimidated not at all by your size, speed, or IQ, so there was nothing to do but watch every step you took so as not to annoy the little critters and find yourself screaming like a banshee as they chased you around and lit you up like a Roman Candle.

Fifth, there was the smell. That's right, the smell. One day I caught the distinct scent of decaying flesh inside my house. Searching for something to explain the stench, such as an overlooked German Shepherd carcass rotting in the middle of the back bedroom, I could find nothing to explain the foul odor. I walked outside to clear my nostrils so I could take another run at finding the source, and was knocked over by an overwhelming, pungent stink. The smell was coming from *outside*. I jumped back into my house to try to make it go away.

After inquiring about what in the world such a smell might be, I was informed by those who knew of such things that the stockyards lay southeast of town. When the wind was just right—about a quarter of the time—the whole town took on the scent of a giant cow chip factory. That was on fire. Being put out by being smothered with horse manure. *Old* horse manure. It was *amazing*.

Finally, there was the culture. I have no earthly idea how to describe the culture, so let me share just a couple of things I found notable.

First, there were the "Blue Laws." So called because they were originally written on blue paper, Blue Laws outlawed the selling of certain products on Sunday. The problem was that the laws were originally written in a very different era—like the week before the Mayflower landed—so their prohibitions no longer made any sense. You might, for example, be able to buy a barbeque grill on Sunday—but not charcoal. Or maybe you could buy a garden hose—but not a nozzle.

Further, the local government acted as though the fate of Western civilization rested solely on businesses' adherence to the Blue Laws. With such vehemence were they enforced that stores were positively phobic about running afoul of them. The result was that places like grocery stores, hardware stores, and discount stores organized their shelves not by category, but by which products they could and could not sell on Sunday. This meant, for example, that cans of paint might be in one place, and paint brushes completely across the store altogether, right next to the baby food. This would allow stores to stretch yellow plastic tape across both ends of the aisles containing the forbidden products in order to prevent the sale of these items on Sundays and risk bringing about the end of the world.

Which meant that when you shopped on a Sunday you'd better watch where you were going. If you were unfamiliar with a store and were distracted by talking to someone, you could easily turn a corner down a new aisle and, like a fly caught in a spider's web, find yourself dangling in a criss-cross of yellow tape that you then found yourself using to pull down shelving on both sides of an aisle as you struggled to extricate yourself. As if the embarrassment weren't enough, it was also potentially painful if you managed to wrap some of the tape around your head and hair and had to rip it forcibly from your body, taking large chunks of your goldilocks out with it.

Then there was the local news. Now *there* was some entertaining television. One weatherman would regularly appear at his weather map clad in all sorts of strange hats and getups. Weird enough. But one day he did the entire weather cast while holding a leash attached to the collar of a chimpanzee that was sitting on a stool by his side. He didn't comment on the monkey, mind you, it was just *there*. And, of course, there was the show when, right in the middle of his weather report he yanked out a fly swatter, and with all his might smacked something in the middle of the weather map and shrieked "Ha! Gotcha!"

But that was nothing compared to the screw-ups. The weekend broadcasts were the best, as they seemed to be run by an inexperienced, part-time technical staff that had just recently learned to feed themselves. I was watching a broadcast one Sunday night where there had already been multiple errors involving switching to the wrong camera or cutting to the active newscaster late, after they had already been talking for several seconds. At one point a newscaster began talking and the camera switched to them—but to their neck, not their head. So as they talked you had the distinct pleasure of watching their Adam's Apple bob around. The camera never did make it to their face. To make matters worse, when their co-anchor started talking, the camera shot suddenly switched all right—to a view of the weather instruments. Over the next several minutes, with the news anchor talking merrily away about some unrelated story, the camera slowly and aimlessly drifted up the row of weather instruments. It was hilarious.

But how weird was the local news *really*? This weird—*I* showed up on it one night. For real.

During my time in graduate school, the original "Alien" movie was released. Directed by (Sir) Ridley Scott, that movie was the one that established his place in history as a singularly talented and gifted director, one capable of making audiences feel as though they had been directly transported to Planet Hell with a significant likelihood of never coming back. (If you don't believe me, go see "Black Hawk Down" and talk to me again.) Well, "Alien" was new, different, and—for the time—an *amazingly* guttural, gory, and scary sci-fi movie. It was rumored that following the preview in Dallas they'd had to cut fifteen minutes because of scenes that were so intense the audience just couldn't take it.

Well, one Friday afternoon, with nothing better to do than try to keep up with a workload that was choking us to death both individually and as a group, a bunch of us clinical students decided to throw caution to the wind, make our lives significantly more miserable by putting off our work until we could feel our eyes pop from panic over trying to get everything done, and go see what all the hubub was all about with this new, "unique," sci-fi horror movie. So off we went.

Entirely living up to its reputation, we gasped our way through the thing and stared at each other, traumatized and wide-eyed, as the lights came up. As we rose and tottered unsteadily toward the exit, we noticed that there was a very bright light coming through the door. Strange. When we got there we discovered that the local news, apparently also with nothing better to do, was interviewing people about what they thought about the movie as they came out.

Being surprised, blinded, and disoriented by the bright lights as I emerged, I ran straight into a local news anchor who began trying to perform a tonsillectomy on me with her microphone. Trapped and uncomfortable, I stuttered out a few comments sufficiently insipid as to ensure that: a) I could get away quickly; b) I would never in a million years be the one to show up on the news.

Unlike me, another student in our group coming out behind me had seen the cameras and was prepared for his moment in the limelite. *He* emerged sounding eloquent and somewhat comical, a shoo-in to be on the show. Fine by me.

That night several of us gathered around someone's TV to watch for the "Alien" review. The student who we were all quite sure would be featured even brought a video camera to record for all posterity his shining moment. Sure enough, the news anchor commented that the movie "Alien" had come to town. They showed a chart of audience ratings, and then said they had talked to some people coming out of the show. Pause. Cut. Me. That's right—me. Huge. Bright. My face. On TV.

Oh, for God's sake.

Then out of my mouth came the following Pulitzer-Prize winning prose: "Well, the special effects were good…and the acting was good…and it *was* scary." Cut to commercial.

Slowly, ever so slowly, everyone turned toward me. Swallowing hard, I stared straight at the television set, pondering under which piece of furniture I should spend the rest of my time in graduate school. The matter was never spoken of again.

Finally, there were the liquor laws. Based on some completely indecipherable logic designed to do—something—regarding liquor consumption, liquor-by-the-drink was legal in the city limits, but *packaged* liquor was not. So you could walk into any old bar or restaurant and get yourself blind, shit-faced drunk, but you couldn't invite your neighbor over for a beer.

Undaunted, the ever-enterprising local business community had managed to turn this absurdity into a booming little cottage industry. Just outside of town lay "The Strip." The Strip was a nearby highway that sported a very long row of very large, very successful packaged liquor stores, open 24 hours a day, seven days a week. Far from diminishing consumption, having to drive to The Strip to buy liquor resulted in *tons* of alcohol coming into town. The logic was this: if you were gonna drive all that way, then you'd better damn well *stock up*. So the parking lots on The Strip were perpetually grid-locked with vans, pickups, station wagons, and other assorted personal cargo vehicles being loaded to overflowing with all manner of packaged liquor headed back into town. Perfectly legal.

The whole thing was really, *really* strange.

You know, my whole introduction to the place was ignominious and should have served as an omen of the traumas to come had I been paying any attention at all. The summer prior to starting graduate school I drove *There* to find a place to live. I was immediately struck by two things. First, the occupancy rate seemed alarmingly low for any place listed in the Farmer's Almanac as capable of sustaining human life. It was not at all hard to find a place, and within about four hours of arriving I rented the duplex where I would live for the next three years. Second, the Taco Bell took checks. Heaven. Or so I thought.

I had planned to spend two or three days looking around. But as the first day wore on I began to feel kind of strange. The feeling was not very specific, though, as I couldn't even distinguish whether it was emotional or physical. But *something* seemed amiss. It worsened through the day, and by that evening I was sufficiently spooked by how I felt that I actually slept with a light on in the hotel room. It was silly, I know, but I found it comforting, so sue me.

The next morning I felt worse yet. By late that afternoon I was becoming increasingly concerned because I was finding it a little bit hard to walk. So I decided to cut my visit short, get the hell out of Dodge, and drive to my parents' house in a city about ten hours away. So, late that afternoon I headed out of town on the nearest highway.

And I went downhill in a big, fat hurry. After a few hours on the road my vision began to blur. I began to feel weaker and weaker. I alternated between shivering and burning up. I struggled to keep awake and stay in one lane. I started having aches and pains of all description and variety. When I stopped for gas at a convenience store I was so wobbly and weak while walking in that I consciously worried about the clerk thinking I was drunk and calling the law on me.

To make matters worse, along about ten o'clock that night, with about three hours yet to drive, my car threw its alternator belt. There was a sudden "whiiirriiiip" under the hood, the engine barfed the belt out a wheel well, and everything electrical in the car suddenly dimmed. It was just me and the battery. To conserve power I turned off the stereo, shut down the AC, dimmed the gauge lights, and prayed very, very hard that my battery would hold out for the next three hours so they wouldn't find the car, and me, dead on the side of the road the following morning.

Luckily for me it did, and at about 3 A.M. I staggered into my parents' house, fell into bed, and didn't get up for the next three days. Since along about day four I still felt like I was going to die— and soon—I wangled an appointment with a local internist who wryly noted the trouble I was having sitting upright on his examining table and said that "I looked like hell." Thank you very much. He gave me a good going over, scratched his head, threw up his hands, and said the medical equivalent of "Beats me." I went back to my parents' house and crawled back into bed, concerned that I would wake up dead at any minute.

Then, the very next day, I awoke with bright red spots covering every inch of my body. I stumbled to the kitchen where my mother took one look at me and laughed out loud. "You've got the measles!" she shrieked.

That's right, I had the measles. The goddam measles. I had the *measles. Real* fucking funny.

And let me tell you something—this "childhood disease" stuff? Don't you buy it. There's nothing in the *least* childlike about that stuff. It is a demon monster from hell. I have never been that sick. (OK, one other time, but it was shorter and induced by Jose Cuervo, so it doesn't count.) I damn near died of that bug with its stupid red spots. Little tip—if you're gonna get the measles, do it when you're a child. As an adult, it's ugly.

GRADUATE SCHOOL, PART II: THE FACULTY

It takes a special breed to be faculty in a graduate program—or a student who manages to get into a graduate program. Having spent way too much time in academic pursuits, neither group was what you might call "well-rounded." I suspect some had no reflection and would have burst into flames if exposed to direct sunlight. For starters, the faculty in my program was an interesting lot.

Take the department chair, for example. Although people occasionally referred to him by name so I have to assume that he was an actual biological entity, I was never quite sure that he really existed. In the three years I was on campus I recall seeing him in his office—which was right off the lobby of the department, so it was hard to miss—a total of twice, and I participated in a conversation in which he was involved a total of once. Looking like a creature on the down escalator of evolution, his mis-buttoned, mis-sized, and haphazard manner of dress gave him the interpersonal feel of an unmade bed, and it was quite easy to imagine him choosing his clothes each morning by smell rather than appearance. He maintained—assuming that he did, in fact, do any maintenance—a goatee of such dubious shape and texture that it had earned him the squeamishly accurate subterranean nickname of "Goatman," although I thought he had a somewhat sinister air, so I tended to refer to him as "Mephistopheles." I never quite figured out what, if anything, he did, or how, in any way, he mattered to what went on in the place. Given that no one much talked about, or to, him, whether he ever did anything of importance—either good or bad—is entirely beyond my realm of knowledge. I never did have a one-on-one conversation with the man, and to this day I have no idea if he even knew who I was.

Another professor was so acutely distractable that during a class on psychological testing he got so enamored with the stopwatch he was using to demonstrate the test that he began timing each sentence he spoke. He was, however, far preferable to his Teaching Assistant, who may have been the single most destructive person I have ever met. Had this person said one more arrogant, demeaning thing to the students in our class, we surely would have been able to raise the money for a hit man.

You think I'm kidding. I'm not. During one class this person responded to my question about an item on one of the personality tests with a dismissive "Hey—like I care. I'm into the Rorschach." This person had already found innumerable ways to demean us as a class and make us feel stupid and incompetent, and as I recall I was in an especially cranky mood that day. At the conclusion of the comment, before I even realized it, I was on my feet preparing to leap over the desk and grab him by the throat. Suddenly becoming aware of what I was about to do, I decided it was not a wise course of action if I wanted to complete my degree. Or stay out of jail. So I sat down. And shut up. And thought I might have a stroke from the resulting spike in my blood pressure.

Then there was the faculty member who appeared to be using classes to audition for The Rocky Horror Picture Show, because his lectures involved prancing about the classroom, performing grand, sweeping, Shakespearean gestures, generating dramatic pauses, and using "stage whispers" to add emphasis. Trust me, this was not a figment of my imagination.

And, of course, there was the faculty member who was so compulsive and concerned with detail over substance that his only comment on my first term paper was that he didn't like the paper on which it was written or the font I had used to print it. This was in the days of typewriters, not word processors, remember, so truth be told I didn't have a hell of a lot of choice about either issue, and he was a complete idiot if he didn't know it.

I guess that explains *that*.

Another faculty member was a full-blown cow-kickin', boot stompin', beef eatin' country-bred good ol' boy who spoke exclusively in country metaphors and who wore cowboy boots and string ties with custom-made thousand dollar suits. Wild and unpredictable in both behavior and language, when walking out of a room where this man had been presiding, people who didn't know him would look at each other and say "What on earth was *that?*" And once that man got to talking, he was a *machine*. He could talk longer and about more subjects without requiring a response from another person than anyone I've ever met. There were times when I thought he didn't even need to *breathe*, he could talk such a non-stop blue streak. Rumors abounded that he was bipolar, steroid-crazed, or had received a sharp rap to the head as a child, if you get my drift. Whatever—once he got started talking, he just didn't stop.

Which made it unnerving just to walk past the man's office. No force in the universe could help you if he caught a glimpse of you. You were dead meat. It was a foregone certainty that he'd race into the hall, call out your name, chase you down, tell you he had a *real* important question to ask you, put his arm around you, and usher you back into his office. Let's hope you didn't have a doctor's appointment, a dinner date, or plans for New Year's Eve, because at that point you were trapped, as his audience, for the foreseeable future. It could literally take hours to extricate yourself. And he was always working on some get-rich-quick scheme that he would undoubtedly want to describe to you in excruciating detail. Various ideas he floated past me included pocket-sized safety seats for toilets, coin-operated air compressors at gas stations, and fiberglass liners for the beds of pickup trucks. God knows what he talked to other people about. I never asked, and I'm not sure I want to know.

Fortunately, he was rarely in his office. In fact, most of the time most of us had no earthly idea where he was—you'd see him dash in and out of the building seemingly at random, for no obvious reason, and with no known destination. That made for an interesting task if, for some reason, *you* needed to talk to *him*. You'd best start searching for him about a week before your deadline, because it could easily take that long to find him. Or longer. A classmate and I were once sitting outside his office waiting to meet with him as part of an independent study project he was supervising when, at our appointed meeting time, he unceremoniously walked out of his office, smiled at us as he walked past, got into his car, and proceeded to drive to the next state.

Absolutely true.

Despite all this, the man could not be dismissed as merely a crazy, because he was probably the most gifted clinician in the place. When he was with patients he was *brilliant*. Even in class, during rambling monologues that were often just shy of coherence, he could, on occasion, spew out an insight or a way of looking at something that changed *everything*. Receiving even one of these precious gems could make the years he took off your life forcing you to listen to him ramble on about this and that and the other thing entirely worthwhile.

He could be a brilliant supervisor as well, assuming you could get him off his topic and onto the subject of your case for some portion of the hour. Once, I managed to interrupt him long enough to describe a patient with whom I was feeling frustrated. The professor asked me what approach I was using. I said that I was being analytic (as in Freudian). He said "show me," and began to play the role of patient. I did my thing as if he were, in fact, my patient. He sat bolt upright in his chair.

"Huh?" he snapped. "That ain't analytic, Bubba."

"No?" I replied meekly.

"Does the sun shine blue over cow patties?" he snorted. "*This* is analytic. Be your patient." I started talking like my patient. He began to respond. But his responses were nothing whatever like mine. Instead, they were as crystal-clearly psychoanalytic and as finely honed and precise as if he himself had been lying on Freud's couch that very morning. Given that psychoanalysis was not this professor's primary theoretical approach, it was an *unbelievable* display of knowledge and skill.

"Oh," I said. "That's very different from what I've been doing."

"As plain as the stink from a pig farm, ain't it?" he chuckled. "Now, whaddya gonna do with that, pardner? You gonna go back to the barn and get ya a new steed, or ya gonna keep on that there nag you been ridin'?"

At other times he could be arbitrary to the point of exasperation. During his course on group therapy, somewhere well into the class and near the end of the semester he suddenly declared that he was considering making us write a term paper (which was shocking in and of itself, as he never assigned such things because he didn't want to be bothered with grading them). Panicked at the thought of having to add this to everything else we were trying to get done, we looked at each other in paralyzed horror. He scanned our stunned faces and bellowed "OK, so whadda y'all think about usin' that as the road we take to the pasture?" Silence. Then, from the back of the

78

room, from a soft-spoken, completely kind student who never had a bad word to say about anyone and who almost never spoke in class, came a barely audible "It's too late, *Buster*." We gasped. But the professor laughed. And he dropped the idea of our doing a paper. And the rest of us bought that student a beer.

But where the guy shined most brightly was when he was ridiculing a mistake. He turned mockery into Shakespearean drama, a literary feast for the eyes and ears. Not only did he get away with it, despite being exceptionally biting and sarcastic he managed to hurt surprisingly few feelings while doing it.

Once, while listening to a tape of a student's therapy group, a manipulative group member made a veiled threat to walk out of the group. The student therapist, clearly rattled by the maneuver, started trying to persuade the group member to drop the threat. Her voice became cloying and pleading. The professor had a meltdown.

"What!" he cried. "Why, you're beggin', honey! Hell, if you gonna beg, you gotta do it right! You got to get yourself down on one knee— like this!"

At which point he got up, knelt in front of the student, and proceeded to look up at her with wide eyes, hissing breathily: "Here's how you do it, little darlin', so take note. See? You gotta just *say* it: 'Oh please, oh please, oh please, I beg of thee do not abandon little ol' me and my little ol' group. I jus' cannot *live* without ya.'"

It was amazing that he could pull these things off, given that his mockery was downright stinging. But he was just too wild, irreverent, and funny to be wounding. It was a gift.

Then, of course, there was the faculty member who *did* hurt people's feelings. Virtually the exact opposite of ol' Bubba, this faculty member was dry, cynical, and not, to put it mildly, given to compliments or encouragement. He seemed to be always looking at you with a critical eye and you always felt, probably accurately, that you never quite measured up. Once, in supervision with him, while listening to a recording of my session with a patient he heard me say something that he apparently didn't like. He turned off the tape, and without looking at me, began shaking his head, mumbling "Oh, Greg, Greg, Greg…" I had no idea what I'd done wrong and I *still* wanted to poop in my pants.

This professor talked very little and stared at you a whole lot. This enhanced the sense that he had a lot going on inside him, it was all negative, and it was about *you*. I had my own personal meltdown over him when I got switched, without my knowledge, out of another professor's class and into his. Fueled by gut-wrenching panic at the thought of taking this particular class from him, I stormed into the division chair's office to demand an explanation and a retraction. He relented and put me back into the original class only after I pointed out that this was not the first time they had done this to me. I had *already* been switched between classes multiple times without my permission, and no one else had. That seemed enough.

My wife, Pam, actually met this particular professor in passing at a professional meeting some years ago. We stopped long enough for me to introduce him to her and to talk to the man for a little while— probably five or six minutes total. As we were walking away she turned to me and said, "Now, tell me again—who, exactly, was that asshole?"

An amazing judge of character, Pam.

We did manage to gig one of our professors *really* good, though. One of our more serious professors served as the consultant to a local television news show when they wanted an opinion from a psychological expert. The show had interviewed this professor as part of their story on a local unsolved murder. In the interview, which aired during the five o'clock news, our professor said "The police are looking at the family because, statistically speaking, you are most likely to be murdered by your family and friends." He was quite right. And we could not let it go.

We got a group together, went to a local engraver, and had a plaque made that said: "To (the faculty member's name), Channel (the local news channel) psychologist, for his quote 'You are most likely to be murdered by your family and friends.' This plaque is presented to him by his family and friends." Then we listed our names.

Now *that* was some good, wholesome, graduate school fun, I'll tell you.

GRADUATE SCHOOL, PART III: THE STUDENTS

As goofy as the faculty may sound, they were a paragon of mental health compared to the students, some of whom set Olympic records for weirdness. A diverse bunch, they came from all walks of life, races, creeds, and solar systems. A few—like the overt psychopath who somehow managed to wangle his way into the program and is by now probably enjoying the hospitality of the federal government in some maximum security facility—didn't last. Others, like the scary, possibly dangerous, borderline personality disorder, (you saw "Fatal Attraction" or "Play Misty For Me," right? And remember my butt-walking patient at the psychiatric hospital? That.) graduated. One student mysteriously disappeared and as far as I know has never been found. Yet another was so charismatic, entrancing, and sinister that it was not difficult to envision in his future a virulent suicide cult pulling off a subway gas attack or initiating war against the ATF. That man scared *me*, and I didn't think anything could rattle me after the things I'd been through at the psych hospital. Wrong.

Another student had a psychotic break and was forced to take a leave of absence. Still another was so hostile and demeaning toward men that it was frightening for any male student to be in the same room with her (and she had a live-in boyfriend, which none of us could quite figure). Another was so head-spinningly self-centered and self-righteous that everyone else's matter-of-fact name for him became "The Narcissist" as in "Hey—has anyone seen The Narcissist?"

Then there was the student who announced that because she felt a need to "get back to nature" while in graduate school, was considering taking some of her menstrual blood and smearing it on her vegetable garden. To everyone else's credit, her comment brought the meeting where she said it to a screeching halt and produced universal resolve to never accept a dinner invitation to her house. To her credit, during the awkward silence that ensued she managed to mumble "Does anyone think that's weird?"

Then there was the wife of a student who, although being a 35 year old professional woman, attended graduate school parties dressed—I could not have made this up if I'd wanted to—like a six-year-old beauty pageant contestant. Clad in little short sailor suits with big lapels in the front and bows across the back and her hair pulled into the top of her head like "Pebbles" in the Flintstones, had she broken into a chorus of "The Good Ship Lollipop" no one would have batted an eye.

Then, of course, there were the more minor oddities, like the two guys with waist-length pony tails and the student who treated sleeping as a competitive sport. His favorite condition was unconsciousness, and my primary memory of him is of his regular pronouncements to the world at large that if anyone wanted to know where he was, he was Going Home To Nap. His day ran from about noon to 4 A.M., a schedule he got me onto for a summer. It was actually quite debilitating, thank you very much, and required several months to get back onto an earthling's schedule. I think he was a vampire.

And let us not forget the student who, on the final exam of a personality research class, completed one of his answers with the statement "I guess what I'm trying to say is that I'd rather kiss a pig than do personality research"—to which the professor wrote in the margin what I considered to be the amazingly restrained response of "WHAT IN THE WORLD...?!" Another student, on a test, listed the way the auditory system in the brain worked as "Sound goes into the ear hole, is transferred to the ear nerve, and goes into the ear brain." And, of course, the student who said that "Romaine" grammar was "a type of lettuce." The grader wrote in the margin "Nice try."

Then there was our obsessive-compulsive. An early and major casualty in the whole graduate-school culture of sadism and assured mutual destruction, with a single utterance that I am sure to this day he wishes to high heaven he'd never even *thought* much less *said*, he managed to ruin his life for the next three years.

To understand the gravity of his comment you must first get a mental picture of this fellow. Small and thin, slightly balding, he had generated nearly a perfect score on his GRE's and was the walking embodiment of obsessive-compulsivity. Remember that Freud called obsessive-compulsive functioning "anal retentive" because he felt that it was the result of a power struggle between the child and the mother over toilet training, with the parent wanting the child to produce a bowel movement and the child exhibiting hostility by passive-aggressively refusing to let fly.

A variety of characteristics go with being obsessive-compulsive, including such things as precision of speech, detail-orientation, stubbornness, ambition, and rigidity. But it is obsession about, trouble with, or some kind of over-emphasis on, all things anal that historically characterizes the condition.

Well—this particular student had it. He fit the whole obsessive-compulsive picture perfectly. And not only did he have the personality elements, he had the physical elements as well. Physically he was, well, *different*. How was he different? To put it bluntly—when he walked, his butt didn't move. Honest. His butt just didn't move. As bizarre in appearance as it sounds in description, he was like a cat with a large turd hanging from his behind—that part of his anatomy seemed to be operating according to its own rules rather than in tandem with the rest of his anatomy. It seemed paralyzed, somewhat disembodied. It didn't seem to be comfortable, it didn't seem to want to go along, and it seemed completely, impossibly, permanently, spring-wound, vault-door, fallout-shelter, clamped-shut *tight*.

Hence the colloquial name for obsessive-compulsives: tight-asses.

Be assured that this man's anatomical and personality characteristics were not lost on the rest of us. He had immediately become the butt (pardon the pun) of our jokes. To his face—and behind his back—we regularly kidded about him "walking like he had a corn cob up his butt." But, kid as we might, we were unprepared for the night he uttered a remark so amazing, so unbelievable, so shockingly *perfect* coming from an obsessive-compulsive, that everyone within its psychological blast radius was changed forever.

It happened during a party at my house. Understand that obsessive-compulsives, God love them, are a highly controlled and controlling lot. But their control is something of an all-or-nothing proposition. As a result, for most of them there are times when the controls just dissolve and out floods all the stuff that has been so carefully stuffed—anger, or sexuality, or some other behavior that is wildly antithetical to the typically prudent, prudish, or controlled nature of your everyday obsessive-compulsive. And one of the times this can happen is when they get a few chemicals in them.

Well. At this particular party this particular student had managed to snarf a few beers—enough, it seemed, to not only slur his speech, but to remove his usual controls. Anyone with half a brain would have read the writing on the wall given the overtly sadistic social system of graduate school and kept his freaking mouth shut. But, chemically altered and now dangerously disinhibited, my classmate began to regale my party guests with a story about something rather unusual that had happened between him and a patient in the clinic that morning. To his ultimate ruin, everyone stopped to listen and he just could not shut himself up.

My classmate reported that he had been trying to empathize with his patient, to communicate that he understood that the patient was having a hard time. He said that he had considered saying "Man, you're getting screwed." But given that my classmate was fairly religious, and that remark was a bit off-color and a sexualized metaphor, he did not feel comfortable saying it. He decided, instead, to say "That's like getting stabbed in the back." So far so good. But, true to the "maybe this, maybe that, maybe this, maybe that" quality that characterizes the thinking of obsessive-compulsives, he could not quite make up his mind *what* to say. The problem was that, despite his uncertainty, he kept talking. As a result he stumbled, and out of his mouth came the following sentence:

"Man, that's like getting *screwed from the back!*"

Now, I'll be honest with you—I am unable to find a phrase that adequately conveys the impact of this admission. And if I ever do manage to find such a phrase, I will be oh, so humble in my acceptance of the Nobel Prize for Literature, because for this there are, in fact, no words. This utterance produced what was, for all practical purposes, the end of recorded history. Someone like *him* saying something like *that?* And then *admitting* it? Really—there are simply no words. People shrieked. They dissolved in breathless, hysterical laughter. People stared at him in awe as tears formed in their eyes and their faces grinned so widely that their lips cracked and blood appeared at the corners of their mouths. People turned to each other, put their heads against each others' chests, and wept uncontrollably. Violently shaking with laughter, people hugged each other through heaving gasps and sobs. Not one single person remained upright.

For myself, I can only be grateful that I was alone, in the kitchen, listening in as I was getting more ice, because I could drop to my knees and roll about the floor, gasping for air in a state of life-threatening hysteria, in private.

The upshot of the whole thing was that it instigated what is to this day the single most relentless taunting of any human being who ever lived. *We never let him forget it.* He would go to his mailbox in the psychology department and find that someone had stuffed it with pictures of pig butts at a trough that they had cut out of some agriculture magazine. When a bunch of us would go to the movies together, one-by-one each of us would refuse to stand in front of him in line. With a great flourish of high, mocking drama, we would each, in turn, grab him from behind us and cry "Oh no, you go *first!*" And we would proceed to pass him to the front of the line. The final insult was delivered when, upon leaving for internship, at his going-away party a student gave him the present of—really, truly—a framed Polaroid picture of his naked butt.

You know, I need to say this to retain my sense of fair play—I gotta hand it to him. Through it all, this guy was incredibly good-natured. He never once reacted badly or got bent out of shape. He took it all as good-natured kidding and laughed right along with us. And, I mean, you cannot *imagine* the creative, sophisticated, cutting mockery that can be concocted by a bunch of clinical psychology doctoral students. But through it all my classmate retained a good attitude, took it in stride, and never once lost it. Because of that he earned everyone's respect, ended up being one of the best-liked students in the place, and became a good friend of mine and someone whose friendship I prized. It might have helped that he's a bonafide genius, I don't know, but I will say this—had it been me I'm not at all sure I could have been as good-natured about it.

So I guess it's a good thing it wasn't me, huh?

Speaking of me—in case you're wondering what cage I inhabited in this richly populated human game preserve, if you think about it, it's a relatively easy guess. Given what it took for me to get into graduate school and what I had been willing to do to get there, how do you think I approached it? That's right, I was Super Student. I was the zealot—the no-holds-barred, balls-to-the-wall, go-everywhere, do-everything student. I compulsively excelled at everything and could tolerate being bested by no one. I did everything, I did it all the time, and I did it over the top. You couldn't turn a corner in the place without me having already gotten there. You couldn't bring up a topic that I hadn't already mastered. You couldn't cite a study that I hadn't already read. Honey, if it had to do with graduate school I was going to do it, I was going to do it before you could do it, and I was going to do it better than you could do it. Think "Mighty Mouse with a beer and an attitude."

In retrospect I can't imagine how others must have felt around me, given my single-minded, shark-like pursuit of overachievement. I went all-out, all the time. I could have made Gandhi feel inadequate. Only one other student even came close to matching my aggressive drive for accomplishment, and she and I reached an unspoken agreement to resolve our standoff at the top of the heap by establishing territories—she would be considered lord and master of research, and I would be considered czar of clinical work. That worked so well that even the faculty came to see us that way.

In truth, though, in no way was my excess fueled by malevolence or a desire to make anyone else feel bad. Believe it or not, those things never even crossed my mind and the few times someone said something alluding to other people feeling bad around me I was flabbergasted. Instead, my demeanor was connected, as usual, to one of my secret internal resolutions, this one having to do with the terror of flunking out that was alive and present every moment of every day of graduate school.

Everyone had to cope with the universal terror of flunking out in some way, and mine was to use the department's pride against itself. I decided that I had not come this far and done this much to get into graduate student just to end up flunking out. So I figured if I were to be a student of sufficiently awesome proportion, if I stood out as a clearly superior specimen, if I were a stellar example of all things excellent as a graduate student, then even if I *deserved* to be flunked out, the program would be too ashamed to do it. So by setting myself up to be the poster boy for superiority, I was essentially taking out an insurance policy. I wanted to make it so that there was no way in hell they could get rid of me no matter how much they might want to. I went there to be a psychologist, and, by God, I wasn't leaving until I was one. So I was going to see to it that they were never—ever—going to be able to find an excuse for preventing me from being one.

While fearing that I might flunk out might sound insane given that I was up to my ears in such hysterical overachieving, (I was the only student in my class to make a 4.0 grade point average the very first semester, and for which one of my more competitive classmates kicked me rather hard when he found out. And I failed to make a 4.0 the second semester only because another one of my more pleasant little professors announced that he had a rule to "never give first-year students an 'A' in his course. Asshole.) the truth was that the program was brilliant in their ability to keep us motivated through terror. So although our fear may have been slightly out of proportion to the actual danger, fear was still the omnipresent feeling. The reality that few people really did flunk out did not diminish the need to cope with how scared we all were.

Okay, maybe we were all a little paranoid, but I think my resolution was at least moderately adaptive under the circumstances. God knows it certainly helped get me trained well.

GRADUATE SCHOOL,
PART IV: RELATIONSHIPS

It was a long-standing, generally accepted truth that psychology graduate school was hell on relationships. But it was equally true that the way our relationships worked were part of what made graduate school hell. I can't say for other departments on campus, but romantic involvements in the psychology department were about as calm and sane as nursery school children playing with weapons of mass destruction. Sex was a commodity, breakups were horrible, public and melodramatic, and partners shifted with the unpredictable momentum of the San Andreas Fault. In one of the classes after mine, every woman entered married—and graduated divorced. One classmate told me that she and her classmate/friend/boyfriend decided they had to stop having sex once they realized that they actually liked each other. Go figure.

Where to start. There were the two students who moved in together toward the end of grad school and whose house I was visiting when I ran across a stash of particularly juicy—and not at all hidden (it was on the living room coffee table, as I recall)—S & M literature. That was fun. Then there was the student who was dating another student who was so awful and so reviled by everyone else (I once saw this man bring an entire continuing education seminar to a complete halt with his offensive, arrogant, and insulting demeanor) that when they ran into classmates in public places she would hide—even to the point of slipping out back doors and diving under tables, if necessary. I am not kidding.

Then there was the couple whose breakup was followed by her making death threats to him and his calling the police—who told him to take the threats seriously, as they had seen this type of thing before and it was *not* good. But that was nothing compared to the student who gave his girlfriend a psychological test "for fun" only to discover that she generated the average profile for women in Mexican jails who had killed their husbands.

And, of course, there was the woman who stole her boyfriend's car and sold it. There was the student involved with another student who made hangup phone calls just to hear his voice and to check on his whereabouts. And there was the student who regularly accused his girlfriend of various infidelities. To her credit, he was probably right only about half the time.

Oh, and did I mention the student who fell madly in love with a faculty member and who did everything short of stalk the man? During a psychology conference several of us attended, this student was so aggressive about walking next to this particular faculty member that several times she nearly knocked one of my other classmates into a river to get her out of the way. *That* was a fun trip. As I recall, I ended up furious and my classmate ended up in tears, and both of us tried to never speak to the student in question again. Imagine what a happy little return trip we had from that conference—four of us riding together in my car for four hours with two of us refusing to speak to one of the people in the back seat. Big fun.

Many years later I talked with this professor at some length about the whole thing because I had felt so sorry for him during that time. It had been viscerally painful to watch. He was an exceptionally decent chap with a wonderful wife and family, and there was absolutely no chance he would ever have been willing to commit de facto suicide by getting inappropriately involved with this student. But he wearily admitted that he had been woefully unprepared to deal with the obsessive zest with which she attached herself to him. He confided to me his feelings of being overwhelmed at the time and not knowing what to do with her. I could understand. It was a terrible position for him to be in, and I'm glad it wasn't worse than it was or that it didn't go on longer than it did.

Then, of course, there was the student and the professor who *did* become involved, and whose relationship essentially forced the department to allow the student to switch divisions lest her faculty paramour also end up being her academic advisor. Switching divisions was generally something allowed only when there was firm evidence of the Second Coming, so this was a *big* deal. But less of a big deal than the inevitable lawsuit, I guess.

Another classmate became infatuated with one of his patients, who he happened to be treating as part of marriage counseling. (Isn't that perfect?) When the marriage of his patient and her husband didn't work out (surprise) and his treatment of her ended, he went through a series of psychological contortions that would have made a gymnast blush to see if he could twist the idea of getting personally involved with his ex-patient into some form of socially acceptable shape. To his credit he ultimately decided it was not OK, but after watching his gut-wrenching machinations I made a decision about how I would forever handle relationships with my own ex-patients: no matter what was permitted by any professional code of professional ethics, for me it was "once a patient, always a patient." I decided that I would never have anything other than a professional relationship with any person I ever saw as a patient. That decision, I am pleased to say, has served me exceedingly well. As far as I know my classmate ultimately came to the same decision.

Now, so far I have talked about other people. Do you think this means I was exempt from the graduate school relationship crazies? *What?* How can you even ask that question? Have you not being paying attention? Have you not been *listening?* Remember me—the virulent overachiever? Do you think I would fail to overachieve in the relationship crazies, too? Not on your life. In fact, some years after graduate school, during one of my not-infrequent episodes of self-flagellation over some of the bizarre relationships and relationship behavior in which I had been involved during graduate school, a former classmate tried to comfort me by saying that I hadn't *really* done anything any worse than anyone else—I just managed to do it all "in public." Oh yeah, that helped. Maybe next time she could just jab me in the eye with a knitting needle and be done with it.

Let's see. There was my relationship with a classmate of whom I was physically afraid at various points during our time together. She demonstrated a variety of worrisome behaviors throughout our relationship, not the least—or strangest—of which was her habit of "playfully" nibbling on my finger with increasing vigor, to the point of chomping on me like an alligator and inducing such terrible pain that you could hear me scream into the next county.

Then there was my relationship with the student whose rage attacks were so fierce that during one of our regular breakups she managed to tear, rip, crack, or destroy nearly everything breakable in her apartment, especially anything related to me. You could frequently hear her scream into the next county, too—without me biting her finger. (Ultimately no one cared, as she managed to systematically alienate everyone in the place—even my major professor, which until that point had been considered impossible.)

Then there was the student with whom I had a delightfully perverse, torrid affair—all while she was in the middle of a particularly acrimonious divorce. It began at my house at a post-final-exams party designed to eradicate the effects of a particularly harrowing semester and where so many shots of Jose Quervo Gold were consumed that no one—myself included—remembered the end of the party. That's probably a blessing, as I awoke the next morning horrified to find myself entwined with the previously mentioned soon-to-be-divorcee with no idea how I got there but plenty of ideas about what I'd *done* there. Shortly after her departure I spent 7 straight hours alternately throwing up—from the tequila, not my encounter with my classmate—while lying on my bathroom floor so I'd be near the toilet the next time I needed it—and quaking in my world-class-poor-judgment boots with fear that I'd get subpoenaed as a witness for my classmate's soon-to-be ex in an attempt to use a claim of infidelity to wrest custody of their kids from her. I was scared. Actually, not true. I was terrified.

That scenario did not come to pass, which is a good thing since it is unlikely that anything resembling good sense or fear of consequences would have stopped us from regularly repeating our illicit activities for some time thereafter. In the end, we managed to have one of the few truly successful, no-strings attached, thoroughly enjoyable (the recently mentioned episode of terror not withstanding), all-too-brief, amicable, and secret affairs I have ever heard of. (So imagine my surprise when, some years later, a classmate confided to me that he had figured out what was going on because he saw my paramour and myself "look at each other" in some telling way during a class. So maybe we hadn't been so clever after all.)

Then there was the teaching assistant from another department with whom a classmate and I became so infatuated that we would station ourselves in strategic positions on campus just so we could watch her walk by. I mean, she was *cute*. But, true to our developmental age, neither of us could ever get up the nerve to talk to her, and instead developed rather wonderful fantasy relationships with her. Besides, a relationship between her and either of us would never have worked out given the severe developmental maturity gap—psychologically, she was in college, and we were in junior high school.

More? OK, there was the student who got herself sloshed to the gills one evening, invited me to her apartment on some pretense (which, like the idiot I was born to be, I never once thought to question the legitimacy of), and regaled me with her overwhelming desire to have sex with me. Flattered? Oh yes I was, as she was as attractive and sought-after as they came. Tempted? Not on your life. Given that she was reputed to have a very—I said *very*—big mouth, and a boyfriend who was said to be so paranoid that he even followed her around (literally, in his car, like a detective shadowing a suspect), and I had a hideously volatile girlfriend at the time, the whole thing smacked of a quick drink of hemlock rather than an enjoyable roll in the hay. So I gratefully, regretfully, and as gently as possible, declined. Whereupon she demanded I leave her apartment "before she tried to rape me." Interesting girl.

Oh, and the next day, along about noon, it was *all over* the psychology department that I had refused her advances. So my suspicions that any, shall we say, "alternate" outcome of the previous evening's festivities would have been all over the department—and her boyfriend's half-functioning criminal brain—seemed confirmed. Now *that* was dodging a bullet. It also inexplicably raised my stock value among the rest of the female grad student population, which was not an altogether unpleasant side-effect.

So like I said, our relationships were more grade-school than grad-school, and as crazy and extreme as they could be. The truth was that we just didn't know any better and it was the best we could manage under the circumstances. Like 13 year-olds we fed on crushes, infatuations, passions, messages through third-parties, hints and innuendos and the other things you see in your average sixth grade class. I'm surprised we didn't actually pass notes. There's nothing like a little arrested development to make for an interesting four years of relationships.

Perhaps the only positive aspect of all the relationship craziness in graduate school was that it made working with patients seem downright easy. After all, with our classmates and faculty we had no special influence, no position of power that would allow us to address or correct their ill-designed behavior. But with our patients we were *therapists*, by golly, entitled to give all manner of advice that they were actually supposed to listen to and maybe even follow. So even if our patients had more loose screws than, say, our faculty, with them we were sanctioned to wield the mental screwdrivers that were designed to help fix things.

GRADUATE SCHOOL, PART V: MERLIN

Bobbing in the middle of this boiling pot of strangely stirred humans was one faculty member who, just by his presence, almost made the insanity of graduate school worthwhile. In order to avoid embarrassing him should he ever decide to go slumming and read this, I'll simply call him Merlin, because as far as most of us were concerned, he was magic.

Deeply unpretentious, balding, physically slight and intensely average-looking, the man had a brain the size of a small planet. A junior faculty member still in his 20's when I started and who had only recently completed his doctorate and joined the department, he exuded a seemingly impossible mix of brilliance, forthrightness, integrity, interpersonal sensitivity, personability and compassion, combined with a work ethic that made Mother Theresa look like a bon-bon eating libertine. At the height of his productivity he published eight research articles in one sixteen week semester. Freakin' *awesome*.

Merlin was so smart that even when he said something offhand and ordinary (once, when a bunch of us were out drinking, he quipped that the bar we were in "looked like a place where you would actually want to get beat up in a bar fight because it would be such a high-class beating") it was so clever that even the students most in need of antidepressants were forced to smile. His clear-headed practicality was astounding and his problem-solving skills were nothing short of breathtaking. When he instituted a research project development team among some students in one of the classes following mine, he responded to his discovery that, as a group, they were rude and repulsive human beings, by moving the meetings to his home in the evenings because that way "he could use the social demand to be polite to a host in their home" to alter their behavior. Wow.

Those of us who succumbed to Merlin's spell came away immeasurably better for it. His intellectual honesty, flawless reasoning, and willingness to matter-of-factly deal with any issue or question no matter how thorny or politically incorrect, set him apart from ordinary mortals and provided value to every student, no matter how deficient or brain-damaged they might be. He is the main reason some of us turned out to be even halfway decent psychologists. I know that mine is a debt to him that can never be repaid.

Merlin's classes were famously fearsome. Treating everyone as though they had the same intellectual capacity he did, he figured out the workload that would kill you and then backed it off a hair. Whether you were taking his course on psychotherapy, psychopathology, personality measurement, marriage counseling, or having him supervise a therapy case, it was best to have cleared your calendar and be caught up on your sleep. You were going to learn that topic inside and out, upside and down, dissecting every nuance to the point where you could argue any position and criticize your own argument. He assigned massive quantities of reading, fearsome research papers, and gave tests that required an unabridged dictionary just to understand the questions.

And we couldn't get enough. Most of us took every class he offered and tried to spend as much time with him as possible. He would assign ridiculous quantities of reading and give exams designed to maim and kill, and we would beg for more. He'd ask us to understand the incomprehensible and we would sooner have contracted dysentery and died a horrible, wrenching death wracked with guilt than to ever let him down by showing ourselves to be short of the task. We would have followed the man into hell and, speaking for myself, I would have eaten whole live chickens if he'd asked me to.

But as much as we may have loved the man, Merlin was not so well received among non-clinical students. You see, it was lost on no one that the other divisions within the department—the ones that did not involve clinical work (seeing patients), were not exposed to anywhere near the same level of demand that we clinical students were. (Remember the 300-applicants-per-opening was for *clinical* psychology—the other divisions were not such a buyer's market. Nowhere near, in fact.)

I still remember—as bizarre as this sounds, it is absolutely true—walking into the computer room in the department, seeing some research psychology students playing a computer game (some kind of "Star Trek" game, I believe) on the terminal connected to the university mainframe computer, and finding it *entirely* and *completely* beyond my mental capability to understand how on earth they could be spending even a moment of their time doing that. I was puzzled into disbelieving silence. It would be like walking into the cockpit of a 747 during a horrible thunderstorm with life-threatening wind shears and the plane tumbling a thousand feet a minute to find the pilot deeply engrossed in surfing porn on the internet. "What the *HELL!?*" would be an appropriate, if understated, reaction, and it was mine as I watched the non-clinical students actually spending waking hours playing a *game*.

It would never even have *occurred* to a clinical student to *play* on a computer. Play was so far out of the question that it was impossible to even consider. Our gargantuan academic demands, like five-hundred-pound duffel bags filled with angry, venomous snakes, required unbroken attention and 24-hour-a-day devotion lest we get eaten alive. They were literally all any of us could focus on at any time of the day or night. I still remember one of my girlfriends at the time saying to me, entirely without rancor or resentment or sarcasm, that she could really use some attention sometime soon—maybe even this month. That was just the way it was.

But for non-clinical students it was not that way at all. I can't imagine what they thought of us clinical students (it was probably no accident that none of us bothered to ask) but my guess is they thought we were all crazy. So, given that they seemed to want to have nothing to do with us and we had no time or energy to be so appropriate as to do anything close to actually relate to them, there was very little interaction between the groups and very few of their students ever showed up in our classes. *Especially* Merlin's.

Except once. There was one non-clinical student, one time, who for some reason found his way into Merlin's den and showed up for one of his classes. And wouldn't you know, it was the most bone-crushing of all of his classes, a course on empirical and statistical measures of personality. This student became the exception that proved the rule: Merlin was not the non-clinical students' cup of tea.

Understand that there is perhaps no area of psychology as difficult and as complicated in both conceptual structure and mathematical process as trying to measure personality variables in an empirically reliable and valid manner. Name an obscure and convoluted mathematical principle, and you'll find it included somewhere in the topic. Multivariate analysis? Yup. Cluster analysis? Of course. Rotating matrices? You bet. Multiple regression? Naturally. It was obvious to everyone that only Merlin possessed the intellectual bandwidth necessary to communicate this level of information to a bunch of drooling graduate students, and that only clinical students were sufficiently fanatical as to be willing to dive into a pool filled with such thickly congealed intellectual content.

Or at least we thought it was obvious. But for some reason this non-clinical student appeared in our room on the first day of class. All of us clinical students thought it was an error or misunderstanding and, of course, we promptly said so in no uncertain terms. But no, the paperwork showed that this was in fact the very class that the non-clinical student was intending to attend and he resolutely assured us he was in the right place. So although we were puzzled, we made summary introductions, recovered from the embarrassment of assuming that no non-clinical student could ever withstand Merlin's Intellectual Kamikaze philosophy of teaching, and we set about the business of preparing to go to war with the daunting intellectual foe he put before us.

Which was when the non-clinical student demonstrated to himself and everyone else that he was, indeed, in over his head. In truth it was heart-breaking. When we would sit in a circle and discuss the concepts and principles involved in the topic, the non-clinical student would try to put his two-cents in. But his comments always addressed something so obvious, basic, and unsophisticated relative to the level of understanding required in order to forward our understanding of the material, that there was no place for any of us to take the conversation when he was finished. So we would look at him, then down, then at each other, there would be an awkward silence, and someone else would basically change the subject and start over.

Trust me, none of us wanted it this way. We were not trying to hurt the man, to be exclusionary or demeaning, or to get rid of him. We just seemed to be functioning in two different space-time dimensions. By the fifth class meeting we were all finally beginning to comprehend the material and the non-clinical student failed to appear. Merlin quietly noted that the student had decided to drop the class. That was that, no one said anything else about it, and as far as I know no other non-clinical student ever appeared in one of Merlin's classes.

THE REBELLION

That the clinical students operated on a different plane and enjoyed a different reputation from those in the other divisions was not lost on anyone, which made for an interesting set of feelings toward clinical students on the part of the faculty in the other divisions. It could loosely be called "malignant hate." And nowhere were those feelings more obvious than in the classes clinical students were required to take that were taught by non-clinical faculty. While allegedly designed to produce "well-rounded" psychology graduate students, it was a public secret that they were part of a shadow curriculum entitled "You Gotta Get Through Us, Hotshots."

The most notorious of these classes was a course in probability and multiple correlation. It was taught by only one professor in the department, and the horror stories about his class—whether or not they're true—were the stuff of legend, the likes of which I have never heard before nor since. People said things like: the workload was crushing—the professor was sadistic—the information was impossible—the assignments were endless—there was no time left to work on any other class—you had to spend hours at the computer center virtually every day.

On and on they went. The bottom line is that whatever may or may not have gone on in his class, students *hated* it. Many seemed to regard their semester with him as their preview of hell, and in any given semester any number of students might find their way to Jesus.

Further, most of us were terrified of the man. He was, as far as I could tell, widely considered to be as arrogant, haughty, and condescending as any defense attorney being interviewed on a news show. (Even a member of the clinical faculty confided in me that he felt this way.) Worse yet, for some reason he seemed to reserve his deepest hostile feelings for clinical students.

For some strange reason, he seemed to *really* dislike us. I could never quite figure it out, but I still have pictures in my head, like little snapshots, of his face—with a disgusted expression—turning away when I would try to talk to him. It was *weird*. At least another professor in his department that I'd gotten crosswise with was finally able to be friendly with me once we discovered that we were both amateur radio buffs. Not this fellow. With him, it was *different*. Sometimes I wondered if he just had it in for clinicians. A desk in his classroom broke one day, for example, and he left a note on the clinical students' bulletin board not only blaming us, but threatening to find and summarily "break" the people responsible for that desk being in his room. Real nice.

No one knew why he seemed to so many of us to be so hostile toward clinical students, but guesses as to the possible reason were the source of much whispered speculation and late-night gossip. The most persistent rumor I heard was that he had long ago started out in a clinical program, been flunked out, downshifted to a non-clinical division, and was ever-after determined to never let anyone in the clinical world live down his humiliation. I haven't the vaguest idea if the story is true, but if it isn't there is surely some equally rational explanation for his demeanor—like he had been cross-bred with a Velociraptor.

Anyway, for whatever reason, he came across as one spiteful little rat bastard, and the situation had been worsened by the fact that by the time I got to the program his actual class was no longer required. Even the other faculty members had grown weary of his arrogant behavior, so in order to dilute his (and, to be honest, a few others') despot-like power positions, they pushed through a brilliantly passive-aggressive plan: Instead of making his class mandatory for all students, they developed a test *based* (at least partly) on his class that they made mandatory for all students. That left his fiefdom largely, but not completely, intact—students didn't *have* to take his class, but they did have to learn the information, and his class remained the only game in town. The solution served everyone—the faculty got a giggle out of taking away his power, no one could say that students were forced to be abused by the horny little toad, he still got to teach the class, and the whole thing validated his self-righteous vindictiveness by convincing him that he permanently resided in enemy territory.

But then, along came—well, me. To this day I'm not sure what it was, if it was arrogance, rebellion, fear, stupidity, grandiosity, good sense, confidence, or all of the above, but for some reason I got it into my head that since the test was required but his class was not, screw his class and to hell with his malevolent assignments—I would study on my own and pass the test without taking the class. I figured that I could learn everything I needed to know for the test by studying the textbook and talking to students in the class, thereby avoid having to deal with the venomous little viper or his ridiculous demands.

Here's what you need to understand—this had never been done before. *Never.* No graduate psychology student in the history of the department had *ever* escaped his class or had even *considered* escaping his class. It had been mandatory until a few years before I started, and even without it being required students were so frightened of the test (and of the smarmy little weasel himself) that they simply bleated and obediently lined up at his door lest they fail the test. Every single student.

Until, well—me. And, as usual for me, (and which, if I had any sense at all, would long before have taught me would undoubtedly bring the roof down on my head) I publicly announced my intention. I said that I was going to skip his class, study on my own, and pass the test.

Perhaps you've heard of this event. It is commonly referred to as "The Laugh Heard 'Round the World." No one believed me. Even those who thought I had only one mental marble to begin with thought I had lost my last one. It was not until I really and truly did not sign up for the class that people even *considered* I might be serious—at which point an interesting thing happened: One-by-one, over the span of about a week, *every single clinical student asked if they could study with me and, when I said yes, dropped the class.* By the third week of the semester not one single clinical student remained in his class. Buoyed by our solidarity—or more likely our shared sense of self-destructiveness—we formed a study group and set out to learn the information on our own.

Are you following along in your songbook? This was not a subtle event. Nor was it, shall we say, an *impersonal* event. *Every single clinical student* dropped his class. No one had ever missed his class and now an entire division opted out. Can you imagine how this went over? No, not like that. Worse. *Much* worse. Suddenly, and without warning, the twitchy little troll found himself being rejected by those goddam clinicians. And, if the rumors about his past *were* true, then he had just found himself being rejected by those goddam clinicians *again.*

I must say that, in all of my historically-validated ability to make proclamations that threatened to bring about the end of the world, nothing had equaled this. My behavior not only ripped open an (alleged) old wound, but realistically threatened a long-standing, if informal, academic autocracy. My actions shook his very roots, and provoked a rage reaction the likes of which the psychology department had rarely, if ever, seen. He was beside himself.

But, as it was, he was stuck—there was nothing he could do. Technically, we were following the rules set out by the program. We just had to pass the test, we did not have to take his class. All he could do was fume, make indirect threats through the graduate school grapevine, and pray that we would flunk the test.

Well, in truth that was not quite all he could do. The man may have been a jerk, but no one said he was stupid. He was not about to sit idly by on his pointy little laurels while we showed him our collective behinds as we marched out the door of his class. No, sir. What he could do was to figure out a way to engineer our demise. And if he wanted to, there was a way. It was already in the works. Here's how he could do it:

Both the formulas used and the mathematical proofs involved in the content of his class were written in a particular type of scientific notation in the textbook that was used. It is a standard and commonly accepted form of statistical language. He knew this, of course, and the usefulness it offered him was the stuff of cleverness itself.

What he did was to use, in his class, a form of the notation that was subtly altered from the style used in the textbook. His own version had the same meaning as the information in the textbook, but was sufficiently idiosyncratic that it would never have been known—or used—by a psychology student who had not been in his class. He didn't mention that he did this, mind you, he just did it. And under normal circumstances the difference in notation between the class and the text would have seemed sufficiently minor and irrelevant, that if you weren't paying attention you would have considered it no big deal.

No big deal? Don't you get it? The test we had to pass was graded anonymously—students were given ID numbers to use instead of names, so no one knew whose test was whose. Well, the slithery little snake had a foolproof way to be able to see through the anonymity to the only thing that mattered—distinguishing those who were in his class from those who were not. The students in his class would use *his* notation on the test, and the students who had not taken the class would use the textbook's notation. Bingo—instant identification.

Now, you might think I'm cynical or overly suspicious to think that he'd actually go so far as to *use* the difference in notation for that purpose, and I might agree with you had he not done something that, to me, demonstrated that he was, in fact, quite capable of such subterfuge: he summarily forbade the students in his class from talking to those of us who were not in the class.

No kidding. His precise words were: "If you talk to 'them,' you will just be hurting yourselves, because anything 'they' get from you can only improve 'their' scores on the test. That will raise the curve and making it harder for *you* to pass."

See what I mean? Not bad for a primitive life form, eh?

Ah, but as dastardly brilliant as the scaly little insect's possible plan may have been, had he poked his head into our study group for even a moment, he would never have bothered with it. We were, as it turned out, our own worst enemies. We discovered—quickly, and in no uncertain terms—that studying the information ourselves was much, much more difficult than any of us had imagined. To make matters worse—let me make this very clear—I *suck* at complicated math. If you knew the deficit in my complex math skills you would understand how completely insane it was for me to think I could ever master the material on my own. I am not a psychologist instead of an engineer by accident, OK? The truth is that I took no math classes at all in college with the exception of one token and very, very basic statistics class that I essentially had to take. And I put that off until my last semester. And here I was trying to learn advanced probability and multiple correlation from a *book*?

Remember that chronic terror of flunking out? Score: terror—one, me—nothing.

Unfortunately, I was as stuck as the professor. I had engineered this rebellion, we were well beyond the point of no return, and there was no way out. So despite the horror of finding ourselves bobbing in a sea of confusion surrounded by the circling sharks of indecipherable statistics, we could do nothing but press on.

So we did. Our study group set meeting times, made assignments for specific people to master specific material and then teach it, and we struggled to help each other try to decipher the indecipherable. But I got very, very worried on the day I realized that while I felt hopelessly lost, somehow I had essentially ended up being the primary *teacher* of the group. Trust me, if I were the person most qualified to teach this stuff, then our butts were about to get very hot because we were going down in flames.

But through stubbornness, fear, or whatever, we kept at it, struggling to learn and understand the information. And, I must say, learn it we did. I have no idea how, but we managed to figure out that damn stuff and cram it into our heads. It wasn't easy. I not only memorized the entire glossary of the text (sixteen pages) I also memorized—and understood—no fewer than 17 pages of statistical proofs. The actual morning of the test, on a lark, I memorized one final proof that I had not bothered with previously because I figured it would be complete lunacy for anyone to put something *that* complicated on a test. It was on the test.

And there was one other thing. I held a wild card that dear old Professor Sewer Rat could never have counted on. He may have been vile and smart, but I was something even more dangerous—I was desperate. I had resolved (yet another of my secret resolutions) that I'd be damned if I was going to have gone through everything I'd gone through to get where I'd gotten just to have some power-mad warthog who was puffed up about a threat to his arrogant little academic empire derail me and my plans to become a psychologist. So I not only studied like a maniac, I hatched a secret plan of my own, designed to deal with his potential treachery.

You might have wondered how I knew so much about what was going on in his class when I wasn't in it and he had forbidden his students to talk to us. (Don't forget how scared everyone was of him and how reluctant they were to oppose him.) It was simple: I had a spy.

Unbeknown to the professor, a student in his division was my tennis partner and a good friend of mine. He was in the class. He was a really good guy who was sympathetic to those of us who dropped the class because he also thought the professor was a lunatic. I had persuaded him to not only keep me informed about what was going on in the class, but to give me copies of his notes. When I noticed the difference in scientific notation between the class and the text, heard about his prohibition against talking to students not taking the class, and remembered the "anonymous" scoring of the test, I had an "ah ha" experience and saw the mischief he could make, if he was so inclined.

So I decided to neutralize any scheme he might have to identify us with one of my own: I would use *his* version of the scientific notation on my test. That way my answer sheet would, from all appearances, be that of someone in his class rather than from the cohort of evil clinical students threatening the world order. After all, *he* didn't know I had the class notes, and *he* didn't know I knew his version of the notation, so he could have no way to guess that my answer sheet was, in fact, *my* answer sheet. In short, I would use the very method that could be used as a way of exposing us, to conceal myself.

Take *that*.

So that's what I did. And say I'm wise or I'm selfish, I don't care, but this time I told no one about my plan. No public announcement. This time it was mine, all mine.

As long as I live I will never forget how it turned out. It all came together in one final scene I like to call "The Great 'Game-Over' Moment."

With the test several weeks behind us, someone wandered into a room where a group of clinical students were studying and mentioned that the grades for the statistics test were in and Dr. Moron-in-a-Bottle had them in his office. The grading wasn't fancy— you passed or you failed. If you passed, fine. If you failed, you got one more chance. If you failed again, you were transferred to your new position at Burger King.

A good friend of mine, also a clinical student (and, I must say, someone far more talented at math than I, a shoe-in to pass the test, the person who really should have been teaching the study group, and someone without whose tutoring I would never have survived the whole ordeal) decided to face the enemy right then and right there. We trotted down the steps to the basement to where Dr. Bloodsucker had his office, and appeared in his doorway. (It was the one and only time that I had even looked into his office. In my three years there I never actually entered it.)

Sure enough, there he was—fangs and all—sitting at his desk. We asked if we could have our scores. He said sure. My friend told him his ID number. The professor looked down at his sheet, looked up, and said he had passed. No surprise there.

I told him my ID number. He looked down at his sheet. He looked up at me. He paused. He looked down at his sheet. He looked up at me. He paused. He squinted. He looked down at his sheet. He mumbled something about being unsure it was really my score. He looked up at me. He asked me my ID number again. I told him. He looked down at his sheet. I prepared to vomit.

Then, right before our eyes, something happened. I'll never know exactly what it was, but I swear to you, at that very moment, that man changed. Right in front of us, his entire demeanor altered. It was as if something inside him snapped, or dissolved, or expired. He began to talk a little strangely—even softly. First, he sighed. Then he said that my scores were "interesting." He leaned back in his chair, absentmindedly rubbed one of his horns, twirled his moustache, (OK, he didn't have horns—but he did have a moustache) and began talking.

He said that I had done extremely well on the part of the test that had to do with another class, (a class on experimental design that I had actually taken) scoring a 96%. But the part based on *his* class had been lower and had received a split-opinion from the graders. The result was that my overall score was precisely on the cusp of passing or failing. It was a toss-up and came down entirely to a judgment call as to which way it would go. He said that he had cast the deciding vote. He had voted to pass me.

Now, I will never know if my masquerade as a class member had anything to do with him deciding to pass me. I will never know if he would have decided differently if he knew whose test it was. But I can tell you this—I saw in his face, and in his eyes, what looked for all the world like surrender. It looked like he understood at that moment, for the first time, that he had been had—*completely* had. I saw in his eyes what looked to me to be the recognition that he had been up against something he had never imagined—not some silly rebellion, not some crazy rogue graduate student, but a heretofore unheard-of willingness to go to any length necessary to do the unthinkable in service of achieving the impossible. I may be way off-base here, but my feeling was that while he didn't *want* those scores to be mine, and he couldn't *believe* that those scores were mine, upon discovering that those scores were, in fact, mine, he realized that for the first time in his life he had been playing out of his league. I mean, what could be worse than finding out the very system you could use to root out your enemies had been used by your enemies to overcome you?

In short, I saw him fold.

Or maybe I'm way off-base here and I'm completely wrong, and nothing of the sort was going on. Who knows. But I do know this—not only could both my friend and I feel something change in that moment, but for my remaining years in the program neither he nor any other non-clinical faculty made so much as a peep about me. (When I invited one particular experimental psychology professor to be on my dissertation committee, he accepted, looked up at me and said, somewhat timidly—and I quote—"I promise I won't make any trouble for you." Wow.)

One last thing. I'll admit this now, for the first time. I have never before, nor since, had the feeling of vindication I experienced that day while walking away from Dr. Single-Celled-Organisms's office. Normally I'd have felt sorely unhappy that I did poorly enough on a test to nearly flunk it. But that time was different. That time I felt—*enormous*. I remember the feeling like it was yesterday. And it wasn't, it was over 25 years ago. God forgive me, it was glorious.

PRELIMS

The statistics test was just the first beast I wrestled in the initial herd of snarling academic threats the program unleashed on us. It was one member of a set of tests called "Prelim" (as in "preliminary") Exams. These were four, four-hour tests designed to test our "preliminary" (hence the name) knowledge of graduate-level psychology. Passing them essentially marked the end of our "beginning" graduate school and our mastering the "general" topics in psychology (again, hence the name). The tests covered four areas: Statistics, Learning, Personality, and Physiology.

Because I decided to face the most fearsome beasts first, after the Statistics Prelim I decided to take the Learning Prelim. Now, "learning" may sound like a relatively straightforward topic, eliciting happy little images of Sesame Street, Big Bird, and Mr. Rogers' Neighborhood imparting common-sense wisdom and understanding. Not hardly. When placed in the hands of experimental psychologists bearing small white rats, large computers, and the desire to make everyone "get through them," "learning" took on a whole new tone. Think "theoretical astrophysics," think "quantum mechanics," think "totally fucking obtuse." In short, when it came to a Prelim exam in "learning," suddenly no issue was too minute and no rat study was too obscure to be required reading as potential grist for the Learning Prelim Exam mill. Put succinctly, the material covered on the Learning Prelim was a laughably vast, unbelievably detailed array of both animal and human learning studies, any one of which could be covered on the test. Further, there weren't even specific courses that covered the material like there had been for the Statistics Prelim. Instead, the test, and the information for it, were simply material that you had to study in addition to your course work. You were on your own.

It's not like there were *no* guidelines, though. There were several "required" texts that formed the core of the information alleged to be covered on the test. I bought them, and decided to start my study with the most daunting of the texts, a book on animal learning (a nice way of saying "rat studies"). It turned out to be a British text and, quite clearly, the inspiration for the saying that "England and America are two countries separated by a common language." It was impenetrable. It might just as well have been written in Pali for all the resemblance it held to any Western language that existed in the late twentieth century. Worse yet, not only was it neigh-on impossible to understand, it was extremely complex, packed with studies and statistics that involved all manner of rat anatomy and esoteric rat behavior. If its weight had been determined by the density of the statistics in the thing, it would have qualified as its own Quasar.

Have no doubt, I found studying for the Learning Prelim to be very, very difficult. Remember that I had never even had a class in animal learning, so I was unfamiliar with even the most basic terminology in the book, and the studies were presented in such excruciating detail that I got vertigo just trying to read them. Further, I had no way of knowing what parts of the book would actually show up on the test, so my most prudent course of action would be to memorize the entire text—like that was possible.

So I was reduced to trying to understand everything I could, and to guess what might show up on the test. Good luck on that, too. I had nothing whatever on which to base my guess about what might be on the test, so the upshot was that I was not only confused and lost, I was—as usual—scared to death. That, of course, served as one more impediment to concentrating effectively, and I consistently felt as though I was frantically chasing my own intellectual tail. As I sat, hour after hour, trying to absorb the book, I could feel myself sinking deeper and deeper into depression.

It got so bad that, beyond the experiences I have just covered, my time spent studying for the Learning Prelim is pretty much a fog. However, there is one incident that is burned into my memory and is as clear and bright as that full-color snapshot your parents have of you throwing the temper-tantrum in that department-store Santa's lap when you were four and that they had *so much* fun showing your friends at your sixteenth birthday party.

It was Labor Day weekend. I had been holed up in my house studying for the Learning Prelim for I don't know how long, but certainly long enough to be able to play a good game of dominoes, had I wanted to, with the accumulated empty pizza boxes littering the place. As I recall my roaches were having a field day.

I probably hadn't talked to another person in days, and my human contact largely consisted of leaving The Jerry Lewis Telethon playing silently in the background on the tiny black and white TV set that sat on the floor in a corner of my living room. I, too, was sitting on the floor a few feet away, and lying on the floor in front of me was the previously mentioned British animal learning text. I was somewhere near halfway through the thing, but I was having so much trouble retaining anything or keeping straight the various terms that sounded like components of alien spacecraft that I was becoming firmly convinced I'd never manage to learn the stuff (how's that for irony—being unable to learn the information in a book on learning) and I was starting to panic. But because I was exhausted from studying for so hard and so long, I did not experience the kind of panic where your heart races and you feel agitated and unable to sit still. I simply did not have that much psychic energy left. My panic consisted of a slow slide into oblivion, a generalized amorphous flattening of brain, body, and mood.

I remember that, at one point, out of sheer frustration and despair, I started to cry, and a single tear slid down my face. At the same time, Charro began to dance the Coochie Coochie on the Telethon. That was the year (perhaps you've heard about it) that during her dance her dress worked its way so far down her chest the camera had to back off into the next county to avoid it looking like she was the featured dancer in the world's first nationally televised topless bar (no, Janet Jackson was not the first). I remember that the tear dropped off my chin and hit the book at exactly the same moment that I happened to look up and see Charro's chest suddenly become exposed and the camera instantly cut to a shot taken from somewhere in orbit. I distinctly remember that I was not amused. Or aroused.

Ultimately, though, somehow, in some way, I did manage to pass the Learning Prelim. And on my first try, no less. I have no idea how I did it because I just don't remember much about it.

After those tests were done, I took the Personality Prelim and the Physiological Psychology Prelim, both of which were far easier than the Statistics and Learning Prelims. We had several classes in personality that covered the information on that test, so it was a done deal, and the Physiology Prelim was based on one relatively easy text. So although I was tired, worn, frazzled, and I don't remember much about that particular time, all told I did OK and made it though Prelim Exams unscathed. Most of my classmates were not so lucky, and most failed at least one Prelim and had to face the unpleasant task of passing it on their second try lest they be ejected from the program. I felt lucky to have avoided that.

PATIENTS

Ah, patients. After all was said and done, after the insanity of graduate school with its shrieking night-terror level of stress was accounted for, the bottom line was patients. Patients were the point. Patients were the reason we were there. Patients were the thing—the only thing, really—that made the emotional shake-and-bake of the program worthwhile. Put simply, we were there because we wanted to learn to help patients.

Whatever other awful things my program may have been or done, on this score it delivered. Although my program resided at a generic and some might say largely unremarkable university, it had a well-deserved, widely-known, consistent reputation for turning out truly outstanding, even gifted, clinicians. Nearly everyone who made it thorough my program turned out to be a really, really fine clinician. Clinicians who could really and truly *help* people.

It might surprise you that many clinical psychology doctoral programs are not like that at all. Many, if not most, programs—at least during the time I was in graduate school—do not emphasize clinical work the way mine did. Some, believe it or not, are overtly and admittedly hostile to the whole idea of psychology being a treatment-oriented "profession," and consider training clinicians to be a violation of psychology's "real" mission. A psychologist's place, according to them, is to remain in the academic version of barefoot and pregnant, working as university faculty or on staff at a research institute. Period. To them, going into "practice" is a sellout, and practitioners are dastardly traitors who have made a deal with the devil—*medicine*.

Medicine, you see, has historically been a treatment-oriented profession. And treatment-oriented professions tend to be as much art as science. Well, psychology has historically been an academic pursuit, and a Ph.D. has historically been a research degree. In scientific jargon that means engaging in the "hard" experimental science of research and data as opposed to the "soft" science or intuitive "art" of a treatment-oriented profession. It also means that you don't *dare* expect your training or your degree to make you any notable amount of (say it softly now)—money.

As a result, many psychologists consider it a ridiculous and catastrophic dilution of psychology to try to turn it into a profession. (This had been one of the hard lessons I learned from my first round of rejections from all of the graduate programs I had applied to. On my applications I had been honest and admitted that I wanted to be a clinician in professional practice. Most of the "big name" programs hated that idea with a blue-veined purple passion, and since that's where I had applied, once they stumbled across the word "practice" in my essays, the flushing sounds began.)

A woman who was an intern with me, for example, came from a very, very high-powered and very, very famous clinical psychology program where, prior to internship, she had never seen an actual patient for an actual therapy session. Nearly all of her work had been with rats, believe it or not.

Up to the time I entered graduate school, a clinician had never even been elected president of the American Psychological Association, and there was all manner of heated debate over whether a clinician ever *should* be its president. Once a clinician did become president and a serious "professional" bent to the association developed, some of the more vociferous opponents of professional psychology got mad, stuck out their tongues, stamped their feet, and decided to take their ball and go home. They quit the APA and formed their own association, dedicated solely and strictly to the "real" psychology of hard, academic science rather than this soft-headed "profession" nonsense.

So *there*.

The other force that opposes psychology as a profession is the universities themselves. The truth is that most universities could give a big ol' hairy rat's butt about the quality of clinicians their clinical psychology programs turn out. They couldn't care less if their students become brilliant clinicians, because there's nothing in it for them. *Medical schools* make their name on the level of practitioners they turn out. Not so universities. Universities make their name on one thing, and one thing only. Sorry to burst your bubble, but it ain't teaching—not even close. No, universities care about one thing, and one thing only—*money*.

Yep, that's right—money. They may consider the idea that an academic degree should enable *you* to make a lot of money to be one notch lower on the moral desirability scale than, say, clubbing baby seals, but they do not feel that way about themselves. Far from it. For them, it all begins—and ends—with *the money*.

You think universities are selfless, altruistic entities whose sole reason for existence is to propagate knowledge and educate the future generation? Confucius say "Make laugh so hard, burst belly button." If that's what you really and truly think, then honey—I got a bridge to sell you. At a very special price.

Universities care about el dinero. And not tuition money, either. For many schools, tuition money is chicken scratch. It comes nowhere near covering their costs, much less allowing them to grow, build buildings, get famous, and take over the world. No, the money that allows universities to grow, the money that makes universities drool, is—*grant* money. Research grant money. And grant money works in a self-feeding cycle: Big-name faculty write big-time grants that bring in big-ass money which allows for hiring more big-name faculty to write more big-time grants that bring in more big-ass money, which allows for more—you get the idea.

You see, grant money is the be-all and end-all because it is the only thing that can pay for itself *and more*. It builds buildings. It buys equipment. It hires faculty and assistants. Grant money buys eternal life as far as universities are concerned. So that's what they want—grant money, grant money, grant money—gimme, gimme, gimme. And that requires big-name faculty writing big-time research.

Well, my program didn't have big-name faculty. It didn't have big-time research. It could not get big-time grants. So it didn't have a prayer of attracting big-ass money. As a result, trying to pass itself off as some kind of high-powered, research-oriented clinical psychology program would have been a full-frontal joke. In the face of that hard reality it did the only reasonable and rational thing it could do and that no self-respecting big-name, big-money clinical psychology department would be caught dead doing: it devoted itself to training clinicians. My program's goal was to train real, honest-to-God, front-line, professional psychologists. The program had been started by a dyed-in-the-wool clinician, and remaining true to its heritage as well as being realistic about its nature, it continued to have training clinicians as its sole purpose for existence.

And, God bless it, it did. Clinical work was what my program was all about. Instead of an emphasis on research and publishing, the emphasis was on lots and *lots* of clinical experience and clinical supervision. As crazy as my program may have been in every other way—and then some—it offered about as much direct clinical training as was humanly possible given its residence within the confines of a university psychology department.

The result was that, in my program, we were all something that we could never have been at a big-name, big-money department: we were all *clinicians*. And goddam proud of it.

Now, as you might expect given its how-hard-can-we-make-this-on-you, baptism-by-fire, throw-you-into-the-deep-end-before-you-know-how-to-swim approach to things, the way my clinical training worked was this: your first semester in the program was introductory. It was all classroom study. That was your grace period. Then, beginning with the first day of your second semester, you were automatically and unceremoniously assigned a day or so per week of "intake" duty in the University Psychology Clinic. That meant whoever had an initial appointment or happened to walk in the clinic door when you were on intake was yours, all yours. You either took them on as your case or you took them to group supervision to try to find someone else who could see them. But they were yours and you had to decide what to do with them.

The point is that after one introductory semester, just like that— you were a clinician. You were entirely responsible for cases. Like I said, you'd better have come to the program to learn to be a clinician, because by golly that's what you were gonna be. Right away. Ready or not.

The clinic where we saw our patients took up a goodly proportion of the ground floor of the four-story psychology department building. There were two hallways of clinic rooms. One consisted of "testing" rooms, each being a relatively spartan space with a linoleum floor and a table with chairs on either side and a one-way mirror for supervisors to observe through. That's where we gave intelligence, personality, and neuropsychology tests. It was also where we took Prelims and Qualifying Exams. The other hallway had rooms off it that were much nicer. These were our "therapy" rooms. They were carpeted, had comfortable stuffed swivel chairs, nice cabinets, and lamps for soft and pleasant lighting rather than the harsh overhead flourescent lighting of institutional buildings. There were also two "group" rooms at the end of the hall, each large enough to hold therapy groups consisting of up to about ten people.

All told, our clinic was very, very nice, and by comparison with most university psychology clinics a veritable Taj Mahal. The only facility nicer than ours that I was familiar with happened to also be on our campus—in the Home Economics Department. I'm not kidding. They had a "family counselor" program, and because Home Ec was the largest department on campus (still not kidding), they had even nicer digs than ours. But even so, our clinic was really, really nice.

Do not, however, let this fool you into thinking that our clinic was nice because it was any kind of university priority. Most of us figured that we had ended up with the nice rooms by accident, or perhaps by some kind of faculty subterfuge that had enabled the department to build the place under the university's radar. In reality the university seemed to not know, or care, that we existed. Or that we continue to exist.

For example: during the fall semester of one particular academic year, we had an unexpected and unusually severe early cold snap, where the temperatures dropped to freezing for extended periods of time. Well, the university had a schedule of when they turned on the heat in our clinic and, by golly, it was too early to do so. So despite persistently freezing temperature *inside* the clinic rooms, they refused to turn on the heat. For a good month our patients, and we, sat through sessions bundled up in down parkas, hats, and gloves. During sessions we—and our patients—shivered, watched our breath, and froze our bottoms off.

Still not convinced? OK, get this—the freezing clinic wouldn't have been so bad except for the fact that, at the very same time we were shivering in our sub-zero clinic rooms and seeking orthopedic consultation regarding the amputation of frostbitten fingers and toes, directly across the street, and in full view of the psychology clinic, the university was busily repaving—at great trouble and even greater expense—the parking lot of the music building. Why? So that it could be lined off like the football field. Why? So the marching band would have a nice place to practice.

I mean, there are *priorities* here.

There were other, assorted indignities as well (such as our clinic's antiquated and nearly unusable videotaping system for recording sessions versus the "family counselor" clinic over in Home Ec with its multiple-camera, motorized, remote-control recording system, complete with a second-floor, glass-front control room that you could have used to film *Star Wars*), but suffice it to say that our clinic was nevertheless a really fine facility—which is good, given that outside of the library and classrooms it was where most of us spent the better part of several years of our lives. One semester I calculated that I actually spent more time in the clinic than I did in my house. Counting sleep.

Our clinic was run entirely by, and for, the clinical psychology department. And our patients came from the entire community, not just from the college campus (we were not affiliated with the student health clinic and as such actually saw relatively few college students). It might seem surprising that ordinary people actually came to a "student psychology clinic" for help, knowing they would be seen by therapists-in-training rather than full-time professional and experienced practitioners. But come they did. Our clinic was well-known, well-reputed, and relatively inexpensive, and as a result we had *lots* of patients. In fact, our biggest problem tended to be too many intakes and too many people wanting to be seen for the number of student therapists available. So in my program we got to see patients—lots and *lots* of patients. Like I said, we were there to be trained as clinicians, and it was there that we got trained as clinicians. Big time.

For most of us, myself included, this was the one—and only—aspect of the program that was truly enjoyable. It was the one part that was exactly what we had hoped for and that enabled us to justify to ourselves the suffering we were enduring. Most of us, myself included, found ourselves falling in love with psychology, and with our patients, over and over again. The clinic was the one thing that reminded us why we had come to this place. It enabled us to thank our lucky stars that we were in this profession, that we were graced by patients who entrusted us with their lives, and that we could live out our dreams of becoming clinical psychology clinicians.

Most of us ate, drank, and breathed our work with patients. For myself, at least, I could never get enough. I relished seeing patient after patient after patient. During my entire time in school I'm not sure I ever turned down a case. I worked with almost every conceivable population—adults, children, couples, and families. Another student and I even formed a therapy group that lasted over two years— after hearing over and over and over from faculty and older students that no one had ever been able to or would be able to form a viable therapy group. Bullshit. We wanted to, we set out to, and we did. And it worked. Other students regularly asked to observe our group because it was something no one else had done and other students were every bit as hungry as we were to learn how to *do psychology*. And to do it well.

So we saw patients. Oh, how we saw patients. We saw them during the day. We saw them on nights and weekends. We scheduled them back-to-back. We scheduled them between classes. And we loved it.

CARLTON

One of my patients was a young man from the local community who I will call Carlton. Carlton came to the psychology clinic because he was unhappy. There was no specific reason he could define for his unhappiness, it was more a general sense of discontent, a low-level, chronic gnawing that he could neither accept nor banish. As a result, he was always uncomfortable. He didn't know why. But he was. And it wouldn't go away.

Clinically speaking, Carlton's condition was not complicated—he was depressed. Most people associate depression with feeling sad, but that's not its essence at all. Clinically, depression is a state of "lowered" functioning—lowered energy, lowered morale, lowered mood, lowered activity. A variety of emotions can go with this lowered state, not just sadness, and in fact it is not uncommon for people who are depressed to be irritable and argumentative, kind of like you feel when you're really, really tired. Often this results in no one realizing that they are, in fact, depressed. They just seem disagreeable.

Carlton's depression, on the other hand, was the long-standing, chronic, and low-grade variety known in the business as "dysthymia." The word literally means "bad mood," but in its technical definition it means at least a couple of years of sub-par mood, functioning, and outlook. People who are dysthymic seem to almost always be "kind of down." They're not feeling so bad as to be standing on the edge of a roof considering a plunge, but they don't find much about life that turns them on, either. Such was the case with Carlton.

Carlton had a fairly mild, generally unremarkable history. An only child, he had been raised by his mother, his father having disappeared long ago and before Carlton could have known him. Living in a fiercely rural setting in upstate New York, Carlton had grown up in the ways and sensibilities of small towns. Everyone knew everything about everyone, he had lots of friends—and a few enemies—and the whole place was, on the surface, reasonably bland and white-bread.

One cannot be misled into automatically thinking that there cannot be strange or notable things beneath such banal exteriors however, and while Carlton's upbringing was nowhere near abusive or criminal, it did have some significant pointy spots in it. His mother, for example. A good woman with a heart as big as Texas, her functioning seemed defined largely by her fear of loss. Perhaps traumatized from her abandonment by Carlton's father, or maybe from some earlier disastrous loss of which no one in her current life was aware, she lived in abject terror that Carlton would be next on her list of disappearances. She was not sure how this might come to pass, but since she feared that she would lose him somehow in some way at some time, she set out to guard against all possibilities.

The result was that she stuck to Carlton like a sticky note. She monitored everything he did, quizzed him endlessly about everything, and sought to ensure that nothing ill would ever befall him. Never really overtly abusive or pathological, her behavior was nevertheless excessive and caused Carlton some significant degree of discomfort, especially as he entered teenage years and began to feel the way that all teenagers feel about their parents—humiliated by their very existence.

To his credit, Carlton was a good kid and handled this whole business with his mom reasonably well. Born with a pleasant disposition and a genuine kindness, he was adaptive nearly to a fault. He made good grades, avoided hanging around with the wrong crowds, and never caused anyone anything that even resembled grief. Eager to satisfy his mother's wishes—and to save her from her fear of abandonment—he made the most of the confines in which he found himself and managed to fit in well. As his teacher, or principal, or baseball coach, you'd never have given him a second thought because he was a fine, mainstream kid. Nothing troublesome or even particularly notable about him, good or bad.

As he got older, Carlton managed to gather sufficient gumption—and to provide adequate reassurance to his perpetually worried mother—to be able to go away to college. He didn't go far, but away he went. The family was of modest means, so he attended a branch of The State University of New York in a nearby city. He graduated in four years with a degree in engineering and took a job with a consulting firm in yet another nearby city. Finally, he changed jobs and moved still further away, to the city in which my university was located. He had been working at this job for about two years when he appeared at the door of our clinic not knowing exactly why he needed help, but knowing that he was unhappy and that he didn't want to be. His appointment happened to be on the day I was on intake, so he became my case.

When I met him, I found that I liked Carlton immediately. His unpretentiousness and lack of driving ambition (something I certainly have never been blessed with) gave him an endearing quality. He did not seem to have a duplicitous bone in his body, and I could not imagine him ever being conniving or scheming. He was a genuinely nice guy. The only problem was that he felt bad, and he wanted that to go away.

Carlton's current life, like his mood, was not terrible, but was not very good, either. He did not dislike his job with the consulting firm. But he did not particularly like it. He was involved in a few social and community activities. But none of these particularly excited him. He had a few fairly casual friends. He read avidly and often.

Despite his apparent ordinariness, three things struck me fairly quickly as being just a bit peculiar about Carlton. First, he looked much younger than his twenty-six years of age. He seemed like a boy of maybe thirteen or fourteen—a nice boy, a boy who wanted to please and be a good boy, but a boy nonetheless. Not a man.

Second, he appeared to have a complete absence of, interest in, or history of dating. He seemed blithely unconcerned with sex, marrying, having a family, or any of the other mating rituals that drive most people of his age. It was as though he had been the subject of some hormone-depletion program, because any time I asked about dating or sex he seemed almost supernaturally blank and noncommittal.

Third, he seemed to have no particular goals for the future. While he seemed to want more than his current career—and life—offered, he also seemed entirely unclear about what it was that he wanted "more" of. He had no desires to be rich, famous, or a community leader. All he really knew was that he wanted to have more than he currently had of whatever would make him happy. That was why he showed up at our clinic asking to be seen in psychotherapy.

OK, so let's talk about psychotherapy.

Psychotherapy is an interesting thing. At its core it is simply a specific kind of conversation. It involves two—or several, if done in a group—people engaging in a conversation that is intended to either provide one of the people in the conversation something they don't already have, or with the ability to go out and get that thing.

In the scheme of things standard and social, psychotherapy, and a psychotherapeutic relationship, is somewhat peculiar. It is an intimacy, but not of equals. It involves the exchange of money for a service, but it is intensely personal. It is a type of "treatment," but it looks and sounds like "just talking." So it lives in a kind of never-never land between "medical treatment" and "ordinary life."

Since its inception, psychotherapy has engendered reactions to it and opinions about it that have spanned the entire range of possible feelings. Some have glorified it, considering it to be "the answer" that spiritual and religious writers were trying to get at in their search for enlightenment before they got weird and detoured off into theological and ontological questions of the nature of the eternal and the meaning of life. Others have vilified psychotherapy, demeaning it as the "purchase of friendship" (the actual title of a book by one of my supervisors on internship) and being nothing more than a silly placebo consisting of verbal smoke-and-mirrors that promises little, delivers less, and is hardly different from talking things over during drinks with a friend.

As if actively trying to fuel its most extreme respondents, over the years psychotherapy has provided much fodder for both camps. Stories of great emotional resolution with amazing results that strain credulity have shown up in the literature. Reports of symptom relief have ranged from the elimination of paralysis to recovery from hysterical blindness. At the same time, stories of outrageous and outlandish behavior in the name of "psychotherapy" have appeared as well, with everything from having sex with patients to performing "past life hypnotic regressions" being justified. In short, during its relatively brief history, psychotherapy has managed to span the extremes, from the sublime to the ridiculous.

Ultimately, after nearly a hundred years of arguing and investigating, the extremes of opinion about (and the actual behaviors involved in) psychotherapy have pretty much given way to the sensible and most likely appropriate middle-ground. First, it is clear that psychotherapy is not "the answer" to anything inherent in the human condition any more than penicillin or any other form of "treatment" is. It is a particular activity, done in a particular way, for a particular purpose. It can work well when applied to certain conditions according to well-established and well-researched methods. But it is not a panacea applicable to everyone or everything. (Once, when I was testifying in a trial about a little boy who had been mauled by a dog, the opposing attorney—an offensive loose-cannon of the worst sort—said "Well, Dr. Lester, isn't it true that *anyone* can benefit from psychotherapy?" Without pausing to listen to my answer of "No, actually, they can't," he fired off a hostile and challenging: "Well what about me, Doctor, do I need therapy?" to which I answered—as sarcastically as I could—"Do you really want me to answer that?" Grinning and self-satisfied, I glanced at the judge—who was giving me a very, *very* dirty look. With my grin gone, I urped up the canary, swallowed hard, turned back to the attorney, and said "Uh, what I meant to say is that I have no idea.").

But as much as psychotherapy may be a disappointment to those who had hoped for a universal cure for human suffering, it is also not the useless activity that its most vociferous critics would contend. While it is not nirvana, it is not just "two friends talking things over," either. It is a legitimate and specific "treatment" activity that is designed to work on the mechanisms of the human psyche in such a way as to give to someone something they are missing, or to enable them to get it for themselves. Things really and truly can be accomplished in psychotherapy that are outside of the normal range of conversation and relationships. In short, psychotherapy can work— for some things, at some times, with some people.

As a result, one of the most important aspects of psychotherapy is determining whether any particular person at any particular time is a good candidate for it. You have to investigate them, explore their history, and evaluate their concerns to decide whether you think a course of psychotherapy would be beneficial for them. If it wouldn't be, you're wasting your, and their, time, energy, and money.

Given Carlton's presenting complaint, his motivation, and his level of intelligence and functioning, I thought he had come to the right place. I thought that psychotherapy could help him. I thought that psychotherapeutic conversations might enable him to go find some of that happiness he was looking for. So after talking over with him his background and his current concerns, I invited him to come back to see me for a course of psychotherapy. He agreed, and for the next year we met for the somewhat standard, although decidedly unmagical, once-a-week, fifty-minute psychotherapy hour.

CARLTON'S PSYCHOTHERAPY

The whole thing started out rather slowly. When we would sit down to meet, Carlton would feel awkward and uncertain and not know where to start the conversation. He would hem and haw and say that he didn't know exactly what to say or what he should talk about.

Now, one of the special qualities of a psychotherapeutic relationship is that the therapist has explicit permission to say things that, due to their intrusive and revealing nature, in normal conversation would be considered rude or socially inappropriate. While the therapist might not say such things "rudely," if they were said, even in a kind way, at—let's say—a cocktail party, it would still be considered rude.

A primary example of this is what is called a "process comment." A process comment is a comment to another person about the way they are being or behaving *while* they are being or behaving that way. It would be like your saying to someone you had struck up a conversation with at a party "You know, your tone of voice with me sounds arrogant and demeaning. Are you always like this, or are you specifically trying to make me feel bad?" You'd get your butt thrown out of that party, pronto.

But in psychotherapy that is the kind of thing the psychotherapist is *supposed* to say. By pointing out such—usually—"unmentionables" about the way the person is behaving, the patient is able to examine how they are being and what that means and where it comes from and how it may be unwittingly driving them and backfiring on them.

So during Carlton's rather frequent episodes of stuttering and stammering for what he should say or talk about, I would often comment that he seemed to be lost without someone else telling him what he should—or should not—do, and that he behaved as if I would come to the rescue and guide him if he were just confused long enough.

In response, he would look at me blankly because, of course, he had no idea of what to do with my comment that he had no idea of what to do. Then I would point out that, like a Chinese puzzle box that has puzzle boxes within puzzle boxes, when I pointed out that he did not know what to do, he did not know what to do with my pointing out that he did not know what to do. And he would look at me blankly because after that comment he did not know what to do.

But after a while, an interesting thing began to happen. Tentatively, in small and uncertain ways, Carlton would inquire as to whether he was really supposed to, in the sessions, talk about things he "really wanted" to talk about. I would respond that there were no particular rules, but that he was certainly welcome to talk about whatever he "really wanted" to talk about. He seemed genuinely thoughtful about this response and he mulled it over repeatedly. It seemed to be a novel idea to him.

This was the first inkling that there was, in fact, *something* that Carlton "really wanted," or at least really wanted to talk about. Because he had seemed so lost and so undefined, the idea that there was something in him that had some energy, some interest, and some spunk, was a refreshing one.

One day, dropped obscurely into the middle of a session like a candy wrapper in the middle of a crowded train station, a seemingly minor and offhand comment pointed the way. He said "You know, I've always kinda wondered what it would be like to be an artist."

Wham. You have to understand that, for Carlton, this minor musing was a statement of interest and intent on the order of someone declaring himself a candidate for president. Carlton generally seemed so lost, so young, and so in need of direction and guidance, that for him to "wonder what it would be like" to be *anything* was a huge statement. So I asked him to tell me more about it.

He said that, as a child, he had gazed with pleasure and interest at works of art—sculptures, to be exact. He had examined the material, the shape, the texture, the color, and the shadow. These objects made him feel—what, exactly, he could not say. But they made him feel *something*. Something he liked. Something he wanted to feel again. So I asked him if, as a child, he had ever tried sculpting.

Oh no, he said, seeming horrified by the question. Never. Never had he done anything with art. Or even said to anyone that he *wanted* to sculpt.

Surprised by the intensity of his response, I asked why. And—just like that—he froze up. He just froze up. He seemed to be unable to generate a response of any kind. He looked at the floor—silent, motionless.

I let him sit for a few moments. Then I said softly, "Carlton?" He looked up at me. I was taken aback to see that his eyes were filled with tears.

"Carlton," I said, "What is it?"

"I don't know," he replied.

"Yes," I said. "You do. What is it?"

"I don't know," he said.

"Yes," I repeated. "You do. Tell me."

"Really?" He asked.

"Yeah, really," I said.

There was a very long silence.

"That's all you have to do," I said quietly.

Another long silence.

"Carlton?" I prodded.

Silence.

"Tell me?" I said.

"Well, " he said. "Because. Because art is for goddam fucking, asshole *sissies*."

Hmm. Now, it is said that during the detonation of a thermonuclear device, atomic fusion creates a blast core that goes from zero to the temperature of the surface of the sun—more than two billion degrees—in less than a tenth of a second, and as a result it is literally impossible to determine where any matter at the center of the blast actually goes, or what actually happens to it. To try to conceptualize something in that state lies beyond the scope or comprehension of the human imagination.

But I'll tell you this—wherever that matter goes, that's where my brain went. In the entire time I had seen him, Carlton had not so much as come close to peeping loudly, much less expressing the level of energy contained in that statement. Further, I had never heard him utter a single swear word, much less an entire string of them in one breath. It was like he had suddenly been taken over by a venom-spitting, demonic entity from another world.

"Really," I said noncommittally, attempting to mask my internal meltdown by tensing my muscles to the point of snapping bones. "How so?"

At which point Carlton unceremoniously got up out of his chair, walked to the door, and left.

OK, now we have to talk about "energy." I have mentioned energy several times because in most theories of human function and malfunction the notion of "energy" takes a central role. Freud conceptualized the core energy of life as "libido," a kind of generalized sexual energy that is applied by the psyche to various activities and interests. Other theorists have slightly different takes on how energy functions in the human psyche, but essentially all talk about how something we have strong feelings about gets imbued with psychic energy. So when a topic is touched upon that has some heightened level of energy attached to it, there is usually a heightened level of emotion attached to it as well—and a corresponding heightened behavioral response. The emotion can be pleasant or unpleasant, but its intensity indicates an issue, a conflict, or an interest—in short, something special about that topic. It means the topic is important.

So for Carlton, something about the topic of art was connected with the topic of "manliness," and it had one jumbo-sized dump truck load of energy on it. At that point I made a silent guess as to what it could be. I also guessed that it was the thing that was sapping the energy from the rest of his life.

Psychotherapists see this kind of thing all the time—a "block" on one's energy, a hot-button issue where one's life-energy is all jammed up. Apparently we'd hit Carlton's block squarely on the noggin, and sooner or later we would have to confront it. Moreover, every therapist knows that when it comes time to confront such an issue one enters a particularly tricky time. It is not at all unusual that at that point all hell breaks loose. Patients can quit, verbally attack the therapist, try to kill themselves, or start distracting the sessions by acting badly or igniting crises. It is unpredictable. In the best outcomes, sooner or later they face the issue.

With Carlton it happened sooner rather than later. In the very next session—which he came to on time and somewhat sheepishly given his previous abrupt departure, he came out with it—he admitted the thing that had been sapping his energy, that had prevented him from having a life, that by failing to face had cost him happiness. You will likely not be surprised. I wasn't, either. Carlton thought that he might be gay.

It was the classic story: He'd known he was different from the time he was very young. He had felt wrong and bad and confused by failing to experience the heterosexual urges shared by his friends. He felt shame and fear as, in his little-town rural culture, gay jokes abounded and euphemisms for being homosexual were hurled as smile-when-you-say-that insults. All told, Carlton was totally, abjectly terrified by the possibility he was gay and had desperately retreated from the possibility.

Unfortunately, doing so required that he retreat from the rest of life as well. For better or worse, such things tend to be an all-or-nothing proposition about how life is for us, and Carlton had ended up with nothing. Later on in therapy Carlton would wryly note that he felt like he had been so far in the closet that he was "in danger of becoming a hanger."

It is often the case in psychotherapy that the task of the patient and the therapist ultimately comes down to helping the patient learn to live with something they didn't ask for, don't want, and fear will be difficult or impossible to tolerate. And whatever your moral stance on homosexuality, even those who believe it to be fully biological and an "orientation" rather than a "choice" admit that it usually makes life more difficult for most people. Or as one of my favorite patients some years later said: "Even those of us who are OK with being gay would have to be complete idiots to have freely chosen it, given how much more complicated it makes life."

True to form, Carlton was not at all pleased with his realization—or his admission to me about it. For many subsequent sessions he struggled with the issue out loud. One week he was gay—hell yes, he was gay, what was he thinking—and the next he was not so sure—wait, maybe he was wrong, how did he really know? Back and forth he went.

Even more notably, Carlton got more depressed. Not overtly suicidal, but certainly in the room right next to it. This is also not unusual in therapy when people finally and directly confront the issue or dilemma they have been spending their time and energy avoiding.

They've been avoiding it because it feels bad, and psychotherapy disables the avoidance.

To his credit, Carlton kept coming to sessions and talking about it, and slowly, ever so slowly, the mysterious process called psychotherapy worked its magic. Slowly, ever so slowly, Carlton began to change. He began to calm down about the whole thing. He began to get used to the idea. He began to think he might be able to adjust and maybe even try to accept it. He decided that, what the hell, there was just not a whole lot he could do about it, so maybe the question was not *could* he live with it, but *how* could he live with it.

That was the turning point. At that point Carlton could start building a life—a real life, a life with some juice in it. At that point I saw a man begin to emerge from behind the timid little boy. I began to feel like I was talking to a real person, not some pale ghost who didn't know what to say, didn't know what to do, didn't know what was wrong. Even when he was upset and disagreeable, Carlton finally started to seem *real*. At that point he began to, as Henry Miller said, "take his life into his arms."

It was painful, touching—and beautiful. Carlton began making friends—gay and straight. He joined some gay social clubs. He went out to dinner with people. He came to sessions and laughed himself silly regaling me with stories about people, about nightclubs, about embarrassing moments, about social screw-ups and ridiculous parties. He laughed and I laughed. There were painful moments as well. The moments of shame. Of rejection. Of isolation. He cried about them. I tried not to cry. But for better or for worse, gay by design and finally filled with acceptance, Carlton was alive—and becoming a full-grown man to boot.

I'll never forget being at a restaurant with some friends during this time, and when leaving noticing a large table at which sat only men—maybe ten or so. They were laughing and joking and generally having what for all the world looked like a wonderful time. And there—at the very head of the table—sat Carlton. I'll never forget the grin on his face, the comfort in his demeanor, the look of being at home and being happy that I had never once seen when he first came to treatment. I remember forcing myself to scoot out of the restaurant before he saw me, because given my druthers I would have gladly stood there for an hour, drinking in his happiness, his acceptance of life, his ability to experience joy and comradery, his finding his place in the world. It was beautiful.

Which brings up one of the more difficult parts of being a psychotherapist: as soon as the patient gets well, the therapist loses them. Their work done, the patient turns their back, walks into the world, and leaves the therapist in their office, awaiting another patient to live with and then lose. So while Carlton's newfound life was good news for him, for me it meant it was time to become his ex-therapist.

We both knew it. He was sad. I was, too. He didn't know how to express affection toward me, to tell me what our work had meant to him. I told him I needed nothing because I saw his happiness, and that was all that mattered to me. But he continued to muse about it out loud with me. How could he—appropriately—communicate his affection toward me?

Then, completely unexpectedly, at our last session, he brought me a present. He presented me with the thing that he said epitomized my place in his life. And he unveiled for me the very first sculpture he ever did—an abstract figure representing growth and change. It was really good, and I liked it. He said that he wanted me to have it for my someday-office. It looked to me like Carlton really had talent, and his gift to me of his very first piece choked me up. But as you might have guessed, it is bad form to burst into tears in front of one's patient, so I maintained my decorum, thanked him, and we simply said goodbye. He hugged me, and off he went—to live life, to gain and lose, to laugh and cry, to love and feel, to succeed and fail. He was resolved. Very resolved. In fact, when we finished there was only one thing that still bugged Carlton, one thing he could not work out, one question that kept him up nights, one question that nagged at him and that our work could not—would not—answer to his satisfaction:

Was *I* gay.

You see, from the time he admitted his sexual orientation to me, Carlton dogged me about *my* sexual orientation. After all: I wore no wedding ring, I was reasonably masculine but also unusually touchie-feely for a mainstream male. Further, to Carlton I had mentioned no girlfriend (if Carlton only knew) and yet I didn't talk much about anything else in my life, either, so it was unclear if my silence on the issue was significant. The truth was that he knew little-to-nothing about me personally. And the issue of my sexual orientation bugged the living daylights out of him.

For a while this was directly therapeutically useful for his work. In psychoanalytic terms, he spent a good deal of time "projecting" onto me his own internal struggle over whether or not he was gay. At first it was easier to wonder about me than about himself. So after he told me that he thought *he* was gay, he spent a not insubstantial amount of time wondering whether *I* was gay. There were several times I was even concerned that he might be following me to try to find out. I don't think he ever really did, but he did manage to pester me, session after session, to tell him if I was gay or straight.

I never would. Even after he was able to focus on his own sexual orientation I still refused to tell him. That's because even though his question no longer served as a projection, my answering it still had at least two problems attached to it. First, the truth is that my sexual orientation was totally irrelevant. So-the-hell-what if I was gay or straight? Neither answer changed his dilemma or the work he needed to do one bit. Second, *either* answer compromised my power to be therapeutic. If I said that I was gay, then he would have either tried to model himself after me or seduce me. That would do nothing to help him build his own life. If I said that I was straight, then he could have replied to anything I said that he didn't like with "How could you understand—you're *straight*." Ditto that for being unhelpful. So although to the uninitiated I may have seemed coy or unreasonable by not answering his question, by refusing to settle the issue of my own sexual orientation I was actually preserving my ability to help him.

But Carlton never did accept it, and to the last he bugged me to tell him. And to the last I refused. At the end it became kind of a standing joke between us—and I became his—quote—"maybe-gay, maybe-straight, unreasonable, mysterious, withholding, butthead therapist." I would just laugh. By the end, so would he.

So, Carlton—if you're listening, just to put it to rest—I'm hopelessly heterosexual. But I still understood everything you were going through, and I still loved you, my friend. You are a good man.

RETURN TO TA

Remember that a theory called Transactional Analysis had started me on the road to becoming a psychologist. I have not talked much about it because up to this point in graduate school I had not done much with it—at least not openly. First, a bit of background:

Technically speaking, TA is more-or-less a form of "object relations" theory. Object relations is a school of psychological thought derived from psychoanalysis that says human beings function by creating and referencing internal, psychological "maps" of reality. It is only by referring to these internal representations of ourselves and the world around us that we know what things are and how to relate to them (hence the name—object "relations"). For example, your internal map contains a representation of something called an "apple," so when you come across a round, red fruit you already know it works better to eat it than to try to wash your clothes with it. By internalizing a stable and consistent representation of "apple," your psyche gives you a resource that allows you to live more effectively because you don't have to relearn what to do every time you run into a round, red fruit.

Object relations theory says that because internal maps of the world are something that every human being requires in order to function, inside everyone's head lies an inborn, automatic, psychological map-creating machine. This machine records what we think, feel, say, and do, and what the world thinks, feels, says, and does, and assembles these words, pictures, relationships, and experiences into the maps that we use to tell us what to do and how to be. Further, because we need these maps right away, our machinery starts laying them down from a very early age—almost from the moment we're born.

As is the case with any collection of information, the data in our maps needs to be organized in some fashion in order to be easily accessible. This is where schools of object relations differ from each other. Each school has a different theory of how the information in our maps is organized. TA divides our maps into three sections based on the source of the data. One section contains the data from how we felt and what we did as children, and is called the "Child." Another section contains the data from what happened around us when we were very young, and is called the "Parent." The third section contains the data about life's cause-and-effect that we learn as we grow up, and it is called the "Adult."

TA calls these three sections "ego-states" (as in the "states" of one's ego), and for all practical purposes they function as three separate, individual experiential entities between which our consciousness travels. When someone's consciousness is "in" their Child ego-state, they feel, behave, and react—*literally*—just like they did when they were a child. When someone's consciousness is "in" their Parent ego-state, they feel, behave, and react—*literally*—just like their parental figures did (or at least appeared to) when they were a child. And when someone's consciousness is "in" their Adult ego-state, they function like a rational, cause-and-effect machine—think Data (sans emotion chip) or Mr. Spock from "Star Trek."

If the implication of all this has escaped you, let me spell it out: two-thirds of your consciousness is out-of-date. *Way* out of date. Two-thirds of your map of how the world works is a leftover from what you did and what happened to you in your early life. That means most of your experience—right now, today—is filtered through information gathered from long ago. As T.S. Elliott said: "You are nothing but a set of obsolete responses."

This strange turn of events—that your current thoughts, feelings, and behavior are largely archaic—is an artifact of the efficiency of our internal map-creating machinery. Because our maps start being drawn very early on, the space in our brains available for recording data is pretty much filled up by the time we're about six years old. There is still *some* space left, of course, and the information that goes into this space becomes our Adult ego-state. But most of our map is complete (neuroscientists might say most of our neuronal pathways are set) before our age is even close to surpassing single digits.

The result is that, without realizing it, throughout our life we all tend to repeat the patterns from our childhood that are recorded and live on wholly intact in our Child and Parent. This fact—that we tend to repeat childhood patterns—was one of Freud's earliest observations about human behavior. It led to one of his very first psychoanalytic concepts, called "the repetition compulsion," which states that human beings are compelled to repeat the same pattern over and over.

And it's true—people really do repeat patterns because the patterns are alive and well and active right here and right now in their Child and Parent ego-states. So, for example, if there was a lot of pain in your childhood and a lot of pain got recorded in your Child ego-state, as an adult you are likely to find yourself getting into recurrent painful situations. If your Parent ego-state recorded a lot of arguing—maybe your parents argued a lot when you were young—even now you may find yourself engaging in frequent quarrels with your intimates.

The problem—the thing that keeps the patterns going—is that our maps don't *feel* like "maps." We don't *feel* like we're "repeating patterns." Not at all. We feel like what's happening to us and what we're doing are unavoidable, accidental, bad luck, or "just the way things are." It's not "us" living out a selectively arranged pattern, it's just "reality." And remember—it is *supposed* to feel this way because our maps are *designed* to feel like "reality." Once, when I noted to a patient that she tended to select men who would abandon her just like her father had abandoned her family, she said, "Huh? No way. The problem isn't that I go looking for men who'll leave me. The problem is that men are a bunch of irresponsible, abandoning assholes."

She was wrong, of course. But try telling that to her Child, for whom her father (whose patterns were still alive and well in the Parent in her head) was—and still is—"all men." So she plays out her early pattern, but experiences it as an unavoidable and objective reality that "men always leave you."

In short, what causes most of our problems in life is that we can't tell the map from the territory.

The power of TA is that it enables you to tell the difference, easily and powerfully. TA stands out among object relations theories because it is so *fast*. It allows you to know a great deal about someone in a very short period of time. Just by observing someone's behavior you can tell which ego-state they're in, and once you know which ego-state you're looking at you can *literally* see their past pass before your eyes. You know *all about* what happened to them when they were young and how it's playing out in their current life. For example, a woman had come to see me about a surprising and sudden-onset depression. I noted that her oldest daughter had just turned thirteen years old, and as my patient talked she looked and sounded about thirteen herself. So I asked "What happened when you were thirteen?" Shocked, she replied, "My mother died—how did you know that?" and burst into tears. We spent the next two years burying the mother and resurrecting my patient.

TA also makes it very easy to figure out what's going on—or going wrong—in a relationship. Fundamentally, there aren't two people in a relationship at all—there are six: the Parent, Adult, and Child in each person. And at any one time each person's active ego-state is talking to an active ego-state in the other person. This is also how people usually "find" each other for a relationship in the first place—by the consistency of patterns in the other person's ego-states relative to their own. If my Child felt abused, I'll "happen" to find partners with an "abusive" Parent ego-state. Then we will fit together perfectly, like two jigsaw puzzle pieces—and hate each other for it.

Using TA you can map the moment-to-moment interactions between people and within people. If I'm in my Adult ego state and I say to your Adult ego-state "What time is it?" you can respond in three possible ways. You can say from your Adult directed to my Adult, "It's three o'clock." You can say from your Child directed to my Parent, "Stop bugging me." Or you can say from your Parent directed to my Child, "For goodness sake, don't you own a watch!" Similarly, if you're "arguing with yourself," your Child and your Parent can be talking to each other inside your own head in an endless round of back-and-forth.

TA has various names for and classifications of these conversations or "transactions" (that's why the name is *Transactional* Analysis) between ego-states along with what they mean, where they come from, and how they play out. It's even possible to draw diagrams of the transactions by drawing three snowman-ish circles representing the three ego-states in each person and then drawing the lines of communication between the active ego-states in each person. It's also quite easy to see how people kid themselves about what's going on and so unwittingly set themselves up for bad things to happen. TA calls this process psychological "games" which forms one of the best-known concepts from TA and became the title of Eric Berne's most famous book, "Games People Play."

The elegance, simplicity, and raw explanatory power of TA are what turned it into the most popular psychology theory of all time. It's fast, effective, and can produce change in a big hurry. After all, it worked on me—just by reading a book about TA I changed my life significantly. It's what got me into this whole psychology graduate school thing. In fact, by the time I started graduate school I had started to think about life largely from a TA perspective.

But once I got to graduate school I was hesitant to do much touting of my devotion to TA. There were several reasons for this. First, my program had no faculty members who espoused a TA orientation. Many other approaches were represented—we had faculty members with psychoanalytic, cognitive-behavioral, family systems, and Rational Emotive viewpoints. This diversity in orientation was certainly a positive thing, as many graduate schools are completely dominated by one particular theory and that's all its students ever learn. Not so with mine, as we were exposed to a variety of different viewpoints. But not TA.

Second, you must understand that within many, if not most, schools of thought in psychology there lurks a subtle—and some-times not-so-subtle—antipathy toward other theorists and their theories. If ever there were a place where "true believers" are made, it's in the followers of psychological theories. As a result, if yours is a viewpoint that someone else does not hold, you can pretty safely assume that to them you will be one thing and one thing only—*wrong*.

It can get ugly. Once, some years ago, the organizers of a large psychotherapy conference managed to get two well-known, fiercely competitive theorists on the stage together. Most attendees, myself included, could hardly believe it, and we crammed ourselves—standing room only—into the hotel ballroom to watch the fireworks. The moderator introduced the theorists, who were both seated at a table on a riser in front of the room, sitting as far away from each other as possible, and never glancing in each other's direction. The moderator invited one of the theorists to begin the session by discussing his approach. The theorist started talking.

And he never shut up. Apparently trying to take the whole time for himself, for the next fifteen minutes the man didn't breathe. He chattered non-stop without a break, preventing himself from ever being interrupted or halted. Finally turning blue from oxygen deprivation, he paused for a microsecond to take a breath to keep from passing out, whereupon the moderator took the opportunity to jump in with "Would you shut the fuck up for just a *second*," phrased as a pleasant "Thank you so much, Dr. So-and-So. Now we'd like to hear from Dr. Other-So-and-So regarding *his* approach." The other theorist started to talk.

Only his microphone didn't work. He spoke, but nothing came out. Puzzled, he picked it up, banged on it a couple of times to no effect, and shouted "We need another microphone." At that the other theorist furiously grabbed his microphone, clutched it to his chest, and shouted "Well, I'm keeping *this* one!" In response, under his breath and loud enough for everyone to hear, the other theorist muttered— completely deadpan—"Trust me, *that* doesn't surprise *any* of us."

Ouch. At that very same conference I, myself, had the poor judgment to get caught in the crossfire. During the question-and-answer section of a particular presentation, I walked to the audience's microphone that was set up on a stand in the middle aisle and asked a theorist if they would comment on their conflict with another school of thought with whom they had been at odds through the years. Given that it had been some twenty years since the height of hostilities, I thought it might be safe—even interesting—to hear some comments that had perhaps been mellowed by the perspective of history. Wrong. In response to my question, the theorist glowered at me, stared a hole through my cranium, and shrieked, "I do *not* comment on *them*! They went *way* beyond the pale and *I do—not—talk—about—it*. Now. Or *ever*!" Then they refused to say anything else. Returning to my chair in front of that room full of people was one of the longest single walks of my life.

Some time later I commented to a friend of mine who knew this theorist personally about my run-in with them. He doubled over in laughter and said, "You have to remember—they know who 'the enemy' is, and they are not shy about saying so." Tell me about it. Apparently I am now one of them.

And listen—that is positively *civilized* compared with the way theorists can go after each other in print. Journals actually publish articles coaching followers on ways to counter the criticism of other theorists. Entire books—even their titles—are based on insulting other theorists. For a very long time, and to some extent to this very day, the rampant, arrogant self-righteousness found in certain fundamental religious sects has got *nothing* on psychotherapy theorists.

So the truth was that while I liked TA, many people did not. Many cognitive theorists thought it was too psychoanalytic. Many psychoanalysts thought it was insufficiently psychoanalytic. Many academics thought it was overly simplified. Many behaviorists thought it was too complicated.

So I did most of my TA work behind the scenes, using it quietly with patients, downplaying it to my supervisors, and reading about it on my own time (read: weekends at 2 AM). That is, until I was in clinical supervision with the one faculty member in the place who I thought might be sympathetic to my interest in TA. He was psychoanalytic in orientation, and while many traditional psychoanalysts held TA to be a bastardization of Dr. Freud's seminal work, others considered it to be a reasonable, if somewhat overly popularized, offspring.

So I decided to take what felt to me like a major risk, and level with the guy about my interest in TA and my hesitance about advertising myself in the place as a TA practitioner. So I did. It took about fifteen minutes of our first meeting for me to recount my history with TA and its place of importance to me. Then I paused, somewhat anxious at my relatively high level of self-disclosure so early in the supervision process. My supervisor nodded, leaned back in his chair, rubbed his beard (yes, he even had a beard), and pondered for a moment. Then he responded—slowly. "Well," he said. "I'll tell you what I think you ought to do." I braced myself.

"I think you ought to go full-blown TA. I think you ought to use it everywhere for everything. That way you can find out—for yourself—what parts of it are useful for you and what parts aren't. You see, no one call tell you that kind of thing, and until you find out for yourself you'll never really know and you will always have nagging questions. So I recommend you pull out all the stops and dive right in."

Picking up the pieces of my brain off the floor, I stared back at him in wonder. I mean, I thought he might be sympathetic, but for him to be completely *supportive* was well beyond my wildest expectations—and certainly unprecedented in any other experience I'd had in graduate school. I didn't quite know what to say, so I thanked him and said that I appreciated his advice, that it made sense, and I would love to follow it. I asked if during the semester I was in supervision with him I could talk in TA terms about my patients. He said he'd be happy to do that, but to remember that he didn't really know TA very well so that I might have to teach him as we went along. I wanted to hug him.

We spent that semester—and the following in which I again asked for him as my supervisor—finding out just how much of TA I found useful. And the answer was—a whole lot. It is likely not an accident that it was at that point I began to blossom as a therapist. It was during that semester that another student and I started the TA-based group that lasted for over two years. I found that sometimes I liked to use actual TA language in conversation with my patients, teaching them some of the theory and even drawing diagrams of their transactions. With other patients I didn't use the terminology, but I continued to think about them and their concerns in TA terms inside my own head.

It was terrific. As time went on I became known around the department as an outstanding clinician, certainly one of the best—if not *the* best—the place had produced. Merlin commented that I presented the best case formulations he had ever seen. I liked it, my patients liked it, and the results of my work showed what I had always thought—TA possesses unique power and usefulness. To this day, after being in practice for over twenty years, I find that I still use TA inside my head any time I'm confused or uncertain. It still works.

And I owe it all to that supervisor. I heard that he died a couple of years back. And you know, despite having had him for supervision for only those two semesters and then not seeing him for over twenty years, I felt profoundly sad. And I'm not sure if I ever adequately thanked him for what he did for me.

RECREATION

Despite everything, we did, in fact, have time for some fun during graduate school. Our recreation—and you must understand that I use the term so loosely as to include such things as taking bets on whose artery will spurt farthest when punctured—was an interesting slice of life. I say "slice" because our fun often resembled a prison-yard knife-fight.

Remember that we were so overwhelmed by our insane level of academic demands that "enjoyment" or "relaxation" was about as readily available as a dry martini at an AA meeting. So our recreation, when we did find time for it, had to be compressed. Tightly compressed. We had to squeeze a year's worth of a normal person's leisure into oh, say, an hour or so. That meant our fun, like the rest of our lives, was ridiculously and absurdly *intense*. We went for broke. For us, when you think "blowing off steam," think "Three Mile Island." Board games became barroom brawls, card games were eye-stabbing voodoo rituals. We didn't throw a party, we threw a spree-kill.

Take ping-pong, for example. In our hands that innocuous little game took on the most worrisome elements of an armed insurrection. There was a whole room of ping-pong tables in the basement of the Student Center, and a few times a week after eating lunch together several of us would descend on the place like a swarm of killer bees. We would commandeer however many tables were required for the number of participants tagging along, and unleash on the place our traveling freak show that went by the deceptively mundane name "Three-Way Ping-Pong."

In Three-Way Ping-Pong a player stands at each end of the table and a third player stands on one side, at the center by the net. One player serves, the player at the opposite end returns the serve, and the player from the center of the table runs to the end where the server was and returns the next shot. At the same time the server runs to the opposite end of the table where the receiver has just been and returns the next shot while the player who just returned the serve runs to the opposite end to take the next shot, and so on. The result is that all three players run around the table to return their next shot from the opposite end of the table from the one where they just were.

The beauty of ping-pong, it turns out, is that the table is exactly the right size to enable three players to consistently reach the opposite end in time to return the next shot—just barely, and only if they run really, really fast. So in this bizarre spectacle that we called "fun," a ping-pong ball would bounce back and forth on the table while three players sprinted around it like drunken planets caught in a frenetic, barely controlled orbit.

But the real fun started about a half dozen or so shots into a point when one or more players would begin to get a half-step behind. That meant for them to retrieve their next shot they had to either dive, head first, at the ball, or sprint so hard that they couldn't stop after hitting the shot and would invariably end up either sprawling across the surface of the table next to them or sliding violently across the floor, on their stomach, until they slammed head-first into the closest wall. And if you were *really* good at it (which I was, given that I invented the game), you could scramble up from the floor, push off against the wall, sprint around the table, and *still* dive to get your next shot.

Overt sadism ruled the day. People would often avoid hitting a clear winner simply so they could extend the point to watch another player suffer. One of the most fun things you could do to a player who was starting to get behind was to hit the ball so softly so that it barely cleared the net. The other player would be running away from the table because they expected the ball to carry well beyond the end of the table. Freaking out at the need for a sudden change of direction when they were already running full-tilt in the opposite direction, they would often turn, slip, and violently impale themselves on the corner of the table as they dove toward the net. Alternatively, they might spin out of control and fall, head over heels, *under* the table.

Now, because you were generally in a pretty desperate spot every time you hit the ball, the truth was that it was hard to hit a clean winner. So if the three players were reasonably skilled, a point could go on for several dozen shots with the number of sprawls, slides, impales, and rolls increasing exponentially as the thing dragged on. And if one player got *real* far behind, two players could start bumping into each other. At that point you could hit a shot on the far side of the wrong player, which would result in the player who was supposed to return the shot physically assaulting the other player as they pushed, shoved, and yanked them out of their way to get to the ball.

Now *that* was some great ping-pong.

As an extra added attraction it was fun to watch everyone else in the room try to ignore us, which wasn't easy given that the game was as loud as it was frantic. Its intense physicality, combined with barely keeping up at every moment, resulted in the game having a loud accompanying soundtrack filled with pants, grunts, shrieks, shouts, "Oh my God's," and side-splitting laughter. Sometimes we'd become so hysterical that we had to stop playing just to compose ourselves. We'd also stop the game when a player on the ground appeared to have stopped breathing.

Imagine the scene. You walk down the stairs into the basement of the Student Center and take a quick right turn into the recreation room housing the ping-pong tables. There you find eight or nine friendly little games going on at the tables in front of you. Then, at the far end of the room, like a scene out of some crazy Monty Python movie or from an alien civilization where time runs at twice the speed of earth's, a group of players are racing around, falling, slamming into each other, sliding across the floor, crashing into walls, and rolling across the surface of the table next to them while shrieking, yelling, screaming, and laughing uncontrollably. It was other-worldly.

Not to mention exhausting. We would regularly arrive at our first class after lunch in a completely offensive state—limping, wheezing, shaking, and completely stinking, covered head-to-toe with sweat. One day after playing, a group of us walked into the psychology department and an undergraduate student looked at me and naively chirped "Oh—is it raining out?"

To top it off, the game was highly contagious. The other students in our after-lunch class would look at us *funny*—until we could persuade them to join us for a game, at which point they would become completely corrupted, hopelessly addicted, and demand that we include them from then on.

On the weekends we had even more fun. One of our favorite past-times was a game we affectionately called "Killer" Monopoly. The name was no accident—at some point during an evening of this fun little family board game for ages 7 and up virtually everyone involved would become actively homicidal. Were we all not so horribly repressed and deeply compulsive, there would surely have been actual gun play.

You must understand that Monopoly was not "just" a game to us. We were so busy pushing, shoving, striving, and being evaluated and tested by everyone at every moment in everything in the rest of our lives that we did not know how to behave otherwise even when the activity was of no consequence. So Monopoly became just another chance to demonstrate our competence and worth as human beings by scratching, clawing, stomping, and biting our way to the top of a pile of dead carcasses in order to howl at the moon and declare ourselves Alpha Dog. If you won at Monopoly, you were God. If you lost, you were obviously a loser who had sex with your pets. It was the law of the jungle and survival of the most vicious, cunning, and conniving. Like the lion who manages to successfully bring down the gazelle, the one with the most blood on their face at the end of the evening won. Everything else be damned.

Oh hell, let's just put it this way—you did what you had to do to win. Period. Losing was not an option. At any time. For any reason. Justified or not. This was all-out war.

In our version of Monopoly, deals weren't made just to try to buy and sell property, deals were made to try to attain such deity-like dominance over the other players that the depth of their humiliation would require them to spend their first three years of salary on psychiatric care. And Lord, Lord, *Lord* help you if you were stupid enough to volunteer to be the banker. It was uniformly assumed that you simply wanted to cheat, so you were never again trusted—anywhere, about anything. You were thereafter accused of malfeasance in all aspects of life, from commingling the Monopoly bank funds with your own, to cheating on tests to screwing your best friend's girlfriend. You would also be the target of blackmail, as other players would demand extra loans at especially favorable repayment terms (such as not having to repay at all) because, after all, they loaned you their class notes from physiology and you kept them a week longer than you said you would so it was your fault they got a "B" in the class so you had goddam *better* lend them the money to buy Park Place. Meanwhile, if you had any sense at all, as the banker you were, in fact, trying to cheat, and you were sneaking money into your pile. But you were well aware that even God himself could not help you if you got caught.

In short, the line between the game and life was gone and everything and everyone was at risk every moment of every game. You could (and were, in fact, expected to) do, and say, *anything* to win.

Herewith is a sample of a typical Saturday Night "Killer Monopoly Rant." Trust me, there is no need for me to resort to anything so crude as "exaggeration." (And pardon the language involved, but you do want the real thing, don't you?) The following would occur after one player made a successful deal to buy or sell or trade property with another player that gave one—or both—of them an advantage over another player who was not involved in the transaction. From the aforementioned third-party the following monologue would spew:

"Jesus fucking *Christ*! What in *hell* do you think you're doing?! Mother of God, I do not *believe* you! You are such an *asshole*! Did your IQ drop fifty points in the past five *minutes*? Have you failed to even *notice*, you blockhead, that the deal you just made with Butthead over there virtually *guarantees* he's going to win? Have you forgotten *he's won the last three games? Hello!?* Do you want anyone else, even yourself, to have a *chance*? Do you *care*? Did he *pay* you to do this? Are you getting blow jobs in the back *room* for this? What in God's name is *wrong* with you? No wonder he wins all the games, you fucking *idiot*, you're the one letting him do it! Maybe you don't want to win because your mommy told you to play nicely with others, but why do you have to ruin it for the rest of us? Oh, wait, no, maybe you're just trying to end the game early because your mommy told you it was time for bed. Is *that* it? I mean, do you need Monopoly *lessons*? Do you even know what the *point* of this game is? Have you even *heard* the phrase 'try to win'?

Dramatic pause.

"OK, so look, *scumbag*, now that you've screwed everything up so royally and ensured that jerkoff over here is going to win so the game is essentially over, the only rational thing to do, the only way to salvage this thing—and to make the game any fun at all—is to give someone else at least a remote chance of staying in the game. Since I'm the only one with even a prayer, you need to sell me your Railroads so that *someone* can make this a game against your diddly little lacky over there. So tell you what—I'll give you a hundred bucks for your Railroads. Here's a hundred bucks. Come on. Give 'em to me. At least make the game interesting for *someone*."

At this point the opponent would excrete the expected retort of profane responses expressing disdain and contempt, which would trigger a continuation of the diatribe:

"What, you think that's too *low?* Too *little* money for a few stupid railroads? Like it's going to make any *difference?* Listen, moron, *you're* certainly not going to win, now, are you? *He* is. You've seen to that. So it's not like it's going to hurt *you.* No one else having a chance is, after all, *your* fault. Now gimme the goddam railroads! Come on! Here's a hundred bucks. Come *on!*"

The accused would proffer a hostile stare or an obscene gesture, at which point the accuser would summarily stand up from the table and declare:

"Fine. I'm going home. What fun is this? This game is over. Shit For Brains over here has seen to that. It's no fun just playing it out when we know what's going to happen. See you guys Monday." And they would head for the door.

That maneuver would trigger a cacophony of begging, pleading, and crying that the player not leave, not abandon the game, not ruin the evening, not destroy the Alaskan National Wildlife Refuge. Everyone turned mediator, everyone offered proposals to resolve the impasse between the combatants, everyone whined and griped and complained. This, of course, would result in both the accuser and the accused turning their venom on the rest of the participants, accusing them of taking sides, turning traitor, and having overriding, covert selfish motives. The others would, in turn, fight back, and a dandy little free-for-all would ensue. Finally, some solution would be reached, the accuser would sit down, the game would go on, someone would manage to win, and everyone would hate each other until Monday morning when all was forgiven and we were best friends again, locked together in mortal combat against our personal Armageddon called graduate school.

Not *precisely* the manner of play envisioned by the creators of Monopoly, do you think?

But as much of a blood sport as our Monopoly games may have been, they could not hold a candle to our card games. These were not "games" at all, at least not in the usual sense. They were satanic rituals, cannibalistic feasts. We ate—and *enjoyed* eating—our young. They were ghastly, violent confrontations using small rectangular pieces of cardboard containing colored shapes as hellmouth-like openings to allow the emergence of whatever primordial urges happened to be the most savage and offensive at that particular moment.

Now, we did not have the time, energy, or mental space to learn to play anything so civilized or technically sophisticated as Bridge, so we settled for more primal and simple games such as Spades or Hearts. But we did not play the "usual" version of either. Oh, no. We played— you guessed it—"Killer" Spades and "Killer" Hearts.

In our version of Hearts, for example, not only was the Queen of Spades 13 points against you, but the Queen of Hearts was, too. So you had *two* "Big Bad Bitches," as they were lovingly known, to watch out for. Oh yes, and the Jack of Diamonds was ten points in your *favor*, so you were desperate to *get* him while *avoiding* the Big Bad Bitches of Death. This kept you scared, on edge, and terrified at every moment because, remember, everything about your quality as a human being was at stake. Your cosmic worth was on the line.

Sound familiar? Yup, the sum-total of our lives, expressed in cards.

The viciousness unleashed in these card games could be downright horrifying. During Killer Hearts, for example, whoever was in the lead at that particular moment would be identified as a common enemy to be chased by the other players into the Hearts version of a blind alley and set upon with the card-game equivalent of bricks and bats. When the current score would be read aloud and the leader announced, the cry would go up to "Get them!" People would point and the chant would begin: "Get them, get them, kill them, kill them!" And we would turn on the leader like a pack of wild dogs. Several outsiders who were brave enough to sit in on a game were so unnerved by the raw verbal violence of it all that after just one experience they thereafter refused to participate in our card games or even be in the same house where they took place.

The single finest moment in Killer Hearts, the event that would move people to tears of joy, elicit screams of delight and high-fives all around, was when the current leader would get *both* queens on the same play. This, in our particular vernacular, was known as the "Double Twisting Back Butt Fuck," or the "Double Twister," for short. (There was a milder version, known as the "Single Twister," when the leader got one queen, but it was nowhere near as well thought of as the Double.) Better still was when the leader got both queens on a hand where *they* led. This pinnacle of self-destruction was entitled the "*Self-Inflicted* Double Twisting Back Butt Fuck." But no matter which version might occur, any night with a Double Twister was a good night (unless, of course, you were the recipient of said event, in which case it was time to excuse yourself, go into the next room, and engage in some serious self-mutilation). And the appearance of a "Self-Inflicted" Double Twister was cause for celebration beyond words—there would be whooping and hollering, glasses being raised, toasts being offered, rounds being bought, ceremonial dances being performed, and fatted calves being slaughtered. Life was *good*. Unless, of course, you were the recipient, in which case the aforementioned episode of self-mutilation awaited.

If our language during our little nights of fun and games seems kind of, uh, "colorful," you are quite wrong. Our language was *awful*. We could make your ears bleed. We invented profanities that sailors would be ashamed to use. Give us a few drinks, put a deck of cards in our hands, and we would find ways to connect words to body parts and give names to intimate interpersonal activities that defy anatomical possibility. To make matters worse, we were endlessly self-congratulatory on any new particularly catchy (read: "offensive") phrase we managed to create, and we repeated them as often as possible in as many places as possible in front of as many people as possible.

The spontaneous outbursts were generally the most compelling. During one particularly contentious Killer Hearts game, a student who had not usually participated in our Saturday Night Massacres was playing and was having some trouble keeping up with the dizzying pace of shifting loyalties, gang-mentality, and vicious personal attacks. At one point she was the recipient of an exceptionally dazzling and unexpected Double Back Twister, whereupon she stared at the cards for a moment and then shrieked "Well, FUCK A BIG RAT!" She promptly turned bright red, slunk down on the couch giggling, and said "I cannot *believe* I said that."

Neither could we. Life-threatening injuries were produced as we fell all over ourselves with glee. Considering this to be the finest phrase ever uttered by a human being, it was thereafter known as "F.A.B.R." and became the standard by which all manner of expressing one's displeasure at anything anywhere at any time was judged.

OK, so I need to admit something here—I'm lying on this one. Here's the truth—she did not originally shriek it. *I* did. Even I'm a little embarrassed about this one. I don't know where it came from, it just kind of came out of my mouth one evening when I got a particularly traumatic hand of cards. But it didn't catch on until the night I just mentioned when this very feminine, rather straight-laced, proper (even uptight), and attractive young woman shouted it. When I said it nobody quite believed I actually said something like that, but it was ultimately written off as just another of Greg's perversely curious behaviors that people had more or less grown accustomed to. But when *she* said it, the sheer outrageousness and incongruousness of someone like her saying something like that firmly established its place in infamy.

Wait—it gets worse. Some time later Killer Hearts and Killer Spades were replaced by an even more heinous game that went by the innocuous name of "Nertz." Innocuous is the last thing it was. Nertz was the ultimate corruption of cards, the final answer to the search for pure evil. Nertz was nuclear war. It was the Four Horsemen of the Apocalypse on a *really* bad hair day.

What was this new-found crime against nature? Basically, Nertz is what solitaire would look like had it been designed by Lucifer himself. In it, each player has a deck of cards and their own solitaire board, but everyone has to try to play out on the same piles of aces in the middle of the table. At the same time. That means you are always in immediate and direct competition with all of the other players for plays on those piles. This produced a new and heretofore unparalleled level of desperation as you played as fast and as hard as you could, ramming your cards onto the piles of aces with sufficiently fearsome force as to terrify anyone misguided enough to try to beat you to the play. Pounding the table to distract, faking plays, shouting obscenities, and pushing other people's hands out of the way were common and accepted tactics.

But the quality of Nertz that raised our card-game fun to a truly delightful new level was the addition of actual physical violence. In the melee caused by this quite ridiculously dangerous game, blood was actually drawn, fingernails were torn, cards were destroyed, and people threw themselves (and others) on the floor, sometimes dragging an opponent out of their chair and tickling them to the point of nausea. And, of course, new and improved profanity was developed specifically for use during Nertz. Let's see, by this point terms like "Butthead" had essentially become terms of endearment, and "Fuck yourself RIGHT NOW" merely a salutation. This new era of recreational warfare substantially raised the verbal bar to the point of creating such happy little comments as "You need to imagine the biggest shit pile in the world and yourself taking a GREAT BIG BITE." Name-calling was elevated to historic proportion as body parts, facial features, and rodents were combined in "You twat-nosed-rat-faced motherfucker!" "Fuck a big rat" even refined itself into "Fuck a big duck," with manic, mass quacking all around. At times it all spiraled into profane nonsense as someone would shout "Well, fuck a double-dicked donkey rat!" No one would miss a beat.

The volume increased as well. A lot. Once, when several of us were on a trip (an actual vacation from graduate school, believe it or not) and engaged in our usual Nertz warfare one evening in a hotel room, it took us over half an hour to realize that our window was open and everyone in the parking lot could hear us. *Big* oops. You don't know embarrassment until you fear that your screams of "You slimy rat bastard motherfucker, evil spawn of the prince of darkness, I command your poison sperm to burn in the ninth ring of cocksucker hell" could be heard by ten-year-olds returning with their parents from a showing of "The Little Mermaid." Ahem.

QUALIFYING EXAMS

If dissertation was like a sinister, foreboding presence haunting you through graduate school, then Qualifying Exams were like a river of molten lava flowing toward you—and gaining. Qualifying Exams were the single most emotionally foreboding event in graduate school. Nothing, not even dissertation, inspired the pure, raw, primordial terror that Qualifying Exams did. Not even close. Qualifying Exams were the stuff of—literally—nightmares. For virtually the entire year before I took my Qualifying Exams I had a recurring nightmare about them: I would be in the exam room busily writing away, and an airplane would fly over, drop a cable with a hook on the end of it, grab me by the collar, and snatch me out of the room.

It doesn't take a Freudian to interpret *that* one.

Qualifying Exams delivered a jumbo, economy-sized case of heebie-jeebies to even the most stable, sane, and well-adjusted student for two very good reasons. First, they stood as the single most significant milestone in the program because they drew the only truly important distinction in graduate school—the difference between being a doctoral "student" and being a doctoral "candidate."

To actually be awarded your Ph.D. you had to first be "advanced to candidacy" for the doctorate. It was kind of like getting engaged—a proposal and an acceptance don't guarantee a wedding, but you're sure as hell not going to have one without them. The way you were advanced to candidacy was to take, and pass, Qualifying Exams. And, just like "no ring—no wedding," it was "no pass—no candidacy" and, of course, "no candidacy—no Ph.D." You couldn't even defend your dissertation until you had passed Qualifying Exams. They stood solidly and resolutely between you and the rest of your life.

Second, Qualifying Exams were designed to test your knowledge about any and all things that you might have, could have, or should have studied during your graduate school tenure. Nothing—*nothing*—in the field of psychology was off limits, whether you had a class in it, had studied it, or had even heard of it. As a result, while they were technically called Qualifying Exams because they "qualified" you as a candidate for a Ph.D., in my program no one actually called them that. The common name for them was "Comps," as in "Comprehensive" Exams. The faculty was fond of reminding us that they were *not* "Comprehensive" Exams, they were "Qualifying" Exams. We were fond of making faces behind the faculty's back and reminding each other that any test covering everything that we had, should have, or could have studied was certainly "comprehensive" in our book.

Comps were a very, very, *very* big deal. Students were often nervous about them from their first day in the program. From the day I started, even before I knew what they actually were, just hearing the way people said the word made me shiver. People said "Comps" in a specific tone of voice—the way one might say "eating ground glass," or "being skinned alive." The tone made it clear that these tests were from the deepest ring of hell, that they were the source of all evil, the mother lode of human agony, the crown prince of pain. It could have raised anxiety in the dead.

It was not at all uncommon for students to begin studying for Comps a full year in advance. I studied for them for just about ten months, and toward the end I regularly spent between twelve and fourteen hours a day studying for them. Furthermore, over several generations of students a set of six huge, spiral-bound notebooks had been amassed, filled to the brim with material to study for Comps *in addition* to everything else covered in the program. These notebooks were passed down from class-to-class in a sort of perverse rite-of-pain passage, perhaps not unlike a ritual handoff of a hari-kari knife from one disgraced Samurai to another.

I'll tell you the truth—Comps remain one of the single most frightening experiences of my life. When I was handed the sheet containing the questions for my Comps, I was shaking so badly that it took me a good five to ten minutes just to calm down sufficiently to be able to *read* the damn things. It took me another ten minutes to calm down enough to actually be able to *write*. The only event in my life that induced anywhere near the compressed intensity of fear that I experienced taking Comps was some years later when, as part of the test for my Third Degree Black Belt in a martial art, in front of a hundred people I was required to break four inches of concrete with my bare hand. At least that, even with the resulting fracture of the bone in my hand and severe sprain of my wrist, was over quickly. Not so with Comps.

Comps were traditionally given once each year, during the spring semester. They were spread over two days. Each day was six hours long. During that twelve hours you were required to answer questions in four areas: Personality, Psychotherapy, Psychopathology, and Ethics. Two areas were included each day. The way it worked was that you had to pass each "day" of Comps rather than each individual "section." So, for example, if the first day consisted of the section on Psychotherapy and the section on Psychopathology, if you flunked *either* section you were considered to have flunked the *entire* day and had to take *both* sections over. Then, when you took the day again, if you flunked either section—even the one you'd *passed* the first time around—you still flunked out because you had flunked the entire "day" for a second time. The bizarre result was that you could actually pass every section of Comps and *still* flunk out of school simply because you failed to pass both sections of the day at the same time. How's that for added stress?

In reality, during my time in the program only two students actually flunked out on Comps, so the odds weren't nearly as bad as the whole aura of the thing might indicate. Irrelevant. The magnitude of the tests' scope, the degree of the stakes riding on them, and the chance that you could pass every section and *still* fail was such a ghastly mix that it universally generated the feeling of being a deer caught firmly, and fatally, in the headlights.

Oh yes, and one other thing—once you successfully passed Comps and were advanced to candidacy, the clock started ticking. From that point you had exactly four years in which to finish your degree, or your candidacy expired. That's right, your candidacy *expired*. Which meant *you would have to take Comps again* if you wanted to get your degree.

I know what you're thinking: "What's the big deal? Four years? What idiot couldn't finish their degree in four freaking *years*?"

I will answer that question: a *whole lot* of idiots.

Here was the problem: By the time you took Comps you were generally somewhere between four and seven years into your doctoral program. While by that time you had likely finished most of the requirements, you had also likely finished most of your savings, most of your spouse's savings, most of your parents' savings, and most of your child's piggy bank. Your years spent toiling endlessly and mercilessly in grinding poverty had worn you down, leaving you whimperingly desperate and jealously eyeing your gerbil's food. You were up to *here* with living on the edge and your family was starting to roll their eyes and treat you like the leech that you were. Patience was wearing thin all around.

Well, by becoming a "Ph.D. Candidate," you actually gained some status and marketability in the field. You even rated initials—you were called an "ABD," which stands for "All But Dissertation," as in "everything finished for the Ph.D. except the dissertation." Of course, that's kind of like saying "the car trip is finished except for backing out of the driveway," but never mind. Being ABD meant that, for the first time, there were people who were willing to *hire* you for a real job in psychology. All you had to do was swear before The Holy See that you would finish your dissertation and complete your degree in a reasonable amount of time.

Ha. The truth was that once you had a job, a paycheck, and a taste of "real" life, all this graduate school nonsense started to look like the ridiculous insanity that it actually was. Only you weren't yet finished with this graduate school nonsense because you still had to finish your degree—meaning your dissertation. Remember that completing a dissertation is an incredibly laborious task, and even under ideal conditions, working on it full-time, it can take a good two years to complete. So if you got involved in a "real" job and a "real" life, and if you procrastinated a little bit here and avoided a little bit there, in no time at all the four years that once seemed like an eternity could dissolve before your eyes and you could find yourself staring into the vacant and hollow, shark-eyed abyss of having to retake Comps to be eligible for your degree. *Very* bad news.

I saw this happen way too many times for comfort. Merlin did, too. One day I was sitting in his office when he marched in, slammed a book down on his desk, looked at me and hissed with a venom *distinctly* uncharacteristic of him: "I am *so tired* of calling up students and begging them to come back and finish their degree! I should not have to be doing this! It is *insane!*"

I could not have agreed more. But I knew that I was no less vulnerable to this danger than anyone else. I knew that if I got even a whiff of normal life after so many years of wading through this hot molten insanity that the effort required to return to graduate school tasks would be so great I was not sure I would ever be able to do it. As a result, very early on in the program I had decided that I would not, under any circumstances, accept a job in the field before I had completely and totally finished my degree. That meant finish *everything*—dissertation included. If I had to take a job standing on street corners passing out leaflets for some lunatic-fringe religious cult in order to support myself while I finished my dissertation, so be it. I was not going to get sidetracked, even if the sidetrack was a real job and a real life.

OK, so back to Comps.

Comp questions were always essay questions, often sweeping in scope and always demanding rigorous thought and the careful construction of a consistent and logical argument. Answers were judged by their accuracy, comprehensiveness, and the quality of your evidence. You couldn't just give your opinion and expect anyone to give a damn about it—you had to cite literature and research so you could report what *real* psychologists thought as support for any position you took. That meant you'd better be able to list studies, names, and data to support your answers. I actually developed a system for memorizing such things, and I managed to pack several hundred studies into my head by the time I sat down to take the test.

The core terror about Comps, though, was that all of your months of attempting to study everything under the sun could be rendered completely useless by the nature of the test questions. Each section consisted of, at most, maybe three or four questions. That meant while you tried to study everything, each section would ultimately focus on only a couple of topics. Well, if the topic that a question addressed happened to be one you'd slighted or missed or glossed over, you were in deep sushi in a big hurry because a good third of your score on that section was now in the toilet. And that's what really scared everyone—there was just no way to know what topics the questions would address. That meant you could study for a year and *still* be unable to answer the questions—ergo the reason I was shaking when I began reading my Comp questions. My fundamental fear was that I would find before me questions that addressed topics where my best answer would be "Huh?"

I remember talking to a faculty member about this issue. I noted how stressful it was not being able to predict what topics would be addressed on the questions. He scoffed, said I was being paranoid, and insisted that the faculty was not so evil as to ask a question that would be so ridiculously narrow that we would have no ideas for answering it. With a dramatic flourish he opened a journal sitting on his desk, pointed to an article and said "Look, if we *wanted* to fail everyone we certainly could, all we'd have to do is ask about one particular article in one particular journal. We know you can't memorize every single article in every single journal, so we'd never do something like *that*." I felt reassured.

What a mistake. On the Ethics section of my Comps, one of the questions—no kidding—*referred exclusively and solely to one particular journal article in one particular journal.* That's right, on my Comps the faculty did the *exact thing* that the professor specifically said they would *never* do, because "they knew it was a sure way to fail people." And I doggone near did fail that section because I had not, in fact, read that particular article. So my answer was completely seat-of-the-pants. I ultimately passed that section by the skin of my teeth—by one tenth of one point. When I think about all that I am *still* incredulous.

Oh—and me, paranoid? My ass.

Worse yet, if you were so close to passing or failing that they could not make up their minds, you were called in for a followup *oral* exam. Oral Comp exams were the single most chilling interpersonal experience I have ever heard described (I escaped that ordeal, thank you, God). There you'd be, on one side of a table, with five faculty members facing you on the other. They would read you a question—and not one from your written Comps, either. A *new* question. One you'd never heard of. Then you were to answer it—orally. And as you talked, the five faces staring at you remained as still and expressionless as figures in Madame Tussaud's Wax Museum. No nods, no smiles, no frowns, no gestures of recognition whatever. Just blank stares. You would talk. Then, when you paused, someone would ask "Does that complete your answer?" You could say "yes," at which point they would read to you the next question, you could say "no," and go back and blather some more in an attempt to keep from passing out, or you could pull out a Glock, put it to your temple, and put an end to the whole charade.

As I said, I studied for Comps for a total of about ten months. At the beginning, whenever I had some moments where I was sick of doing everything else I would pull out some Comp materials and work my way through them. As time passed I tried to be increasingly systematic about how I approached it. Sometimes I would study from the ring-binders. Other times I would work my way through research journals. Then I would review notes from classes. And I would read textbooks. I also tried to be reasonably conscientious about making lists of the specific references I ran across so I could periodically encode them into the system I used to implant them in my head. Sometimes a few of us would study together, but in general studying for Comps was a solitary task. No one could learn the stuff for you.

As Comps grew closer, I studied longer. I spent most of my time in cubicles in the library, as there were fewer distractions and temptations to do other, less important things—like eat, sleep, or bathe—than there were at home. Occasionally I'd study in one of the clinic rooms where I'd actually be taking the test so that I would be reviewing information in the same room in which I'd need to recall it (an attempt to engage a version of "state-specific" learning). By cutting down on external stimuli I found that I could concentrate for increasingly long periods of time.

As the exams became weeks rather than months away, I started spending essentially all of my time studying. And I began to experience delightful new feelings—like how after seven or eight straight hours of studying my eyeballs felt like they were going to fall off my face and I no longer had any discernable sensations in my butt. Or how the feeling of being so tired that you can't stand up also seems to destroy your ability to tell time. It was often only after waking up with my head lying on a journal that I would realize I had fallen asleep while studying.

Ultimately, I had to set up a systems of bribes to keep myself going. Just one more hour, and I could do fifteen minutes of recreational reading. Just one more hour, and I could get a hamburger at the commissary. Just one more hour, and I could fantasize about rubbing Cool Whip on the Dallas Cowboy Cheerleaders. Just one more hour.

As it turns out, I am indeed, apparently, eminently bribable, because it worked to keep me going through what became a rather terrible state of chronic and unrelenting fatigue. I just kept at it, studying hour after hour, day after day.

Then, about five or six days before Comps, all of a sudden, out of nowhere, I crashed. I woke up one morning and could not get myself to do it. I could not get myself to go to the library. I could not get myself to open the ring binders. I could not get myself to memorize citations. I could not get myself to do *anything*. It was as though my psyche was out front, on the sidewalk, with a picket sign. And like pulling the leash on a dog that has laid down and is *not* gonna budge, I tried everything I could think of to cajole, intimidate, or coax myself to study, all to no avail. I could not get myself to work on Comps for even one more minute.

Stranger still, my fear of failing, generally my most loyal companion throughout grad school, had completely disappeared, at least as regards Comps. In its place lay a deep weariness that contained an odd and unfamiliar sense of peace. I was no longer scared of failing them. In fact, I no longer cared about the outcome of Comps at all. All I cared about was not having to keep studying. All I cared about was not having to go to the library. All I cared about was not having to read one more goddam journal article, memorize one more fucking study, learn one more indecipherable theory. All I cared about was taking the tests *so I didn't have to live like this anymore.* If I flunked, well, it was just meant to be and I'd go learn to make Secret Sauce. But no matter what happened, I was *done*.

Which was when it hit me—this was what it felt like to be "ready" to take Comps. Normally, you'd expect a feeling of "readiness" to involve things like feeling prepared, or confident, or well-practiced. Well, when it came to Comps those kinds of feelings were just not on the menu—not if you studied for every moment of every day for the next hillion, jillion years. There was just too much information to cover combined with too many uncertainties about what questions would be asked. In the face of something that onerous, "readiness" was never going to feel like, well, "readiness." Instead, it felt like "resignation." Like surrender. It felt like no longer caring about passing, only about getting the goddam things over with so you didn't have to do this any more. Then you could crawl away, hide, and sleep for a month.

Interestingly, this condition has a name—Buddhists call it "nonattachment." It is considered to be a highly desirable state because by eradicating attachment to the outcome you are rendered both free and peaceful. And I gotta say that I think they're onto something, because—at least until the moment the questions were actually handed to me at which point my heart rate went off the scale—I no longer felt afraid. Of course, *getting* to that state rendered me so dark-eyed, ghostly pale, and ghastly thin that the sight would have terrified small children, but at least I wasn't *scared* anymore. I guess even the Buddhists don't say it's gonna be easy.

As a side note, I learned that reaching this state of sudden onset, resigned, "can't-study-one-more-minute" nonattachment was common when studying for Comps. I saw it happen often enough that I started telling students in classes behind me that this was the state they should actually *try* to reach. I told them to understand that when they said to themselves "I no longer care if I pass or fail, I only want to get it over with," they were as fully prepared as they were ever going to get. The key—as is the case for so many things—was timing. You didn't want to hit the wall a month before the test. You wanted to crash just as you walked into the testing room. If you did that, you succeeded.

My crash came about six days early. When my testing days came, three of my classmates, a student retaking Comps due to an expired candidacy, and I resigned from the human race, put a carpal tunnel surgeon on retainer, and sat down to write—for twelve hours. And I found that nonattachment really was a good emotional state to go into the tests with, because except for the first five or ten minutes when I was hyperventilating over whether the questions would cover topics I was familiar with, I felt pretty calm the whole time. I knew the whole ordeal would soon be over and I would no longer have to spend every waking hour studying. Beyond that, I cared not at all.

The upshot? I passed the damn things. And that's all I care to say about that.

INTERNSHIP: PART I

I hope that by this point you have not been lulled into thinking that graduate school was awful and nothing could possibly make things worse, for it is not so. Even with all the mind-numbing emotional contortions and bone-jarring humiliations experienced to this point, there lurked yet a fresh opportunity to experience life as lived by disgusting and unidentifiable viscous fluids at the bottom of a crackhouse dumpster: internship.

Healthcare professions, bless their pointy little heads, provide not only classroom instruction on what-you-are-supposed-to-do-to-people-that-will-help-and-hopefully-not-kill-them, but full-time, on-the-job training as well. This is called "internship." Internship actually goes by various names depending upon your particular profession. In social work it is called "placement." In medicine the first year of full-time work while still a student is called internship and subsequent years are called "residency." In psychology the first year of full-time student work is called internship and the second year is called "supervised experience." But to make things simple you can just call internship, or interns to be specific, by their formal name: pond scum.

I checked recently to be certain it is still the case, and it remains true that archaeologists have identified interns (and residents) as the lowest form of life ever discovered on planet Earth. Trust me, they are a low form of life. Real low. Excruciatingly low. How low? Amoeba and spores kick sand in their faces. Slime towers over them. We're talking *low* here. Interns and residents are not high enough on the socioeconomic status to be considered slaves—slaves have *some* value—you have to actually pay for them. Not so interns. Laughable stipends, schedules designed to induce emotional and physical breakdown on the molecular level, arrogant supervisors who torture them for sport, and constant terror because their careers are still on the line, interns and residents are not "low man on the totem pole." They are the dirt dug out of the ground to enable the totem pole to be planted.

OK, so I exaggerate. Well, actually I don't. There's nothing like being an intern or a resident to learn what the term "humble" means. To learn what the term "start at the bottom" means. To learn what the term "scut work" means. To learn what the term "Hey you, yeah, you—whatever your name is, YOU—getcherassoverhere RIGHT NOW and do this thing to this patient that I don't feel like doing" means. Like I said—*low*.

Internships are performed at the various hospitals, clinics, universities, and other institutions that maintain formal, structured, "internship programs." Because internship is supposed to be one of, if not the, final step in completing your degree, you had to be pretty close to finishing your academic requirements to be eligible to apply for internship. The requirement in my program was that you complete *all* academic requirements (classes, preliminary exams, qualifying exams, diagnostic comp, therapy comp) prior to attending. The only thing you did not have to have completed was that mother of all black holes, your dissertation. That meant, joy of joys, you could leave that cold dead zombie tucked away in the back of your mental closet so it could fall on you just as you tried to open The Door of Real Life the day you completed internship—just to remind you that things only get worse.

Wherever you decided to apply for internship, the only place you could be relatively assured you would go was called "someplace else." That is, if your university or medical school maintained an internship program, you had about the same chance of gaining admittance to it as you had of being interrupted by The Prize Patrol on Super Bowl Sunday while making love to Cindy Crawford. It just wasn't going to happen. Programs wanted to cross-pollinate, so even if you liked where you went to graduate school and they liked you, you were out of luck—you were gone. So to do your internship you were required to leave your program and once again uproot yourself, trek off to God knows where, and start over as a stranger with people you didn't know. Best yet, to get there you had to endure yet another bloodletting application process.

Fortunately, the internship application process involved a more humane method of kicking you to the curb when you were considered an undesirable than did applying to graduate school itself. Here's how it worked: all clinical psychology graduate students everywhere in the country who were ready to go on internship applied at the same time, generally in late fall of their last academic year. In most programs that was during your third or fourth year. In my program it was not infrequently during your seventh or eighth year. Anyway, internships would review these applications, cull out the applicants to whom they wanted to make an offer, keep a few extras in case their first choices flamed out, and burn the rest in effigy. The result was that if they didn't want you, they simply didn't reply. There were no formal "fuck you" letters sent, there was just silence.

Then, at 9 AM on a single day, (the second Monday in February to be exact—go figure) every internship in the country would begin calling their desired applicants and offering them positions. Some applicants would accept, others would decline, and each internship would go down its list of desirable candidates offering positions until their slots were filled. Then it was done. So the pleasant part was that you never actually had to *hear* a program say "drop dead," because if they didn't want you they just didn't call. The unpleasant part was the haunting possibility that you'd be sitting alone in your house, in the dark, at midnight, polishing off a case of beer while staring at a telephone that has never rung once. That rarely happened, but because it was at least technically possible, the idea freaked everyone out. Our solution was to try our best not to think about it—but of course we did. One of the first things you learn in psychology is that denial is never entirely adequate.

When my classmates and I were ready to apply for internship, we set about the task of once again opening a vein and rearranging our blood on seemingly bottomless application forms while trying not to act too desperate and hoping we'd get a decent offer from someone, somewhere. While the odds of getting an internship—*some* internship—were generally pretty good when you came from a decent graduate program (which mine was), the reality was that it was not so simple as that. Of course not. Other important factors came into play.

For example, *where* (as in what city and state) you went on internship took on special importance. This time, you see, it was for real. What I mean is that when you became an intern you would be working with the professionals in that particular community. You would spend an entire year with them. You would become known by them. So it behooved you to try to snag an internship where you wanted to end up living, as being a known quantity in the community would help you get a job. After all, assuming you still registered a pulse after finishing graduate school, the next round of applications would be for a real-life job. So the pressure was on to decide where you wanted to live in order to decide where you wanted to go to internship.

But that wasn't the only consideration. Internships, like graduate programs, varied in their reputation, quality, and the level of student attracted to it. They also varied in their stipend, which ranged from almost nothing to virtually nothing. I think, as I recall, I was paid 3500 dollars for my internship year (the better the internship, generally speaking, the less they paid). Nevertheless, they did vary some, so this was an additional consideration. I think the largest stipend paid by any internship I applied to was about 8000 dollars. So you had to consider your level of financial desperation in addition to other factors.

At this point I must say one thing for my graduate program that I have thus far failed to mention: in general, my program did have the good graces to not set graduate students at each other's throats, as some programs did. Against the faculty's throats, yes. Against each other in Monopoly and cards, yes. But academically there was little or no backstabbing or maliciousness. Any competitive scratching and clawing (by yours truly and others) was understood by everyone to be simply a good-faith attempt to make it through, not an attempt to beat up or beat out anyone else.

This, and probably this alone, was the only reason I actually had friends during graduate school. Given the scorching excess of my drive to achieve, had the place set us upon each other I can assure you that I would have been the target of every other student's venom and I would have been socially ostracized and most likely mysteriously spirited away and replaced by a blood-soaked cardboard cutout with a target painted on it. As it was, one of the few bright spots we could count on was that as a student body we genuinely felt "all in this together." So when it came to applying for internship, we were actually on each others' sides and worked to help each other out.

To prepare to apply for internship we hunkered down with trusted faculty and tried to devise ways to improve our chances of gaining acceptance to good programs. For example, we talked over how much our interest in various programs overlapped because, we figured, the fewer of our students who competed for slots at any one program the better were the odds that we would each get into the program we wanted. Fortunately, during the year I applied for internship, as a group our interests, desires, and future plans were sufficiently diverse as to give us little overlap. Some people knew where they wanted to live, so they wanted to apply to programs close to that place. Others had specific topics they were interested in, so they wanted to apply to programs that specialized in those. A few didn't particularly care one way or the other about where they went, so they had a lot of flexibility.

I largely fell into the last category. With the possible exception of the Pacific Northwest, I had not been anywhere that I had a strong yearning to settle after graduate school. So I had no particular geographical preference. And I didn't really care about searching out programs with a specific area of specialization, so I didn't really care about the particular type of program I attended, either. As a result, I figured I'd apply to one program in the northwest, and choose my other applications strictly by the internship's quality and reputation. My reasoning was that if I wasn't going to end up living where I was going to be an intern, I would be best served by completing an internship with "name recognition" to help me when I applied for a job.

A sensible decision, no? But of course. And, consistent with most of the major decisions (sensible and otherwise) throughout my life, what initially seemed like such a good idea turned around and bit me—hard—in the ass.

You see, my graduate program, while well beyond rigorous in its training and truly inhumane in its zealous over-the-top intensity, was nevertheless neither a particularly famous nor a "name-brand" place. You might call its reputation "solid," but it was certainly not renown. So by applying to high-powered internships I was once again taking the chance of experiencing quarantine as an untouchable, getting rejected by everyone, and facing the dreaded dead telephone line on the second Monday in February. This, despite the fact that I was said to be the top student in my program in the previous ten years. (You might wonder if this statement is simply another example of my self-aggrandizing grandiosity or, if it is not, how I could possibly know it to be true. Here's how: I read the letters of recommendation my faculty wrote about me to internships. Wait, weren't those letters supposed to be confidential? Yes, they were. Wasn't the whole point for them to be sent without our reading them? Yes, it was. So how did I pull off reading mine? Let me put it this way—it was not rocket science. One file cabinet, one key, one desk drawer, and one thoroughly charmed and schmoozed secretary later, and I not only knew what everybody had written about me, I had photocopies of the letters to call my very own. Whether this means I also read other people's letters must be left to your potentially scandalized imagination.)

But, fortunately—leave it to me—I had planned for the eventuality that applying for a big-name internship would be problematic. In preparation for, and in response to, my worry about being uniformly rejected by such programs, I had surreptitiously commandeered a secret weapon, an ace in the hole, a Weapon of Mass Rejection Destruction:

Merlin.

Through my time in graduate school, Merlin and I had grown pretty close, both personally and professionally. Well Merlin, God bless him, with his flawless competence in all things academic, *had* graduated from one of the top clinical psychology programs in the country and *had* attended one of, if not *the* top internship in the country. And he had done so recently, only three years previously. That meant he was still known by the faculty of that internship. Add to that the fact that Merlin seemed to not only like but to actually respect me, (no accounting for taste, even among the brilliant) and it all added up to a very good thing—not to mention my only leg-up on anyone else trying to gain admission to a top-drawer program.

Merlin's own multi-engine-freight-train-like drive to achieve, combined with the fame of his graduate program, had enabled him to land an internship at no less than the hallowed halls of The University of Minnesota Health Sciences Center. You have no way of appreciating the magnitude of this, of course, but at the time The University of Minnesota Health Sciences Center was considered holy ground in clinical psychology circles. Its name was uttered in hushed voices and reverent tones because in its history lay an accomplishment so enormous that it endowed the place with mythical status.

What was this divinely inspired accomplishment? The University of Minnesota had begotten a psychological test called the Minnesota Multiphasic Personality Inventory.

The MMPI, as it is commonly called, is a test that was first designed in the 1940's and that was for all practical purposes the world's first "empirically-based" instrument designed to measure psychological conditions and disorders. So what, you say? So this: an "empirically based" test was a genuinely revolutionary concept in psychological testing, one that changed the history and face of psychology. By basing a test on its empirical qualities rather than the content of its questions, a whole host of problems that commonly contaminate and invalidate the results of psychological testing is circumvented. The MMPI led the way in doing this, making it a true and revolutionary original. It is not an overstatement to say that it changed the entire field of psychological testing by entering the world as the first data-based, empirically valid measure of psychological characteristics. In short, the darn thing actually worked.

The problem with most psychological tests (especially those found in magazines and on the internet, sorry to disappoint) is that there is more driving someone's responses to the test questions than "the truth." People consciously and unconsciously alter their responses for a variety of reasons, and these contaminating factors can throw off the test scores so much that the results are essentially meaningless. For example, if a question is designed to measure paranoia and says "True or False: I am afraid people are out to get me," even if you are paranoid and it's true that you are afraid people are out to get you, you still might answer "false" for any number of reasons. Perhaps you don't want anyone to think you're paranoid. Maybe you are afraid the test results will be used against you. Maybe you feel guilty that you feel this way, or think you shouldn't. Maybe you don't want the examiner to think badly of you. In any case, due to such distortions the scores on personality tests can be so contaminated by response biases involving social conformity, fear, unrealistic self-image, outright lies, and attempts to make yourself look good—or bad—that they are practically useless.

The people who developed the MMPI figured out a way to get around all that. With the simple cleverness characteristic of true genius, here's what they did: instead of giving people "meaningful" questions that were scored relative to the question's content (and hence were vulnerable to the aforementioned contaminants), they took different groups of people who were *already* and *independently* diagnosed with different types of psychological disorders. Then they took literally hundreds of true/false questions and gave all of the people all of the questions. Finally, (here's the brilliant part) they analyzed the answers to see which questions were consistently answered "true" by one group and "false" by another. When a question was reliably answered one way by one group and the other way by another, the answer to that question credibly differentiated between someone who belonged in one group as opposed to the other. And here's the kicker—the actual *content* of the question was irrelevant. So the question itself may appear to have nothing whatever to do with the psychological condition being measured. That meant you couldn't fake, distort, or contaminate your answers because you couldn't even tell what the question was trying to measure; its content was irrelevant. All that mattered was that for some reason, *any* reason, one group reliably answered the question one way and the other group answered it the other way. So a question could—literally—be "I fear that in my next life I will come back as a slightly obese and socially awkward groundhog," and if people with schizophrenia consistently answered "false" while people with depression consistently answered "true," then that question could differentiate schizophrenia from depression. Pretty cool, no?

Actually, more than cool. Stunningly brilliant. As a result, with the MMPI there was little or no concern over anyone successfully faking their answers. Furthermore, because of the empirical nature of the test, you could actually *measure* someone's attempts to lie. (There are several scales on the MMPI that are designed to measure attempted deception, and they work.) So the MMPI turned the mental health world on its head. It was that level of genius that The University of Minnesota Health Sciences Center had wrought, and everyone in psychology knew it.

Over the ensuing decades since its inception in the 40's, the MMPI had become the most standard and well-studied psychological testing instrument ever developed. It had been used so often by so many clinicians in so many settings that it had long since become the gold-standard of the industry, the CAT scan of psychology. And because I was interested in quality of internship rather than geography, I had a perfect opportunity given Merlin's recent history: I decided that I wanted to go to Minnesota.

So I approached Merlin with what was, for all practical purposes, the entirely insane idea of my getting into Minnesota. To his credit, Merlin was not appalled. In truth I think he was pleased, even flattered, at my interest in attending the same internship where he went, and perhaps he got a kick out of my chutzpah as well. Merlin was like that. So he and I carefully, and in secret, began hatching a plot designed to do the impossible and get me, an unknown student from a relatively unknown graduate school, admitted to the almighty University of Minnesota Health Sciences Center Clinical Psychology Internship Program.

In case you're wondering, we met in secret for several very good reasons. First, we didn't want anyone else getting the idea that applying to Minnesota was realistic and thereby have more than one person from my program applying. That would have provided competition for my application as well as put Merlin into the distinctly sticky position of possibly having to write letters of recommendation to his alma mater for more than one student. A bad thing. Second, we figured that we would cause injury to anyone who found out what we were up to when they fell on the floor laughing at the idea that we actually thought we had a chance of pulling this thing off. No one in the history of my program had ever gained admittance to an internship anywhere close to the stature of Minnesota, so trying to do so was, as they say in jolly old England, "just not done." We also met in secret because, quite frankly, I still had a sore spot on my butt from my not-too-distant-past experience of being repeatedly bounced on it with rejection after rejection from graduate programs. I felt no great desire to relive that experience, especially in public. So if it ever looked like we were sure to fail, I could pull the plug without anyone being the wiser—except Merlin, of course. But I trusted Merlin. And I knew where he lived.

We hatched a four-part plan. First, I would apply to a variety of internships representing a variety of qualities, with The University of Minnesota Health Sciences Center being—obviously—the highest one. (Quite frankly, there weren't any programs of higher reputation to apply to even if I'd wanted to—Minnesota was that highly thought of.) That would maximize my chance of avoiding a repeat of my first-round graduate school application experience where nothing panned out and I was left high and dry. Second, Merlin would coach me on how to complete my application to make it attractive to Minnesota in ways not known to your garden-variety applicant who did not possess his inside information of the program and the faculty's interests and biases. Third, he would call anyone and everyone he knew in Minnesota who had any influence at all to talk me up so my name would be familiar to them and they would know Merlin liked me. (After all, *they* liked Merlin—I'm telling you, you could not *not* like the man). Fourth—and this was the big one—on my application I would tell them that if they offered me a position, *I guaranteed I would accept it.*

Merlin, once again showing his boundless compassion and stunning observational capacity, let me in on a secret that few others knew: internships, it seemed, *hated* being turned down by applicants to whom they offered positions. They were hungry to get not just slave labor, but *good* slave labor, so they tried to choose a set of applicants that they thought would make a good "intern group." If several of their offers were declined, they had to go back to the drawing board—and fast, because they had to make all of their calls on that one day—to try to whomp up the names of some new applicants they could call that would still give them a fighting chance of forming an intern group that did not resemble a herd of slightly brain-damaged locusts. So if I told them that I would *absolutely* accept an offer, they would have to take that seriously, as it was one decline from a good applicant they could count on avoiding.

So I did that. On my application I told Minnesota that they were my first choice of internship and that, if they offered me (oh please, oh please, oh please) a position, I'd accept it.

I ultimately applied to eight internships in total, one in the Pacific Northwest, the others at pretty good hospitals and health science centers, and of course Minnesota. And on the second Monday in February, in unison with every other internship-ready clinical psychology graduate student in America, I swallowed a handful of tranquilizers (I wish) and sat down by my phone, which to my great relief rang promptly and precisely at 9:00 AM.

Upon answering, I found on the other end an affable and pleasant psychologist who was the head of the internship program that I had applied to in the Pacific Northwest. Given that his was the only program besides Minnesota that I had a specific interest in attending (for its location) the call put me into ecstasy—and a bind. I would love to have accepted their offer, as I could envision myself living happily in Washington State. *But,* I had not heard from (or, alternatively, I had not as yet realized that I was not going to hear from) The University of Minnesota. What to do? The psychologist yakked me up for a few minutes in a very pleasant and even humorous manner, talking about the weather, telling me a joke (a pretty good one), and inquiring about how my "internship day" was going. Then he offered me a position. I gulped, thanked him, and asked—timidly—if I could have a little time and call him back to give him my answer. He said sure, five, ten minutes enough? No, seriously, he was very decent and said that I certainly could, to call him whenever I was ready to respond, and that he'd look forward to talking to me again.

Now, despite his pleasant demeanor, this guy was no fool. He had to know what was up. The only *possible* reason I could have for wanting to call him back with my answer was that I was waiting to see if a program higher on my list called me. So at the conclusion of our pleasant little conversation he most likely hung up, uttered a few words that graphically described solid male Bovine waste products and disputed the certainty of my paternity, and began flipping through his list of alternate candidates just to get ready. But God bless him for his professionalism, he was completely kind to me and displayed no ill temper or hesitance at my request to call him back. For that I will be forever grateful to him.

As for me, I hung up secure in the knowledge that I had at least one offer, and one that I liked to boot, in the bag. My anxiety dissolved. And my phone rang again. This time it was a staff member from a medical school in the Midwest. He was also very nice and quickly came to the point and offered me a position. I thanked him and turned him down, saying that I had already accepted another position. This was not technically true you understand, but the only two programs I specifically cared about were The University of Minnesota and the program in the Pacific Northwest, and since I knew I was accepted at the program in Washington State, my only question was whether The University of God—er—Minnesota—would offer me a spot. If they didn't, as was most likely, then everything was still OK and I would happily toddle off to the land of trees and rain and scenic beauty.

The phone rang twice more, with offers from two more programs. I turned them down as well, and in the process decided that maybe I'd have to apply to internship next year, too, that this was just too darn much fun—turning *them* down for a change. After all, I had applied to eight programs and I had received offers from four of them in the first twenty minutes. Life was good.

Then the phone went silent. I hung around, had something to eat, and began musing about my life in Washington State. Along about 11 AM it rang yet again. When I answered, the man on the other end identified himself and I immediately recognized the name—he was the director of internship at none other than The University of Minnesota Health Sciences Center. "Oh my God," I thought, "it's really going to happen." And it did. He offered me a position. I thanked him and accepted. He said he'd send a letter of confirmation to me. I thanked him again and we hung up.

And that was that. It was over in less than two minutes. Maybe a minute-and-a-half. But it was done. Surprising even to myself, I didn't have much reaction. Then I realized why. I had one task left, and I didn't want to do it. Given that it had been a couple of hours since my offer from the program in Washington State, I had unconsciously decided that I was going there and had already started painting pictures in my head of what my life might look like up there. And I had started enjoying the pictures. Now I had to undo all that. I forced myself to pick up the phone, and surprising even myself with my degree of my reluctance and regret, called the psychologist at the program in the Pacific Northwest to decline his offer. I got his voice mail, so I left him a message saying that I had received an offer from another program and thanking him—no less than three times, if memory serves me—for his offer and regretting that I had to say no but that I'd told the other program if they offered me a position I'd take it, and that had happened. I told him I was sorry. And I meant it.

Then, my call finished, I hung up and was suddenly overcome with emotion. I collapsed in a heap on my floor. I didn't know what to do, I was so filled with feeling. I started giggling. Honest to God, I giggled. Then I cried. Wait—maybe I laughed. I don't remember. No matter—whatever I did, it was from excitement, disbelief, and joy. Mostly pure, unadulterated joy. I had done it. Holy Mother of God, I had done it. I was in. I was going to Minnesota. No one in my program had ever accomplished anything that even resembled this. I had done the impossible. I didn't know what to say, even to myself. But I knew that I was thrilled beyond words and it was one of the high-lights of my life.

Which, of course, as you might be able to predict by now given how these things tend to go for me, led quickly and directly to a full-blown, all-out shit storm. When I told other people, (remember—I applied in secret) their reactions were universally negative, ranging from disbelief to outright resentment. That very evening, in fact, when those of us applying got together at a local pub, as we had pre-ar-ranged to do in order to compare notes and offer congratulations or condolences, the meeting went well initially because most everyone who applied got good offers. Most were admitted to solid programs that they liked and wanted and that had a history of taking students from my program because they appreciated the high quality of our training. No real surprises, good or bad.

But when it became my turn and someone said "So, come on—tell us—where did you accept?" I swallowed real, *real* hard and said "Uh—The University of Minnesota Health Sciences Center." And—just like that—there was a chill in the air that could have flash-frozen live turkeys. Silence. Long, loud, icy silence. Several people at the table turned and looked at me. They just *looked* at me. Then the com-ments started.

"Did you say Minnesota?" someone asked.

"Yeah," I replied.

"Whoa," someone sighed.

"Shit,"someone else smirked.

"That's a first," said another.

"Oh man, this sucks," said someone else.

"Goddammit," another voice chimed in.

"All I have to say is that you are one lucky bastard," said another.

"You sure are," said another.

"I guess some people have all the luck," someone else said.

And that, by golly, did it. That tore it. That put me over the edge. I don't know why, but for some reason it was the wrong time and the wrong place and one wrong comment too many. Maybe I was tired, maybe I was irritable, or maybe I was just sick of it all. But for the first time since the day I decided to go to graduate school, for the first time since I began the ridiculously daunting task of getting a damn Ph.D. from that damn Ph.D. program, and perhaps for the first time in my entire desperate little life, I felt a full-blown attack of High Horse rise within me. And not just any High Horse either, mind you—a thoroughbred, Triple-Crown, Seattle Slew, foaming-at-the-mouth, blood-doped, amphetamine-laced, feral High Horse. A High Horse with *attitude*. I could feel its rage rise within me as it shook and it foamed, as it snarled and it growled, as it grew and it glowered, as it bubbled and it boiled, as it hissed and it screamed. It formed words inside my brain in a frenzied, shrieking, billowing torrent.

"So I'm *lucky*, " I thought. "Is that it? It's about luck? Fucking *luck*? You assholes feel bad that I got into Minnesota and you didn't because I'm *lucky* and you're not? Is that what you think? Well, let me tell you what *I* think.

"I think you're a bunch of ignorant, self-pitying, self-righteous, sniveling little vermin who have no right to complain—none, zero, nada—that I got into Minnesota and you didn't. You feel bad because I'm *lucky*?! How in God's name can you even *have* that thought, much less say it to my *face*? How can any one of you have failed to notice that for the past three years I've done nothing but work, nothing but strive, that I have consistently driven myself one tiny iota short of *death* to get where I am? Have you bothered to open your lunch boxes for even a *nanosecond* to look out and see that I have done things no one else in this program has *ever* done or ever thought *could* be done or in a hillion jillion years in their right minds would even be willing to *try* to do? Are you really so stupid that you fail to realize that I have risked *everything* to get where I am? That I have worked my *ass* off, night and day, day and night, without break or pause or respite for *three goddam years* to get where I am? That I have paid for where I am with my life, with the marrow of my bones, that I have sacrificed *everything*, that I have nothing of value left in my life but my desperate, single-minded, monomaniacal pursuit of achievement? Have you failed to grasp *at all* that I have moved heaven and earth, that I have done everything short of sell my soul to Lucifer—and sometimes I wonder if I may have unwittingly done that as well—to become someone who could land this kind of internship?"

The silence at the table was deafening, and the words would not stop coming.

"Do you really and truly not understand, my blind, deaf, dumb, and empty-headed so-called friends, that *you* failed to get this kind of internship not because of bad luck, not because of some lousy twist of fate, but because you were unwilling to do what I have done, to go to the lengths to which I have gone, to sacrifice what I have sacrificed, to endure what I have endured, to give up what I have given up, to risk what I have risked? Do you?

"It is not luck, you cretins. It was *never* luck. It is the farthest thing from luck you can possibly *imagine*. That you think, somehow, it has something to do with luck shows you to be complete, total, blind, fucking *morons*. You are missing the single most obvious thing in the entire universe—the simple, unvarnished fact sitting atop your very own eyeballs that it is your own goddam fault that you didn't get an internship at Minnesota because *you weren't willing to do what it took*. So don't you dare—don't you fucking *dare*—blame me for your feeling bad that I got it and you didn't. *Don't you dare*. You go back and look at the difference between what you've been willing to do and what I've been willing to do and *then* you try to tell me you're as deserving as I am and *then* you try to tell me that I'm "lucky" for getting admitted to Minnesota. *Then* you try to tell me you have any right, *any fucking right* to use my name, The University of Minnesota, and the word "luck" in the same sentence. The short answer, my friends, is that *you don't*. Not now. Not later. Not fucking *ever*."

Yeah, I know—it was over the top. It was insane. It was *way* out of proportion, bordering on the psychotic. You think I don't know that?

Listen, you gotta cut me some slack here. Having been, in my view at least, tolerant to a fault through the entire razor-wire experience of graduate school, I clearly had feelings long cooking inside me, long festering under the terror, the desperation, the fatigue, the drive, the relentless burning and slashing my way through the program, that came spewing into my brain over comments that were at best a backhanded acknowledgment of the magnitude of my achievement and were at worst mildly annoying. I am well aware how inappropriate my reaction was.

But—I will tell you this—that does not change one tiny bit the fact that, while the intensity—and language—of my reaction may have been excessive, I was *right*. Furthermore, I knew that if I'd actually said what I was thinking, if I'd gone crazy and actually *said* all that stuff, *they'd* know I was right, too. I knew that even a tiny portion of that rant would forever shame my classmates into silence and show them up as the rats they were being.

172

But I also knew it would hurt them. I knew the only purpose served by my saying all that stuff would be to make them feel bad, to be vindictive in service of trying to salve my own simmering pain. I knew that they were just like me, that they had done the very best they could to survive the horrible ordeal of graduate school, and that they had done it their way just as I had done it mine. And I knew—I really knew—that while it wasn't *my* fault they had been unwilling to do what I had done to get the kind of internship I got, it also wasn't *their* fault that I *had*. They had nothing whatever to do with my choices, nothing whatever to do with the terrible prices I had been willing to pay, nothing whatever to do with my losses or my sacrifices or the excruciating depth of emptiness my striving had induced. They were, to the last, self-inflicted. So they did not deserve to be the target of my terrible venom. Not one little bit of it.

So I didn't say a word. I chuckled, ordered another round of beers, stood and toasted to us, to our survival, and to our futures, and along with my classmates proceeded to get gleefully, giddily, smashingly, hopelessly drunk. We made complete fools of ourselves that night, my classmates and I, as in front of God and everybody we whooped and we hollered and we sang and we laughed and we toasted and we partied and we were a complete pain in the ass to everyone around us. And we deserved it. Every little bit of it.

THE DEADLINE

So I was off to this high-powered mucky-muck place called The University of Minnesota Health Sciences Center. With that acceptance in hand, only one hurdle remained: my—gulp—dissertation.

Never being one to have life roll over and play dead for me on even the best of days, at this point fate decided to pull the pin and toss me an armed and live, potentially catastrophic problem. Merlin, who was my dissertation chair (as well as my mentor, savior, and role-model—I'm telling you, the man was from another planet) was leaving my program. Unbeknown to us lowly graduate students, he had applied for, been offered, and accepted a faculty position at the very graduate program from which he, himself, had graduated. (Remember it? That super-high powered place full of brilliant and world-changing people just like him? That one.) It turned out that Merlin's secret plan all along in taking the faculty position at my program was to use it as the vehicle through which he could amass sufficiently awe-inspiring credentials as to enable him to return to his alma mater as a faculty member. (He ultimately ended up running the place—how surprised are we?) His program, interestingly enough, was rumored to have a hard-and-fast rule against hiring their own former students as faculty. But, like all things Merlin, once he set out to make something happen, it just didn't matter what the world had to say about it—it happened. So he got the job. He was leaving.

That meant if I wanted to finish my degree without changing dissertation chairs (which would essentially mean starting over from scratch, and I cannot even *begin* to tell you how horrible changing dissertation chairs is—students had literally given up on *ever* completing their degree when they had to change—it probably put you back a good two years under the best of circumstances, it was that

174

disruptive) I was in trouble. Given that his last day as a faculty member in my program was exactly one week after I was due to finish internship, if I was reading the calendar right and planning to complete my dissertation in the normal and expected time frame, I figured I was somewhere between oh, say, about two and five *years* shy of the time I would need.

This was, far and away, the worst problem I had yet faced. It was the worst problem I could *imagine* facing. It was, by all accounts, a problem of insurmountable and hopeless proportion. Even in the most optimistic of scenarios I could dream up, the outcome was the same—I was fried. Worse, nothing I'd accomplished to this point made any difference or helped me out one bit. Even my prized status as Super Student was neutralized because the university's position was "It's really nice you can walk on water and all, and we've certainly enjoyed the show, but you know the drill—no dissertation, no degree. Any questions?"

Shit. As I was sorely reminded, the single biggest factor preventing people from graduating from my program in a timely manner—or at all—was failure to complete their dissertation. Well, it looked for all the world as though I was about to join that select group. The only possible way out was, in fact, not possible at all—to try to complete my dissertation *while* I was on internship. That notion was so laughable as to not even qualify as something remotely resembling an unlikely possibility. Internship was—at least—a full-time job. Writing a dissertation was—at least—a full-time job. So dissertation was a "before" internship or an "after" internship task, not a "during" internship task. Add to that the fact that I would be doing my internship at least two thousand miles away from my graduate program, at least two thousand miles away from my research subjects, and at least two thousand miles away from my research facilities, and my guess was that I was at least two thousand *light years* away from being able to make something like that happen.

The whole thing was not just horrifying, it was, well—really, *really* horrifying. I didn't know what to do. As best I can recall, I wandered aimlessly for several days, trying to figure some way, any way, out of the mess. I could find none. For the first time in recorded history I was even, God forgive me, mad at Merlin.

Which lasted about two seconds, because as soon as he and I sat down to begin talking about the problem, he declared, in the blithe and casual way that only Merlin could pull off when talking about something so grave that nuclear war seems like a preferable option, that the whole thing was really no big deal at all—if there was only one way we could get this thing done, well, by golly, we'd just do it that way. And he matter-of-factly informed me that we were going to set up my research project, perform the study, analyze the data, write the document, and have my defense meeting—all while I was on internship.

Wait—let me be more specific: he matter-of-factly informed me that *I* would set up my research project, *I* would perform the study, *I* would analyze the data, *I* would write the document, and *I* would have my defense meeting—all while I was on internship.

Funny man, Merlin. "Har, har, har," I started to say. "No, seriously, do you think there's some way we can do this?" Only Merlin wasn't laughing. Merlin wasn't smiling. That's because Merlin wasn't kidding. Merlin was dead serious.

Which was when it hit me: the nonclinical students had been right all along—Merlin *was* crazy. The man was psychotic. Insane. Booga-booga bonkers. I mean, demanding that we work twenty-four hours a day, seven-days-a week to master indecipherable personality measurement statistics when we already lacked the time to brush our teeth for a full 3 minutes, or requiring that we read what amounted to a textbook-a-day for an entire semester just for *his* class when we had five other classes, a caseload of ten patients per week, and intake duty three evenings every week in the clinic was one thing, but *this* was unreasonable. This was excessive. This was *bizarre*. Clearly, Merlin had been reading his—and apparently my—press clippings for too long and had managed to come completely unhinged. He had lost touch with reality. This was *not* something that was possible. This was not even *close* to possible. This was ridiculous piled atop preposterous plopped upon ludicrous. It didn't even register on the reality *scale*, much less rate as a serious consideration. And here he was, talking about it as calmly and matter-of-fact as if we were hangin' out in Momma's kitchen with Auntie Claire, drinking jasmine tea and musing about what kind of cookies to make for the bake sale at church next week. As Merlin and I continued to talk I found that I was spending rapidly increasing amounts of energy trying to keep from bursting into tears and running from the room.

Now, just to ensure we're on the same page: understand that not only had no one ever gone to Minnesota on internship, as far as I know, no one had ever gone to *any* internship *and done their dissertation at the same time,* much less from two thousand miles away. Hell, people had gone on internship in the nearest city and *still* had never done their dissertation at the same time. Wait—people had *returned* from internship, started work on their dissertation *full time,* and were *still* not finished *four years later.* What part of this did Merlin not understand? What part of "reality testing" eluded him?

But you know, I'll be damned if Merlin didn't talk about it all in such a matter-of-fact way, and if he didn't present the whole thing as such a fait accompli, that after a while even *I* started to think it might somehow be possible. And that worried me even more, because I knew *I* was sane and I knew for a *fact* this was impossible. For me to start thinking it might be possible most likely meant I was losing my grip, too, and soon there would be no one left whose judgment could be trusted. Then I was really dead meat.

Nevertheless, to be a good sport about it and, quite frankly, to humor Merlin, I continued to meet with him and talk as if we were discussing something that was actually possible. But I knew that our conversations were about as reasonable as discussing the status of the little green men inhabiting my sock drawer.

And then, son of a gun, I'll be damned if one day, out of nowhere, I didn't have another of my life-changing internal seismic shifts. Something in me snapped. I remember looking up and saying to myself "Well, *fine.* You know what? Fuck this. Fuck *all* this. We're gonna do this thing. We're just gonna *do* it." And I actually began preparing myself to do the impossible and take on two simultaneous full-time jobs, two thousand miles apart, with a deadline of exactly twelve months, three weeks, and two days. And five hours. As if graduate school itself hadn't been hard enough.

I had no idea.

DISSERTATION

The topic I chose for my dissertation was depression or, more precisely, a model of depression. It seems a fitting enough topic, don't you think, given the emotional state induced by graduate school. Enough to make a Freudian blush.

The model grew out of the work of a bright young psychologist who had burst into academic prominence after identifying an interesting—and puzzling—phenomenon. When animals were exposed to aversive stimuli (research lingo for "painful shocks" or "really loud, scary noises") and could not escape from them or turn them off, at first they freaked out, ran around, struggled to get away, and basically did all the things you'd expect them to do. But then, for some reason, after a little while some animals did a very strange thing—without warning they stopped. They just stopped. They stopped trying to escape, they stopped trying to turn off the shocks, in essence they stopped trying to do anything at all. Instead, they seemed to "give up" and would unceremoniously plop themselves down in the middle of the floor and sit, silent and immobile, while the experimenter continued to shock the living daylights out of them. And there they would stay.

Stranger still, if the experimenter then opened the cage door so the animal *could* begin escaping the shocks, they *still* didn't move. Even with an open avenue of escape staring them in the face, they continued to lie completely still like inert, furry lumps while the experimenter merrily shocked the crap out of them. The only way the animal would ever again begin trying to escape was if the experimenter repeatedly and forcibly dragged the animal out the open door of the cage to show them that they could now get away. But it didn't always work and it wasn't easy to get them to do it.

The intriguing thing about this phenomenon was not just that some psychologist was crazy enough to have come up with the idea in the first place ("Hey, I've got an idea—how 'bout we go lock some animals in cages, shock the floor, and not let them out!") but that the animals' behavior when they entered the "give up" state looked amazingly like the behavior of people who are clinically depressed. The animals showed slowed movement, loss of interest, and passivity in the face of even avoidable aversiveness—all things that depressed people do. The similarity even extended beyond the actual time the animal was in the cage being shocked. Afterward, back in their safe little home cages, they showed behavioral changes that seemed like an "animal" version of the kinds of things depressed people do—they stopped grooming, stopped relating to other animals, even stopped moving around very much. All signs suggesting that the animals had, in fact, become depressed.

The exciting thing about this finding was that it looked quite possible that the psychologist had stumbled across an actual laboratory model of depression. His findings could explain both the cause of some depressions (repeated experience that one's behavior is unrelated to results) and help find ways to treat depression by finding ways to bring the animals out of their state of "giving up."

The more research the psychologist did, the better it got. He proved that the same thing happened in a variety of animals, so it was a general behavioral phenomenon rather than something characteristic of one particular species. He showed that the depression-like behavior was not due to some kind of physical injury or brain damage from the shocks. He showed that he was not simply teaching the animals to lie still. Further, when he induced the state in rats, snatched them up and cracked open their heads to slice up their brains, he found that their neurons showed some of the same biochemical changes that people with depression show. So not only did their behavior mimic "real" depression, the biochemistry of their brains did as well.

The psychologist completed his magic show with the long-anticipated grand finale: he demonstrated the effect in humans. He gave human subjects a problem-solving task which, no matter how hard they tried, they always failed (because the task was secretly rigged to make their behavior have no effect on the outcome). Then he measured their mood with a depression test and their thinking and problem-solving abilities with thinking and problem-solving tests. Bullseye—his human subjects showed diminished mood, impaired thinking, and reduced problem-solving abilities. All elements that mimic depression.

Buoyed by his success, the psychologist dubbed the phenomenon "Learned Helplessness" and wrote books about it, describing it and hypothesizing that it was indeed a model of depression. And it caught on. Oh, how it caught on. Before long the theory became *huge* in academic psychology circles and began spawning some very serious and very high-quality research by some very serious and very high-quality researchers. The psychologist who developed the concept went on to become so prominent that he was elected president of The American Psychological Association, authored some very popular books, developed some widely-used tests designed to predict human performance, and received a variety of awards that declared him to be a very smart and very clever man indeed.

Learned Helplessness caught Merlin's eye. He decided he would like to study it. So he asked some graduate students if they would like to study it with him.

Now, an invitation like that from someone like Merlin was something on the order of God inquiring as to whether you'd like to be the sole person to whom he reveals the meaning of life. You'd have to have monkey grass for brains to turn it down. So a hoard of graduate students eagerly fell in step behind him and marched with Merlin into the land of Learned Helplessness. I, of course, was one of them.

Merlin and his disciples created a "Learned Helplessness Research Team" that met at regular intervals at Merlin's house in order to steep ourselves in every nuance of Learned Helplessness. We discussed readings, hashed out ideas and interpretations, looked for unanswered questions or flaws in the model, and tried to design studies to find out new things about it. All told, the team met regularly for well over a year and developed an extensive series of Learned Helplessness studies.

Do let me note that because being on Merlin's Learned Helplessness research team was: a) voluntary, and; b) in addition to everything else we were required to do, I am aware that deciding to join it may sound a tad, shall we say, imprudent (even given Merlin's magnetism) what with the truly freakish level of demands that were already being put on our time, energy, and intellects. Taking on an additional demanding—and optional—task certainly does not, on its surface, sound sane. But being on the Learned Helplessness research team actually served an important practical purpose. My program required students to complete one formal research project prior to undertaking one's dissertation. This research project was a somewhat more informal affair than a thesis or dissertation, (my program did not require or grant a formal Masters degree on the way to the Doctorate) so it did not require throwing onself on the bed of nails called a "committee" to oversee the project and ensure that it took several years off your life. Even so, the project had to be a formal piece of research complete with a cohesive topic, a literature review, an experimental design, subjects run through protocols, results reported, and an interpretive discussion.

Being on the Learned Helplessness team created a perfect opportunity to design a research project that would fulfill the research requirement. As a result, many of us on the team were able to parlay our participation into the creation of our required project. In addition, a few of us went so far as to also use Learned Helplessness as the topic for their dissertations. I, of course, was one of those, too.

For a clinical psychology graduate student such as myself, Learned Helplessness had two qualities that made it a very appealing topic for research. First, it suggested that there might be a behavioral cause for depression that could be studied and understood. If depression really was a kind of "discouragement-on-steroids" where the cause was repeatedly failing to get results that are related to your behavior, there might very well be behavioral ways to prevent it and to treat it. Consider, for example, how it works when you push the button for an elevator and it never comes. First you punch the button and you wait. No elevator. You push the button again, and you wait some more. You push the button again, but now you start to get agitated and walk around, maybe even grumbling to yourself. Then you push the button a bunch more times in a row, and you get even more agitated. You begin pacing, looking around, mumbling to yourself and complaining to others who are also waiting. Then you get angry, irritated, and annoyed. If the whole thing goes on long enough you finally give up. The Learned Helplessness model suggested that depression might be caused by a process like that, only happening to someone in a really, really big way.

Second, Learned Helplessness was relatively easy to study in a laboratory setting. It made for research projects that were manageable in scope and size. Understand that the practical "testability" of a psychological model is no small matter. Many theories of psychological function and malfunction are logical and appealing, but are also so huge, esoteric, subjective, and abstract that it's hard as the dickens to design an experimental protocol that will tell you with any credibility if the damn thing is right. I mean, how on the earth do you measure an "Id?" Or study an "introjected self-object?" Learned Helplessness was a gem not only because it offered a possible backstage glimpse into an emotional disorder that is common, painful, and disabling, but because it was born in the lab and so was testable in the lab.

Merlin's research team, although not a formal "class" with grades or tests, was nevertheless typically Merlin. It was demanding. We read lots and lots of stuff. He presented theoretical issues and quandaries for us to think about and fret over. We formulated research ideas and critiqued each other's experimental designs and statistical procedures. As our work progressed and we felt that we were mastering the information, several of us began trying to design the studies that we would use to fulfill our research requirement.

Which was when we smacked head-long into a methodological brick wall. How, exactly, we asked ourselves, did one induce the "Learned Helplessness" effect on human subjects? None of us were animal researchers, and putting human subjects into cages and shocking the floor was out of the questions for (what should be) obvious reasons. Interestingly, in his articles and books the psychologist who had developed the theory was repeatedly circumspect about the type of problem-solving task he had used on his human subjects to induce the Learned Helplessness effect. Whatever the task was, it had to be a pretty neat trick because it had to allow the experimenter to choose whether a subject succeeded or failed while making it seem to the subject that he or she had actually succeeded or failed of their own volition. We were stymied about how to do it, and we spent increasing proportions of our time sitting around, looking at each other, saying a fancy academic version of "Huh?" We were stuck, big time.

And it started getting to me. I tried to tolerate it, I really did, but as time went on the pressure built inside me. Like a suspect being grilled by the police, sweat beaded on my forehead. My nerves began to fray. I started to shake and quiver. I asked for a glass of water and stared at the lights glaring in my eyes. Finally, consistent with my predictable level of idiotic excess and apparent complete denial of the personal and physical limitations inherent to the state of being human, I'd had enough. I broke. I caved. I gave in, I cried "uncle." I said that I would do it, that I would take on the task of figuring out how on earth the psychologist who invented the theory did what he did to his human subjects. I would find a way for us to replicate the effect.

Well, I swear—roasted pigs with apples in their mouths fell from the sky onto serving platters if I didn't hear an actual audible, collective sigh of relief from the rest of the research team. What, I asked myself, just happened? Had they been stalling, waiting until I cratered? Did they know it was inevitable? Or did they consciously—or unconsciously—figure that I was the only one stupid enough to *volunteer* to figure out the induction task? Or were they really all so lost that they didn't think they could do it and so were just relieved that someone offered to do it for them? I wasn't sure I could figure the damn thing out either, you understand. I was just stupid enough to say I'd try.

Now, I needed another thing to do like I needed a hole in the head, of course, but the fact was we were stuck and I wasn't about to sit around until someone else finally decided that, gee, maybe they'd get on it *before* they entered the retirement home. To hell with that. So I took a deep breath, put toothpicks under my eyelids, changed my mailing address to the library, filled my head with accelerants, and set out to figure out how to make our subjects succeed and fail at will.

I gathered every study on Learned Helplessness using human subjects that I could lay my paws on and scrutinized them for clues about the task that was used to induce the effect. All told I found one perfunctory explanation of the problem-solving task and one drawing of one "card" used in the task. It was all very obtuse. I began to wonder if it was no accident that the task was never quite described. Did it really exist? Could the researchers be wanting to prevent others from replicating their studies? Were they fame and glory hogs, treating the procedures as proprietary? Or was I getting crazy? Maybe it was simply a repeated oversight. On the other hand, maybe we were all just stupid and they figured it was obvious from their studies. All I knew was that it wasn't obvious to me.

I read each study over and over and stared at the lone sample "card" long enough to burn a semi-permanent image of it on my retina. I tried to reconstruct what they did, how they did it, and why they did it. I slowly began putting the pieces together as best I could to come up with at least a general idea of how they seem to have proceeded. Here's what I concluded:

The task appeared to involve showing subjects pairs of cards—an "A" card and a "B" card. Each card contained a combination of four or five symbols—say, the "A" card contained an "A," a circle, an "X," and a star. The "B" card contained the opposite set of symbols—say, a "B," a square, a "Y" and a triangle. The subject was supposed to figure out which symbol was the "correct" one by choosing the card he or she thought contained the correct symbol. The experimenter would tell them "right"—it was on that card, or "wrong"—it was on the other. A series of six pairs of cards were then shown to the subject, with the symbols occurring in different combinations on each pair. The result was that through a process of elimination the subject could use the feedback as to which card of each pair contained the correct symbol to deduce by the end which symbol was the correct one.

I know how confusing it sounds in the retelling. But while describing the task is somewhat laborious, practically speaking it was a relatively easy test of logical deduction. But that's not all it was—the parts that seemed to make it work as a Learned Helplessness induction task included: 1) it required the subject to keep track of several symbols at once while he or she used subsequent card choices to pare down the possibilities to the final one. This meant that although the task was relatively easy, it still required a relatively high degree of concentration and juggling several ideas at once. So you could easily assume that if you got the wrong answer it was because you got confused somewhere along the way; 2) success at deducing the correct symbol depended entirely on the experimenter giving accurate feedback about which card contained the right symbol. If the experimenter gave incorrect feedback, no symbol would be consistently correct and there was no right answer. But because the inconsistent feedback would most likely confuse the subject rather than sound like inconsistent feedback, they would likely assume it was their own fault that they failed.

See the point? The experimenter could choose who succeeded and who failed without it ever appearing that they were doing so. By

giving accurate feedback, a subject could fairly easily succeed in identifying the correct symbol. By giving inconsistent (incorrect) feedback,
the experimenter could ensure that a subject would fail. But the subject would not experience the *feedback* as the reason for their
failure—they would feel that they had simply gotten confused and
screwed up the darn thing all by themselves.

The problem for me was that this was my own conclusion about
how the task worked. In reality I didn't really know for sure because
the literature did not describe the task in such detail. So I wasn't
100% sure it would work. Further, beyond the one card drawn in the
one study, I didn't know what the cards really looked like or what
particular sequence or groupings the symbols appeared in. I might
have developed an idea about how the task worked, but I was still on
my own. I was uncertain.

So I set about trying to construct the task—and the cards—in
some version that would work. I drew various versions of the cards
and got other students to help me test out their ability to provide
success with accurate feedback and failure with inaccurate feedback
while at the same time giving the impression to the subject that they
succeeded or failed due to their own intelligence or incompetence. I
tried out several versions of the task until I refined a version that, son
of a gun, worked. It really worked. It worked beautifully. It was so
effective that when we used it in our studies we could prove to subjects that it worked by starting them out with accurate feedback on a
couple of "practice" trials to teach them how the task worked. The
subjects were able to succeed at those. Then, to the "success" subjects we continued to give accurate feedback through the rest of the
trials and they successfully identified the "correct" symbol on each
trial. To the "failure" subjects we started giving inconsistent feedback
which screwed with their heads so much (especially given that they
had succeeded on the "practice" trials) that they felt their failure
represented such a sudden attack of idiocy on their part that they'd
better hit the Yellow Brick Road in search of a brain.

I'm telling you, it really did work, sometimes too well. One of my
"failure" subjects got so angry and frustrated that he picked up the
cards—and threw them at me.

Anyway, on to dissertation. I chose Learned Helplessness as my
dissertation topic—in addition to my initial research project topic—
for two reasons. First, as I mentioned previously, it seemed a

worthwhile topic of investigation. If it really did describe how people got depressed, then investigating it might produce some information that contributed to human welfare. The second reason, though less obvious and seemingly less noble than the first, was actually the more important reason for my picking the topic: because I had experience in the area and knew how to design and run a Learned Helplessness study, I knew that it would be sufficiently manageable in size and complexity that I could complete it in a relatively short (in dissertation terms when I say "short," read: "only" two or three years) period of time. In other words, it would be an easy study to complete.

To understand why this mattered, you have to understand that the whole issue of dissertations and dissertation topics was the one place where I was at odds with nearly all of my classmates. They and I saw the issue from entirely different perspectives—different planets, in fact. Pardon my bluntness, but as far as I'm concerned my point of view was from planet Earth, and theirs was from planet Shit-for-Brains.

I came to graduate school for one reason, and one reason only—to do what was necessary to become a psychologist so I could go do psychology. It was not my goal to be a "student." That was simply a necessary evil, the thing you had to do if you wanted to get that Ph.D. and become a psychologist. So everything I did in school was designed to as efficiently and effectively as possible ensure that I would successfully get my degree and *get out*. Even my malignant overachieving was just my way of trying to guarantee that I would get my degree. As far as I was concerned, my actual "life" started after I was done and, Ph.D. in hand, was being a psychologist doing psychology. Everything before that was just hoop-jumping to fulfill the requirements for admission to the party. So I was never out to excel in graduate school for its own sake. My eyes were always on the prize—that Ph.D.

Because I had observed in the students who came before me, as well as some of those around me, that a cumbersome, complicated dissertation was *repeatedly* and *predictably* the element responsible for people taking six, seven, eight, or ten years to finish their degree (or never finishing it at all), I decided that I'd best make absolutely certain that my dissertation wouldn't snag me. Because I had already run a study on Learned Helplessness and had, in fact, *designed* our helplessness-inducing task as well as the structure for performing such research and some of the statistical procedures to analyze the data, I had the entire methodology for a Learned Helplessness study down cold. I knew the ins and outs, I had worked out all the kinks, I could do one in my sleep. That meant all I had to do for my dissertation was develop a research question of sufficient substance as to satisfy my dissertation committee, and I was off to the races. I could get it done with a minimum of muss and fuss and neutralize any evil notion my dissertation might have about making mischief with me completing my degree.

Most of my classmates did not see things this way at all and found it endlessly puzzling that I thought expediency was such a vital consideration in choosing a dissertation topic. Instead of doing everything possible to get *out* of the program, they seemed to be focusing on their time *in* the program doing something they felt "mattered." They wanted to do things they were interested in, to do things that they felt were important. Because such opportunities were, in reality, few and far between in the real-life world of graduate school, most students ended up focusing all of their unmet desires for gratification and significance on their dissertation. They wanted to do a dissertation that was *a big deal.*

Please know that I had then, and have now, nothing whatever against doing things that "matter." The very reason I went to graduate school was that I felt (and still feel) that being a psychologist and doing psychology *are* things that matter. But that's the whole point—I saw *being a psychologist* as what was important, not *being a student.* I figured that once I was out in the real world doing psychology there would be plenty of opportunity to do important things. My classmates, on the other hand, had no such desire to delay their gratification, and honey—they did not want to wait. They wanted to do significant things and things they were passionate about *right now.* That meant while they were still in graduate school.

For the life of me I could not see how their position made a lick of sense, and they seemed to feel the same way about mine. When we'd talk about it we'd go 'round and 'round. They would wax eloquent about their interests and how they wanted their dissertation to speak to their passion. I would counter that speaking to their passion would inevitably add two, three, four, or more years to finishing their degree and how that did not seem like the best of all possible choices given the house of horrors that we were living in and its corrosive effects on our bodies, psyches, and liver enzymes. They would look at me blankly. I would point out that many students had "mattered" themselves into dissertations that were darn near impossible to complete and as a result never did finish their degrees. They stared at me like I was from Mars. I pointed out that delaying one's Ph.D. on account of a huge, "meaningful" dissertation pushed back getting a job, getting paid, and having a real life. I even drew charts of how much money each year a "significant" dissertation topic would cost them. They didn't seem to hear a word I said. I pointed out that they could do studies that "mattered" after they had crawled out of this hell hole, completed their degree, and were doing things that normal people did, like earning a living, enjoying life, and doing something besides bitching that the library closed early on Saturday nights so they couldn't study until 3 AM one night of the week.

It was like I was speaking Greek. I named all the examples I could think of where previous students had gotten bogged down for years and years and *years* trying to complete some misguided magnum opus dissertation instead of their degree. I went over it again and again.

And no one bought it. We simply did not understand each other. So I gave up, they went their way, and I went mine. As it turned out, of the 11 students in my class who graduated (we started with 13, but two had already been overcome by sanity and quit) only one other student besides myself (another Learned Helplessness dissertation, I might add) graduated in four years. One or two others finished in five years, and the rest took somewhere between six and twelve years to get their degrees. And not to be smug or self-righteous, but I do hope my classmates' dissertations were, in fact, sufficiently meaningful for them as to be worth it, because it is now more than twenty years later, and so far as I know not one of them has achieved prominence or renown or has broken new ground in psychology based on their dissertation topic. In fact, so far as I know, not one of my classmates has even *published* their dissertation. (I didn't either, so it's not like I'm throwing stones. It's just that I never kidded anyone that I *intended* to.) I could be wrong about that, but I keep my eyes and ears pretty darn open, and so far I haven't seen it.

MY DISSERTATION PROPOSAL

OK, so for my dissertation proposal to fly I needed a research question that was sufficiently profound as to qualify as a "doctoral dissertation." That meant I needed a question that would address a significant issue in the Learned Helplessness literature.

I found one. I uncovered what I considered to be the major theoretical and research flaw in Learned Helplessness that no one else seemed to have identified. That flaw was a consistent confounding of the issue of "loss of control" with the issue of "failure." In 99.99 % of the Learned Helplessness research the two terms were used interchangeably, and subjects in the experiments experienced both. Uniformly, however, the Learned Helplessness effect was attributed to loss of control, not to failure.

The problem was that, both theoretically and practically, "loss of control" and "failure" are two entirely different things. Failure is a "bad outcome," an inability to achieve one's goal. "Loss of control" is when an outcome is unrelated to your behavior. But loss of control does not inherently imply a *bad* outcome—it means simply an "uncontrollable" outcome. So according to Learned Helplessness theory, technically someone should still experience Learned Helplessness if they get a *good* outcome, as long as that outcome is unrelated to their behavior. Whether the outcome is good or bad should be irrelevant. For example, in our problem-solving test, "loss of control" combined with a *good* outcome would be one where the subject would receive the phony feedback so they would get confused during the test, but when asked for their answer as to which symbol was the correct one, the experimenter would tell them every time that they were *right*. So they would succeed, but the success would be unrelated to their behavior.

In short, winning the lottery should depress you just as much as having a meteor crunch your house, because it is equally out of your control.

Not very sensible, is it? But no one had ever looked at that. In fact, nowhere in the literature or research had anyone even distinguished between failure and loss of control. Every study confounded the two. As a result, it was unclear whether the Learned Helplessness effect was due to loss of control or to failure. This, in my view, was a major theoretical and methodological flaw and this, in my view, was a question well worth examining.

So I designed a study where I gave our Learned Helplessness induction task to subjects and had half fail and half succeed, as per usual. That was my "success" versus "failure" condition. In addition, within each condition I gave subjects a range of expectation of how well they would perform on the test—due to, I told them, "the design of the test." I told them that the test was rigged to produce a particular level of success. Some I told had a 0% chance of success because the test was rigged for that outcome. Others I told had a 25% chance of success, others a 50%, others a 75%, and others a 100% chance. This gave the subjects varying experiences of "control" over the outcome. Subjects in the 0% expectation of success condition who actually succeeded would be obtaining a result that was unrelated to their behavior—but a good outcome, or success. The subjects who were told they had a 100 % chance of success would obtain a result that was related to their behavior—and a good outcome. The subjects in the failure group who were told they had a 100% chance of success but failed would obtain a result unrelated to their behavior—but failure. And the middle-level expectation groups (25%, 50%, and 75%) would experience varying degrees of loss of control. This design allowed me to tease apart the two different conditions in order to ask the question what produced Learned Helplessness—failure or loss of control.

It is not an understatement to say that my dissertation question examined something at the very heart of Learned Helplessness and that for all practical purposes had the potential to shoot down the whole theory. If Learned Helplessness was simply an artifact of failure rather than the result of loss of control, then the whole notion that "loss of control" was the central issue was, essentially, nonsense. The whole theory was wrong. Pretty neat, huh? You just wait.

This is the way a dissertation works—first, you write a "proposal," which is a formal document consisting of a review of the literature in your area (mine was a dual review—one of the literature on depression in general and the other on Learned Helplessness specifically), an explanation of your research question and why you considered it to be important, a description of the experimental design you would use to test your question, and an outline of the statistical procedures you'll use to analyze the data. This document also forms the first half of the final document. Then, after you've completed the study and add sections that contain the data analysis and a discussion of the results, voila—a dissertation magically appears.

Once you finish your proposal you hand it out to your committee members and schedule a time and date to meet with them to review your proposal to find out what they didn't like and want you to change. It was a given that there were *always* changes of some sort that your committee wanted you to make. Maybe they noticed something you missed, or they wanted you to add an analysis that they thought was important. Maybe they didn't like a statistic you were using, or they thought your proposed sample size was too small, or some such thing.

Alternatively, it was possible that they could laugh their heads off and send you slinking back to the drawing board, tail between your legs, to create an entirely new study because they thought the one you were proposing was ridiculous. It didn't happen often, but it did happen.

Now, nowhere do universities have as strict rules about how things are to be done as they do for the dissertation process. Considered the pinnacle of academic achievement, a doctoral dissertation is the single element in all of academia that perhaps stands most firmly rooted in the tradition of the great scholars and their academic debates on which the whole idea of a university is built. The tradition goes back to ancient Greece, with Socrates and the "Socratic Method." The tradition of academic knowledge is free dialogue, free exchange of ideas, and free thinking.

Which means "in public."

As a result, not only did you have to schedule a meeting with your committee to discuss your study and get them to OK it, but the meeting had to be open to anyone who had a mind to attend and wanted to put their two cents in. So the university required that you create and post, at various places around campus, (they even had a minimum number of places you had to post them) an announcement of your proposal meeting. The announcement listed the topic of your proposal and the time and location of your meeting. That way, anyone could attend your meeting to watch the fur fly as you and your committee fought it out over the brain matter you had arranged on paper and called a "proposal." In short, your potential humiliation at being told your study was asinine and you were a moron would occur in front of anyone sadistic enough to attend.

Most of us made it a point to attend at least a few other students' proposal meetings, if only to get a preview of what ours might be like. Most were a mixed bag. The committee would take issue with a little thing here and a little thing there and the student would unsuccessfully argue his or her case and then finally throw his or her hands up and agree to go make the changes that the committee wanted. Then they would resubmit the proposal for approval, their committee would sign off on it, and the student would proceed to actually perform the study in order to finish painting the target on their back that would form the basis of their "dissertation defense" meeting.

Although it was less formal than the "defense" meeting following the completion of the study, the proposal meeting was, in many ways, more of a danger. Once your committee accepted your proposal and signed off on your study, it had their formal stamp of approval. If they'd wanted to take issue with anything, they'd had their chance and should have taken it. So if at your defense meeting they decided you had rocks for brains and this was, in fact, the single most asinine study ever performed, they were in essence indicting *themselves*. If it was so darn bad, why did they approve the silly thing in the first place? So the proposal meeting was the place where they could go after you if they wanted to, and thrash you good if they felt like it.

Occasionally it would happen. I witnessed a friend of mine endure a meeting where one faculty member (who was on my committee, too, I noted with significant anxiety) continued to ask the same question over and over and over and never seemed to understand the answer that the student was giving. I could tell by witnessing the thing that the problem was that the faculty member and the student were, without realizing it, defining a particular term two different ways and would never, as far as I could tell, come to a meeting of the minds until that fact was brought to light. It never was. The darn thing went on for hours until someone (the student, I think) wore out, said to hell with it, and agreed to change the study to satisfy the professor. That worked.

When I had completed my proposal I handed it out to my committee and dutifully walked the campus putting up announcements all over hell and back just like I was supposed to. On the day of the meeting I walked into the room where it was to be held and discovered, to my horror, that the place was *packed*. To the gills. People *everywhere*. It looked like a prison riot. For some reason, everyone and their dog seemed to want to watch my proposal meeting. Talk about feeling like an object of public curiosity—I couldn't decide why so many people had come. Were they there to get ideas about how to handle their proposal meeting? Were they there because they were actually interested in my dissertation topic? Or were they there (call me paranoid, but this is the one I decided it was most likely to be) because they were hoping that this, at last, would be the chance to see Mr. Super Student finally get handed his head? In any case, there was a whole crowd of spectators present which was completely amazing, as most proposal meetings drew maybe three or four spectators—on a good day.

As I remember, upon seeing the standing-room only condition of the room I had only one clear thought: "Shit." Further, as I entered Merlin pulled me aside and said "Hey, what's the deal with all the people? I mean, 'Heap big crowd!'" (Only Merlin.) He seemed to be amused. I was nervous.

Merlin, as my committee chair, was in charge of the meeting. He welcomed everyone and in short order turned it over to me. I stood up and set about trying to explain the background (depression), the model (Learned Helplessness), my research question (failure vs. loss of control), the experimental design (2 X 5 factorial), and the statistical procedures (multivariate analysis of variance with followup a-priori mutivariate t-tests). It took me, oh, probably half an hour or so to outline it. As I talked I wrote most of it on the blackboard so it could be seen graphically. When I was finished I sat down and looked at my committee. They looked at me. They were silent. Once again I had the clear and distinct thought: "Shit."

One of my committee members asked a question. I answered it. There were a couple more questions, which I also answered. Then, as was required for the meeting, the spectators were invited to ask questions. A couple of them did. Because they were less familiar with Learned Helplessness than I, the questions were basic and theoretical rather than specific to my particular study. Then there was silence. Again. At that point Merlin asked if anyone had anything else to add or ask. No one spoke. So he summarized the study. Then he adjourned the meeting and everyone got up and left.

That was it. In a few minutes, Merlin and I were alone. I looked around the empty room. Merlin looked at me.

"How," he said, "did that happen?"

"What?" I asked.

"No revisions. That never happens. I've never seen that happen."

I didn't know what to say. I mumbled something like "Yeah, how 'bout them Yankees?" Merlin ignored me. He got up to leave.

"Amazing," he muttered. Just amazing." The door shut behind him. I was alone.

(PRE) POST-PH.D. DEPRESSION

With a successful proposal meeting behind me, I was formally ushered into a new era of graduate student existence, technically called "maybe you'll really graduate." The big hurdles, the ones that had "real and present danger" stamped on them, were: 1) Prelim Exams; 2) Qualifying Exams; 3) dissertation proposal. Once you completed those, getting your degree rested almost solely on one factor: staying power. If you could keep your head above water long enough to finish your internship and dissertation, you'd make it. It was still no guarantee of success, of course, as attempting to finish a dissertation had resulted in more than one student picking up a fork and digging into a plate of highly seasoned crow. But if at this point getting through was still not quite a done deal, its scent was at least detectable.

As for me, for the first time since I signed on for this festival of pain I felt justified in allowing at least a twinge of optimism for one very good reason—I knew that I had nothing if not staying power. If all I had to do was endure, nothing short of an active volcano appearing in my bedroom and covering me in molten lava as I slept could stop me. And because the last realistic opportunity for the faculty to flunk me out was history, I felt as though I had finally climbed down from the academic version of a fortieth-floor window ledge and stepped into the relative safety of a hotel room that was simply on fire. As a result I was able to breathe a deep, if tentative, sigh of relief.

I retain a vivid memory from that time: shortly after my proposal meeting I was walking down the street with my arm around my then-girlfriend and I had the conscious thought: "I've passed comps, my dissertation proposal has been accepted, and I'm going to internship in Minnesota. All I have to do is finish the things already in progress, and I'll graduate. For the first time in three years, I can actually see the possibility of making it through. Life is good." I remember the moment so clearly because it was such an unfamiliar experience—commonly referred to, in the world outside graduate school, as "feeling happy." I liked it.

Unfortunately, liking something does not necessarily endow it with longevity, and shortly after the walk upon which my happy little memory was based, an emotional wing came off my mental plane and, in midair, I came apart at the psychological seams and for all practical purposes disintegrated.

Why? Because there is a well-documented and justifiably feared phenomenon in academia that no one much likes to talk about, called "post-Ph.D. depression." It is the graduate-school induced version of a state that not uncommonly befalls people who have completed a goal that has consumed the major portion of their life for an extended period of time. In a truly sinister twist of irony, upon the successful completion of an all-consuming task, life often does not deliver euphoria, or even pleasure. Instead, it provides the person who has completed the goal with the experience of suffering a major loss. By finishing the goal, everything their life had been concerned with up to that point is suddenly gone, and even though they may have succeeded at what they set out to do, they are now missing the very thing that had served to structure, define, and bring meaning to their life. And as anyone even remotely familiar with psychology knows, a major loss is one of the most consistent and significant risk factors for depression.

And that's what happens—when people have completed a task to which they have devoted their life, they often get depressed. Sometimes seriously. Even catastrophically. Versions of this have been reported by such diverse people as Buzz Aldrin following landing on the moon and Jon Krakaur upon reaching the peak of Everest.

Post-Ph.D. depression is one of those. And as is the case with any "Major Depressive Episode," it can be profoundly debilitating. I had already heard heart-wrenching stories of peoples' lives, marriages, and jobs falling apart after completing their doctorate. While in the grips of post Ph.D. depression people often found themselves unable to function, emotionally numb, and tormented with feelings of emptiness, guilt, regret, worthlessness, and even recurrent thoughts of death.

Which is *exactly* what happened to me. Once I knew for certain (at least pretty well) that I would finish my degree, lucky me—continuing in my role as the perpetual overachiever, it turned out that I did not need to actually finish my degree to descend into a full-blown, all-consuming, debilitating case of post-Ph.D. depression. The result was that I spent, give or take, nearly three months sitting on my couch, staring into space. I mean this literally. I just sat on my couch staring into space, often with my tiny black and white television—which continued to sit on the floor because I *still* lacked sufficient furniture to provide it with a table—blaring in the background in an attempt to drown out the terrible emptiness that consumed me.

During those three months I did little, felt less, and made virtually no progress on anything worthwhile. I was almost entirely incapacitated. It was *awful*. Depression, as anyone who has had it can attest, is a very painful thing, a deep, abiding, aching void. And I sat on my couch with it, feeling completely alone and inert in the face of the emotional void of having, for all practical purposes and by most external standards, "made it."

Lucky me.

All things considered, though, I must say that I actually *was* lucky in having the thing hit me at that time. First, it meant that I *didn't* get it after I actually finished my degree. Second, short though that period may have been, the time between my dissertation proposal meeting and beginning internship was the only time I can recall during graduate school when there was relatively little pressure on me. I had not planned to start work on my dissertation yet, there were no fearsome exams lurking before me requiring me to stay up all night every night studying, and even the faculty seemed tired of tossing their career-threatening curve balls at me. The tasks during that time were fairly mundane and, certainly in comparison to the exertion required to that point, relatively easy—finish a few classes and see my patients, with whom I would be terminating soon anyway (isn't it ironic that seeing patients was a *low* stress activity compared to the other parts of graduate school). Beyond that, the demands on me were significantly less than at any other time I can recall.

It's a good thing, too, because I was as nonfunctional as anyone suffering from a terrible case of the flu. My version of chills, fever, and body aches may have been emptiness, angst, and emotional pain, but they were no less acute and debilitating than a terrible physical illness. As a result, there is precious little to report from that time, since I basically could get myself to do nothing beyond the absolute necessities required to fulfill on my current responsibilities and the tasks required to keep myself alive. I don't have much else to say about it except to note that it was a very unpleasant experience, not one I'd wish on anyone else, not one I'd care to repeat, and one that I'm glad lasted only three months.

INTERNSHIP: PART II

Internship was completely unlike graduate school. Well, except that you got paid like a dung beetle. And people treated you like an idiot. And you were expected to do everything and anything at any time. And you weren't, yet, a "real" doctor. And no one could remember your name. And you were uncomfortable all the time. And no one much cared.

Come to think of it, internship was *exactly* like graduate school. The only real difference was that in graduate school it was clear how you should behave—snot-nose sucking-up was a good choice—while on internship it was unclear exactly what demeanor was appropriate. Were you supposed to act like staff, or like a student? Should you behave like you knew what you were doing, or like a neophyte? Did you give instructions or take them? So although internship was allegedly an advancement and a step above being an on-campus academic student, the promotion was, in reality, to a never-never land of professional identity where you were an undefined entity, neither staff nor student, neither professional nor beginner, neither fish nor fowl, not really this and not quite that.

As a group, those of us who found ourselves interns at Minnesota had one other thing to contend with—we were interns at Minnesota. *The* Minnesota. We were painfully aware that we were a select group, a chosen few from the unchosen many. So we were not quite sure how uppity or humble we ought to be. But we knew that we were fortunate indeed, seven people being trained at the best place by the best people in the business.

Which is not to say the most sane. High-powered academic medicine is often awesome to behold—in ways both good and bad. On the positive side, at that time Minnesota led the way in a variety of areas, including such esoteric (at the time) procedures as bone-marrow transplants, behavioral treatment of chronic pain, and family therapy with welfare families. As interns, we had the good fortune of being able to work in virtually any and all such areas, serving variously as therapists, consultants, and treatment team members. A dizzying and delicious banquet of opportunities for clinical experience was ours, and we were dazzled by the rich variety of training available to us. It was truly the opportunity of a lifetime.

Further, just being accepted as an intern at Minnesota carried as one of its perks de facto evidence of competence. As such, the program felt no particular need to keep us terrified with the looming specter of failure should we walk the training tightrope with anything less than perfect precision. Instead, our competence was assumed and we were all considered to be intelligent, mature, self-starting, and fully capable of being worked completely to death.

On the negative side, high-powered academic medicine that *knows* it's high-powered can develop a bit of a—how should I say—"superiority" complex. And Minnesota, being the prominent place that it was, had found its way to having on staff even more than the usual share of well-entrenched academic, medical, and professional prima donnas. The result was an ongoing and sometimes vicious series of clashes between, and within, departments. For us, as psychology interns, the significance of this was that we inherited the legacy of psychology's having been at the epicenter of one of the most violent and legendary turf wars ever seen in academic medicine, and certainly in academic psychiatry. The shadow of the whole thing hung over both the psychology and psychiatry departments like Great Caesar's Ghost.

By the time I got there, stories about the whole affair were available only in bits and pieces here and there, but it seems that some years before I arrived, the prominence of clinical psychology had produced what some at the place considered to be a truly cataclysmic event. I cannot vouch directly for the accuracy of that somewhat hysterical description, for I was not there to see it and have to go by the rumor, innuendo, and gossip passed to me in back alleys and dark corners of obscure bars by confidential informants I recruited with multiple rounds of caustic liquor, unsalted peanuts, and promises of anonymity. But the event, as best I can make out from the snippets of anonymous inside information passed on to me, was that a long-brew-ing turf war between psychiatry and clinical psychology erupted into a miniature, three-dimensional, animated, and holographic preview of the end of the world, complete with surround sound.

Originally, and for many years, as you might expect and which certainly sounds (superficially at least) logical and appropriate, clinical psychology was a division within psychiatry. You know—psychiatrists, psychologists—the terms flow together pretty well, kinda go together, and to the uninitiated might even appear to complement each other. After all, there is perhaps more similarity than difference between the two professions. Psychiatrists may prescribe medications and psychologists may administer psychological tests, but excepting the random birthmark here and there, in most other respects the two are more or less reasonably identical twins. Both do psychotherapy, both do other types of treatment, (group, family, couples) and both are scorned by other areas of medicine as being soft-hearted, soft-headed, and not quite "real" doctors.

But academic medicine functions smoothly only when there is a clear pecking order and the white-tailed deer at the bottom of the faculty food chain knows their place and fully understand that they are never to upset, challenge, or otherwise compete with the cheetahs at the top of the food chain, lest their untenured throats be torn out and be giddily gobbled as dinner in the staff lounges and steering-committees that meet in the surprisingly smoky back rooms of a teaching hospital.

Generally this is not an issue when it comes to psychiatry and psychology, because everyone knows that the game is played on psychiatry's turf, and that determines the rules. Hospitals are, first and foremost, *medical* facilities, and this means that those with the word "medical" in their degree title are lord of the manor. "M.D.," of course, means *medical* doctor, and Ph.D. means doctor of *philosophy*, so if the implication escapes you, you clearly did *way* too many drugs in the 60's and should consider a course of treatment with antipsychotic medication or perhaps electroshock therapy which might very well be of help. Put simply, psychiatry rules the roost in teaching hospitals' departments of psychiatry, and that is generally that.

Except at Minnesota. Remember—Minnesota's Department of Clinical Psychology fathered the MMPI, and as a result had attained a degree of stature and prominence essentially unparalleled in any other medical institution—or department of psychiatry—in the country. And like the indentured servant who becomes the sudden and unexpected heir to previously unknown riches left them by some eccentric and reclusive relative, the power and newfound autonomy can result in a reaction to any previous humiliations that borders on full-scale insurrection.

Nobody really wanted to talk much about it by the time I got there, so the specifics are largely speculation on my part, but the shards of information I picked up suggests to me that psychology did just this—that it flexed its uniquely-large-for-a-psychology-department's muscles, and brought itself into a direct power struggle with psychiatry in ways virtually unheard-of in the land of large medical schools and that produced in psychiatry a level of self-righteous outrage that was terrible to behold. I guess the power struggle steadily escalated, and given that neither group was about to back off, it is my—admittedly eighteenth-hand—impression that the situation deteriorated into a Theater of the Absurd as might have been choreographed by a third-world dictator's personal death squad. I was told that faculty members refused to talk to each other, meetings erupted into shouting matches, accusations and counter-accusations flew, and all-out war was waged over faculty positions, consulting contracts, fees, patients, teaching appointments, and students. I gather that it got worse and worse and began to involve more and more people, money, and staff. I was told that it got so bad that the president and upper administration of both the hospital *and* the university (which were normally such separate entities that during my time as an intern I set foot on the actual university campus only once) were called in to try to stem the bloodletting before the entire department self-destructed, taking half the hospital down as it imploded on itself in a frenzy of vicious and increasingly personal inter-professional urban warfare.

Alas, apparently no negotiated solution was possible. It seems that tit-for-tat had become bang-for-buck, hit for slap, backstab-for-backstab. The professional positions were solidly entrenched, and psychiatry and psychology resembled fully committed and zealous, permanently armed enemy camps. I guess the administration could figure only one possible solution to this insane and out-of-control sibling rivalry: the two kids could no longer be allowed to play together and would have to be sent to their respective rooms. So psychology was summarily yanked out of the department of psychiatry and delivered—ready or not—to its new home: The School of Public Health.

That's where the psychology department resided when I arrived for my internship year. As clinical psychology interns we were not associated with, under the influence of, or otherwise connected to psychiatry. We were students in the Department of Clinical Psychology in The School of Public Health. That did not mean we didn't associate with psychiatry, and in fact as interns we did lots of things in conjunction with the psychiatry residents, but the frost between the faculty in the two departments was still palpable by any estimation, and the one simple rule for keeping your head connected to your body was unstated but seemed abundantly clear—*don't talk about it*. So no one did. I probably shouldn't have here, either. Oh, well.

The truth is that whatever unpleasantness had come before my arrival in Minnesota had either dissipated or gone underground, so it was not a factor in my experience. The result was that I liked my internship. I liked my internship a lot. I got to do all kinds of cool stuff. I got to work on addiction treatment units, in chronic pain programs, at the student health service, in the Child Communication and Behavior Disorders Clinic, and to attend seminars on everything from the Rorschach test to psychoanalysis to medical consultation to attitudes about sex. Furthermore, as interns we pretty much had the run of the place and access to all the technology available, such as the free use of photocopiers (a very big deal at the time), a WATS telephone line to call anywhere we wanted, and grants for use of the University's mainframe computer for research. So Minnesota was, for me, pretty much everything it was cracked up to be, and, once again, Merlin had given me a gift impossible to repay. I got great training by top-drawer faculty and had opportunities that many of my classmates didn't. In fact, I remember being surprised when talking to some of my classmates who had accepted an internship at a Veterans Administration hospital that they had *despised* their rotation on their chemical dependency treatment unit. This blew me away because I had *loved* my work on the chemical dependency program I consulted on. It was one of my favorite rotations. Some of this may be because Minnesota in general, and a place called Hazelden in specific, were central figures in creating the inpatient AA-based model of treatment intervention, so I was being trained by the very people who invented the model and essentially getting my information straight from the horse's mouth by the people who had discovered the horse. It was great. I still look back on it fondly and I still use things that I learned there.

THE CHRONIC PAIN PROGRAM

Internship worked like this: When we first arrived, we spent two full days with the hospital trotting in front of us representatives from the different services where we could chose to work, or do what is technically called "a rotation" (as in "rotate" through the service). Then we decided which programs we'd like to work with and submitted our choices to the internship administration. Most rotations were 3-months long, so if you did full-time rotations you would work on four different services during your intern year. Some placements, however, were 6-months and others were only part-time. As a result, if you were so inclined you could design for yourself a truly complicated year of multiple opportunities differing in length and hours.

I was so inclined, of course—you know me—and one of the first rotations I picked, and one that Merlin had promoted to me with such zeal that I feared he was going to require me to sign an affidavit that I would sign up for the rotation if I got into Minnesota, was working in the Chronic Pain Program. It was an innovative, powerful, and fun program to work on, so I signed up for it first thing. I noticed at the time that my fellow interns seemed a bit puzzled by my zeal to do that particular rotation. They, it seems, had not been the target of Merlin's substantial powers of persuasion and thought that working in "chronic pain" sounded rather dry and boring.

It was neither. Chronic pain, you see, is a devilish and wily thing. It is, in many ways, an entirely different animal from "acute" (read: intense and short-term) pain. It may even use different neurological pathways in the body. As a result, it often does not yield to the same anti-pain medications that acute pain does. While substantial advances in medical treatment for chronic pain have been made in the time subsequent to my being an intern, at that time medication for pain was limited, dangerous, and often impotent in the face of enduring and unrelenting pain. Worse, over time people almost always built a tolerance for, and an addiction to, pain meds. After a while the drugs didn't much stem the pain anymore and the patient either took more and more or continued to take the same amount to at least avoid feeling *worse* by having the pain increase, not to mention going into withdrawal. In extreme cases the chronic use of pain medications actually *increased* pain. In a somewhat bizarre biological phenomenon known as "hyperanalgesia," over time the cause-effect of pain and pain meds can "reverse" and the body actually begins generating pain in order to get the pain killers. At that point the use of the drugs increases pain rather than reduces it. Nice, huh?

So, all in all, chronic pain—as anyone who has it knows—is beastly. At that time the University of Minnesota Hospital was one of the pioneers in treating chronic pain in a new and exciting way, given the medical limitations back then. Once every medical procedure to reduce someone's sensation of pain had been tried and either failed or could no longer be used, they became eligible to be seen in our program, the Chronic Pain Program. Ours used a non-medical, entirely behavioral approach to treating chronic pain. And when it worked, it worked beautifully.

Our program did not treat the "sensation" of pain. Our program treated the "disability" of pain. What we tried to do was to get people to be non-disabled even though they had pain. Whether or not they still *felt* the pain was not our concern. We tried to take their pain out of the center of their life and to move it to the side, to a place of lowered importance. We tried to make their pain irrelevant to their life.

The significance of this approach was that it was designed to give people back their lives. It got people off disability, got them back to work, and resulted in their living virtually normal lives where they could derive the greatest possible satisfaction and joy—certainly more than they had been, what with sitting around in the dark focused on how much they were hurting. Many sufferers of chronic pain who came to our program had virtually given up living life and were existing only in service of focusing on their pain. We tried to change that around 180 degrees, to where their pain became as irrelevant as possible. A perhaps surprising, but not at all uncommon, side-effect of our program was that despite the abandonment of any "medical" treatment for their pain, the sensation of pain often did, in response, diminish as well—sometimes significantly. But that was considered a lucky accident, it was not our goal.

The way we accomplished this "nondisabling" of pain was to work with the patient, their family, and anyone else significant to their life to completely eliminate pain as the cause or reason for doing, or saying, anything. This was a behavioral procedure known as "extinguishing pain behaviors." That is, any behavior—verbal or nonverbal—referencing, attending to, or relating to the pain, was ignored by everyone—family, staff, and friends. There was to be no discussion of pain. Ever. Any behaviors arising from the pain were not to be responded to. Ever. If, in response to pain, the person laid in bed—they were ignored. If they limped around, no one asked about their pain or reacted as if they were, in fact, limping. Our motto was "The sensation pain is strictly yours, and you must keep it as your private business because no one can have it for you." So we worked with the family and the patient and trained everyone in the extinction procedure. We made sure there was a whole lot of ignoring going on.

All of this was done with the full knowledge, consent, and participation of the patient. There were no secrets. We even had the patient sign an agreement where they acknowledged that they knew everyone was going to ignore all of their "pain behaviors," and that they agreed to this procedure.

To get the whole thing off to a good start, the patient was admitted as an inpatient to the Physical Medicine and Rehabilitation unit of the hospital and was treated like any patient recovering from an injury or other musculo-skeletal problem. They were involved with a wide variety of rehabilitation activities—including physical therapy— designed to improve their physical condition to the point where they could be involved in a full range of normal physical activities. Throughout, the physical therapists who did the physical exercises, the psychologists who administered the program, the social workers who worked with the family members, and the patient's family, friends, and coworkers, all studiously avoided responding to the patient like they were, in any way, at any time, in pain.

While this may sound cruel or unkind, the results of our program were often little short of miraculous. The primary patient I worked with, for example, came into the program on crutches and unable to work, and left the program running three miles a day and employed full-time in the job he'd had before the accident that had caused his chronic pain. During the exit interview with the staff, his wife broke down in tears and thanked us for "giving her husband back to her." If that kind of thing doesn't move you, you've got no pulse.

A special area of concern was that many patients came to the program seriously addicted to painkillers, perhaps even suffering from hyperanalgesia. Because we needed to get them off the pills—especially if hyperanalgesia was involved—we told them that we would be steadily reducing their dose of pain meds until they were completely off them. The hitch was that we needed to make sure the patient didn't know when, or by how much, the medication was reduced, so there could be no placebo effect of apparent increase of pain resulting from their awareness that today their pain meds were, say, only half of what they had come to believe they needed to get by. So when the patient started the program, (and, again, they knew exactly what we were doing—there was nothing secret or underhanded in anything) we would dissolve their usual dose of pain meds into a small vial of thick, sweet, cherry-flavored syrup and give it to the patient to drink. Thereafter, the patient was given the same amount of syrup every day, but we steadily mixed in less and less of their medication. Since the amount of syrup was always the same and the disgustingly sweet taste masked the taste (or absence) of any pills, the patient never knew how much medication they were (or were not) getting. Finally, one day—usually after about a week or ten days—the nurse would hand the patient the vial of syrup and say "You can drink it if you want, but there are no longer any meds in it." At that point the patient was successfully weaned off the drugs.

It was a fun program because everyone involved *wanted* to be involved, and the program could work brilliantly. In addition, three days a week we evaluated potential patients, and the cases we evaluated were frequently fascinating. Because it was a highly regarded program we had lots of people applying for admission. But we didn't take many. The requirements to enter the program were stiff—the patient had to be in chronic pain, had to have exhausted all possible medical treatments, and had to be psychologically intact except for their pain. We were not doing psychotherapy. Further, they had to be disabled by the pain and someone (generally their disability insurance company, who would much rather pay for our program than for the next twenty years of disability) had to be willing to foot the not-insubstantial bill of an 8-week inpatient hospital stay and a rehab program involving a wide variety of health care professionals.

Most patients we evaluated were not appropriate for the program, and a few were bizarre or psychotic. But once in a while we'd get one we thought we could help, and at that point everyone in the place salivated like Pavlov's dog at the prospect of having a real live patient to work our magic on. During my rotation we had two patients admitted which, given the intensity of the program, was a full program and plenty for us to handle.

What was most fun for me, though, was that even though I was "just" an intern, because the program was actually administered by psychologists through the Division of Clinical Psychology, I was, for all practical purposes, the day-to-day director of the program. I basically ran the place. It was heady indeed, and I relished the role. In fact, my only real problem was my boss, the "real" head of the program. He could be difficult.

The program had for many years been run by a psychologist who had retired some time before I arrived. This particular psychologist was widely acclaimed as a brilliant and talented clinician. He was world-renown for his work in chronic pain, and he had done much to build Minnesota's into a world-class chronic pain treatment program. People came from all over to study with him. In the world of chronic pain he was a full-blown, sought-after celebrity. In fact, there was apparently only one problem with him (or so I was told—I never met the man and I don't even remember his name, so my information is based on reports from Merlin and sundry others)—he could rage like nobody's business. Apparently he could, and would, throw world-class temper tantrums. So if you worked with him you moved heaven and earth to stay on his good side and not become the target of what was said to be his screaming, table-banging, fist-shaking, ear-splitting wrath. Again—I can't personally vouch for the accuracy of the impression, but given that it came from more than one or two people, I tend to think it might have some truth to it. Nevertheless, everyone seemed to tolerate his reputedly outrageous behavior because he was so brilliant and talented and worked such magic with patients suffering from chronic pain.

He had retired, as I said, and by the time I got there the program had been turned over to a man who had been a student of the former director. This man was understandably flattered to have been hired for what was a high-profile, plum position that anyone in the know would have *killed* to get. It was a high compliment, and he had undertaken the job with great enthusiasm and vigor—as well as some quite appropriate nervousness. After all, he had some mighty big shoes to fill, and if he wanted to get noticed he'd have to shine pretty darn bright given the shadow he was standing in.

His response was to put his nose to the grindstone, buckle down, and work *hard*. He arrived at his office early in the morning, and he left it late at night. He held seminars and in-service trainings. He read everything available on chronic pain. He wrote articles, he consulted on other services, he hobnobbed and he politicked. He was a one-man dynamo. I admired his energy and commitment, and I thought he showed signs of having a long and successful tenure as director.

But—when it came to supervising an intern, it was a different story. In that task he seemed, shall we say, a bit lost at sea. He seemed unsure about what to do with me, and how, where, and when he should do it. So he fell back on the only thing he knew—how he had been supervised—and tried to copy the supervision style of the famous director.

The problem was that my boss was nothing like that man—or at least nothing like the descriptions I had heard of him. My boss *wasn't* naturally prone to rages. He *didn't* have an inherent tendency to scream and yell. He *wasn't* unpredictable and arbitrary. He wasn't someone who "laid down the law." He was a pretty darn nice guy. But for some reason he seemed to think his style wouldn't work to successfully supervise me, so he tried to copy his former boss's style. Unfortunately for me, he seemed completely incapable of distinguishing the parts of the retired director's personality that had worked to build a world-class program to treat chronic pain from the parts that were simply a world-class pain.

It's like the story of the company that shipped off a teacup to be duplicated by a factory that had never seen a teacup: unbeknown to them, the bowl and the handle of their sample teacup broke apart in shipping to the factory. As a result, they received back from the factory a shipment of a million teacups—with detached handles. Same thing for my boss. When supervising me, he essentially tried to copy everything about how his former boss had done things, right down to the temper tantrums.

It just didn't work. First, my boss couldn't throw a temper tantrum worth a damn. His personality leaned more toward the compulsive, polite, and restrained than to the impulsive and abusive. Not rage material. And while he was certainly smart and was fully capable of running a successful program—and supervising an intern—he was neither as brilliant nor as talented as his predecessor. That was hardly a mark against him, because neither was anyone else, myself included. But it meant that when *he* behaved badly it could not be dismissed as the tolerable quirks of a genius. Instead, it showed up as exactly what it was—the behavior of someone acting like a flaming asshole. I remember one of the other interns seeing some of his behavior with me, and commenting that the man "Had better change that, or he was going to get himself into trouble one of these days."

But not with me. I wasn't out to cause trouble, and in truth I actually thought the whole thing was kind of sad. Here you had this nice guy, energetic and enthusiastic, gung-ho and committed, nervous about succeeding, and who I think would have done just fine if he'd let himself be himself and supervise me *his* way, but who seemed to be afraid that he wasn't doing it right unless he did it like someone else.

I don't know how this might have affected a different intern—maybe they would have done OK with it—but I can tell you that it was hard on me. The problem was I didn't know what to expect. Sometimes he seemed to "just be being himself," and we did well. At those times I found him to be informative, knowledgeable, and helpful. But then he would slip into what I came to call his "Former Director Mode," and he became awkward and difficult. It was this unpredictability that made him difficult for me and that made me want to file his supervision style under "T" for "Toxic."

Despite it all, we got along pretty well most of the time. I was generally able to manage his awkward attempts at copying his former boss's pompous hostility and to avoid becoming too much of a target of his lame, put-on, unnatural, and-forced-to-the-point-of-laughable temper tantrums. And he really did try his best to help me gain competence in the areas in which I was inexperienced. So for the most part we seemed to have arrived at a pretty good gentleman's agreement about how to relate to each other.

In fact, the whole thing got out of hand only once, and I think he ended up sorry for it. As I mentioned, the man was an incredibly hard worker, and at times this could lapse just over the line into compulsivity. And although I was supposed to be running the daily operations of the program, sometimes he just couldn't help himself and he would stick his fingers a little too deeply into everything I was doing.

There was this one time when his butting-in had shifted into overdrive, and when I would arrive at the hospital in the morning at the usual time and go to the ward to check on our patients, read the charts, make notes, talk to staff, and do the other things expected of me, I would discover that my boss had always already been there and had always already done all that. There was nothing left for me to do. My initial response was to shrug my shoulders and retreat to my office to work on other things.

This went on for several weeks and I kept kind of passing it off, figuring it was just another part of his overcompensation for feeling insecure in his role as my supervisor. That, as it turned out, was a mistake.

One day, out of nowhere, he summoned me to his office. Closing the door, he launched full-force into his "Former Director Mode" and lit into me with a screaming tirade about what a bad job I was doing because "I wasn't even *doing* my job." I was flabbergasted, I could not believe my ears, and I felt that he had crossed the line in a *big* way by going blitzkrieg on me without ever having addressed the issue—which I didn't even feel was mine—in a reasoned way. Nevertheless, for a while I sat quietly and let him blow off steam.

Then, during the first appreciable pause, I said—slowly, with teeth clenched, and in as seething a tone as I could manage—"So please tell me how, exactly, I'm supposed to do my job when you're doing everything I'm supposed to do before I even get the chance to do it? You're undermining me, my position, and my ability to work with both patients and staff." Then I detailed for him—slowly, painstakingly, and without ever unclenching my teeth, blinking, or breaking eye contact—the specifics of the past few weeks where he had completed everything before I even arrived in the morning—at the time I was supposed to get there, I might add, so it wasn't like I was late and he needed to pick up the slack.

As further evidence that he was not, in fact, his former boss, my reaction took him completely off guard. The wind went right out of his sails. His face fell, he seemed lost for words, and his fit shattered into embarrassing bits on the floor. (Note to self: when throwing a tantrum, never do it half-assed. If you give up too easily you just look pathetic.) He was dumbstruck. He seemed to have never even once entertained the idea that his own behavior might have something to do with the upset he was experiencing. Nor did he seem to have any idea what to do when someone pointed it out instead of cratering in the face of his supposed-to-be-intimidating-but-actually-forced-to-the-point-of-being-embarrassing, pseudo-rage-attack. As far as I was concerned, his nasty confrontation of me in the face of his own bad behavior was an act of self-destructiveness, because it made my blood boil more than any other single event I can recall during my year of internship. He could have talked to me in a reasonable way about his concerns and we would have had a productive discussion. Instead, he ambushed me.

Big mistake.

When I feel that someone has crossed the line that separates the appropriate from the egregious and outrageous to the degree that he did, a less-than-completely-attractive part of my personality can surface, a part that I sometimes call my "tactical verbal nuclear strike capability." Normally I am, I think most people would agree, a reasonably pleasant and agreeable sort. But there is an old Chinese saying: "Beware the anger of a patient man." That's me. When someone crosses the line I don't become hysterical, or crazed, or out-of-control. I go the other way. I become a cold-blooded, predatory, psychological and conversational killing machine. I zero in on the most sensitive spot, drag out the most damning data, present it in the most pointed way, pry open the largest jugular, and impassively comment that they might want to fetch a mental rag to mop up their growing pool of psychological blood collecting on the floor. I am well aware that it is neither pretty nor nice, that it violates entire chapters of principles governing appropriate interpersonal behavior, and that it can permanently damage a relationship. I know all that. I also know that it happens to be brutally effective. So when I find myself so offended that I no longer care about consequences or the relationship and I feel inclined to use it, well, let me put it this way—I have seen people shake. Uncontrollably.

I got it from my dad, in case you were wondering.

Well, this guy had gone well into that range, and I stopped caring if it was just an imitation of the way he was supervised. There was no excuse for his treating me like that. So I raised the threat level to red, went into full cruise-missile mode, and decided to take him down. Perhaps it was the intensity, the suddenness, or the unexpectedness of my counterattack that did it, but whatever it was, as I stared unblinking into his face, my jaw set, my eyes squinting, leaning forward in my chair and carefully laying out the iron-clad case for the inappropriateness of his behavior and the outrageousness of his attack on me, his tantrum dissolved into thin air.

In response to this unexpected strafing run across his psychological landscape, he meekly agreed that maybe he *had* been a bit controlling and that he *should* leave things to me. I responded by saying I thought that would be a really, *really* nice idea—but only if he really *wanted* to act like a supervisor and really *let* his intern do his job to really *learn* something. And be sure that the tone in which I said this was so blindingly sarcastic as to make it an even more personal and pointed dig than the words alone suggest. (Like I said, I was really, *really* mad.) I said a few other similarly vicious things that I don't care to repeat, and concluded by saying that if he preferred to run the program all by himself it was OK with me, given that I had *lots* of other things I needed to do, but if he decided to do that, he'd be *much* better off not blaming me for *his* pattern of controlling and sabotaging behavior—oh, and perhaps he would also like me to recommend to the Director of Interns that I be the last psychology intern ever assigned to work with him.

That fixed things. I got to run the program for the rest of my rotation, and my boss expressed no subsequent complaints about my work.

But there was one final tantrum.

Even at the time I was aware that the final thing I said in my counter-attack might have been somewhat gratuitous, and I suspect it was what resulted in his never forgetting, or forgiving, his wounding at my hands. So before I left Minnesota he managed to find a way to avenge his hurt by attempting to wound me back.

I won't bore you with the details except to say that I said something, in jest, that this man took seriously. His response was to become "completely enraged" (his words) at what he felt was my slight. I felt that his reaction was so grossly out-of-proportion, given that mine was one of the *least* serious of many kidding things said by many people in the situation, that it was likely fueled by something else. I concluded that he was either being stupid or he was getting back at me. And since I knew he wasn't stupid, I decided it was the latter—hence my conclusion it was redress for my previous attack on him.

Sensing, this time, a fight I could not win, and perhaps even an understandable payback for my going one sentence—or two—too far in my previous verbal nuclear strike, I responded to his cartoonish, breathless, sputtering rage by apologizing without defense, rebuttal, or attempt at justification. It simply wasn't worth it. Besides, I was leaving Minnesota at the end of the year and, quite frankly, I was off his rotation and I gave not a good goddam about what he thought of me once I walked away from the place.

But, you know, when all was said and done, I really was sorry that it ended like that. I really do think he was a decent fellow and that he never meant me any harm. And I learned a lot from him. So I was sorry it ended badly, and I'm glad that my bad feelings did not endure. I hope his didn't, either.

MY OTHER JOB

In case you have forgotten, I did not go to internship "just" to go to internship. I went to internship to finish my dissertation as well. And remember—there was a not-insignificant threat looming should I fail to get the thing completed during my time in Minnesota: it was called "not getting my degree." So while I worked at the hospital during the day, my evenings were devoted to trying to assemble the document that would serve as the crowbar needed to pry loose a Ph.D. from the greedy and grasping fingers of my graduate program.

Before I left for internship I had hired a highly competent class-mate to oversee my research assistants in running several hundred subjects through my research protocol. By the time I got to internship I discovered that she was doing a terrific job. I was regularly receiving packets in the mail containing dozens of scales, ratings, and forms, resulting in a stack of needing-to-be-analyzed raw data steadily growing out of the corner of the bedroom of my apartment, threatening to consume the place. That meant I needed to get started analyzing it.

To understand what this means, you have to remember the era. This was the late 70's when essentially no one had ever heard of, because no one had yet invented, the personal computer. The only computers available for performing the fairly complicated level of data analysis required in my dissertation was a university's mainframe. Further, in those days there were no such things as computer termi-nals or disk drives, so in order to enter data it first had to be punched onto cards that were then organized into stacks and fed into card "readers" which flipped through the stack and converted the punches into electronic digits to enable the mainframe to know what the num-bers were and what it should do with them. Then the computer analyzed the data and spewed out the results by way of a teleprinter.

As you can likely tell from the description, the whole process was about as efficient as rubbing two sticks together to make fire, and the time required to do even simple data analyses was little less than that needed to catalogue the entire Library of Congress. In braille. So the steady stream of raw data arriving by way of my able research assistant made it increasingly clear that I needed to start analyzing it already, lest I leave it to the last minute and have to do the equivalent of aging hundred-year-old Scotch in just under forty-five minutes.

Fortunately, Minnesota was generous with their computer time, and as interns we could fill out one simple form and receive a grant that paid for a not-insubstantial amount of time using the university mainframe. (What? They actually *expected* interns to be doing their dissertation during internship? The logic baffled me, especially given that I was the only intern during my year trying to complete a dissertation while on internship—further evidence of the insanity of the situation in which I had found myself, thank you, Merlin.) No matter. Having access to the mainframe was a godsend, and I had submitted the proper form and received a large wad of computer time. All I needed now was a card punch machine, a card reader, and a teleprinter—all of which, to my relief, were present in a room in the basement of the hospital. I was set. So, beginning at about the third month of my internship, I started spending many—if not most—of my evenings in a basement room of the hospital punching cards for my data analysis.

If any of you remember punching data cards then not only are you as old as I am, but you are also familiar with a level of frustration that by comparison makes trying to convince airport security guards that the Luger tucked in your waistband was put there by accident and without your consent seem like an absolute *breeze*. Because with punch cards, you see, any error—any error at all—resulted in your having to redo the *whole* card. That may not sound like a big deal, but because each card—in my study, at least—carried probably fifty data points, one false tap of the keyboard and you just added about twenty extra minutes onto your time in order to redo just *that* card. Multiply that by over two hundred cards, (that's right, we're talking thousands of data points) and you can see that the possibility of the time required for just punching the cards—much less getting them into the right order so the computer would read them—could be roughly equivalent to the span of the most recent ice age.

I spent *literally* dozens of hours punching cards. It took weeks to complete. That meant most every night when I finished work on whatever rotation I was on in the hospital, I would slip off to the computer room in the basement and punch cards until I could no longer stay awake, focus, sit upright, or speak any known language. Then I would go home, flop into bed—often fully dressed—and get up the next morning to once again go to internship and then to the computer room to punch cards.

Although the room with the punch card machine was tucked away in the basement and (thankfully) unknown to most people, occasionally I would arrive and find, outrageous and offensive though it might be, someone else using the punch card machine. The nerve. And unless I could make them sufficiently uncomfortable by standing over them, haunting them like an incontinent, toothless great-grandparent sitting across from you at Thanksgiving dinner spewing half-chewed turkey and dressing out their partial dentures, so they would get the hell up and *leave*, I would have to wait until they decided to stop or forego the evening altogether and lose an entire night of card-punching that I would have to make up at a later date. Given the deadline I faced, missing an evening of punching my data cards would make me feel unhappy. Very unhappy. Occasionally homicidal. Fortunately, it was rare. For some reason few people seemed inclined to punch computer cards in the dark, deserted basement of a large university hospital at 1 AM after working all day. Go figure.

And that was not the half of it. Getting my data cards successfully punched was just getting the data analysis ball rolling. *Then* I had to sequence the cards correctly, feed them into the card reader, wait until the printout came back, and see if I had done it right. If there was an error in any way with any card or with its placement in the pile, the printer would simply type the word "error" and I would get to try to figure out what might be wrong. Then I would redo the whole thing—repunch the card if there might be a punching error, redo the order of the cards if there might be a stacking error—feed the cards in again, and see what news the teleprinter brought me. Add to this the fact that at busy times the university mainframe piled up literally thousands of computing jobs and it could be forty-five minutes or even an hour (occasionally even overnight) before my readout would print out after I put my cards through the reader. Given that I had several dozen analyses to run, each of which required feeding different cards through the reader in a different order, and the time required for the analyses seemed to stretch endlessly before me. Over and over I would stack the cards, run them through the reader—and wait. And wait. And wait. The printout would finally come, I would try to find the mistakes I had made, do what I thought might correct them, and go through the whole process again. And again. Between correcting errors and reordering the card stack over and over the whole thing turned into an enormous job.

I recall one night when I got lucky. Not only was no one using the card-punching machine, but the university mainframe was unusually available and prompt in producing results. I would put my cards through the reader and, within two or three minutes, the printer would urp out my numbers. Unheard of. Nirvana. It was a moment of such miraculous good fortune that I tried to do as many of my analyses as possible, and I stood at the card reader, without a break, from six in the evening until two the following morning—eight straight hours without once stopping or sitting down. When I left I could hardly walk and my legs felt like they had been beaten with a large polo mallet, but I had accomplished so much in my analysis that I left the place at 2 AM feeling entirely and completely euphoric.

And that, my friends, is what passed for "pleasure" on internship.

Once my data were analyzed, the next part of the process began—writing up the results. So, after my several months of running data analyses were finally complete, instead of retiring to a basement room in the hospital after my shift at the hospital I retired to my bedroom, where I had my typewriter. Remember—this was in the pre-word processor era, so happiness was having a *correcting* typewriter. Which I did.

At that point it was also time to bring Merlin into the loop to review my writing to see if it was well done, made sense, or might pass muster with my committee. And Merlin, remember, was not about to let anything half-done or slipshod get through. Oh, no. He made it very clear that were his name to go on the document listed as the dissertation "Chair," then by golly the document was going to live up to his Olympian standards or you were going straight to hell, and your little dog too. So I began typing sections, putting them into the mail, and then either calling Merlin to see what he thought or looking for return mail for the manuscript I had sent him—which not infrequently arrived spewing so much red-ink that it looked like it was bleeding.

Now, I know that all this doesn't really sound terribly complicated—punch cards, feed them in, get the data, write it up and send it off, but the amount of time required in each step was so large, and given the technology of the time the procedures so inefficient, that the whole process could easily eat up every waking hour for many months, even years. Remember—students in my program often worked for years, full-time, on their dissertations, while I essentially had to complete mine (counting from the time I got enough data to start my computer card-punching jag) in less than nine months—all while working full-time at a hospital. I am not trying to belabor the point or be melodramatic about it (OK, maybe just a little) but it is very difficult to communicate how intense the whole thing was and just how much of my life it consumed. It was overwhelming.

For weeks and weeks, I kept at it. I would finish at the hospital, scurry home, pull myself up to my desk, and type until 2 AM. Sometimes I would write a new section, and sometimes I would retype a draft as per Merlin's comments.

But despite my best efforts and burning multiple candles at multiple ends, it was not enough. Merlin and I were running out of time. It seems that in my time calculations I had failed to account for one very important thing—you had to submit your final document to your committee members *well* (as in 6 weeks) in advance of your defense meeting in order to give them time to actually read the silly thing before your meeting. And you had to have the final document professionally typed according to extremely exacting standards of margins, page numbers, and typeset. That by itself took (at the time) nearly a month. All of this meant that I was off in my estimated time for completing the thing by nearly three months. So it turned out I didn't have 12 months in which to complete my dissertation after all, I had more like eight months. Subtract the three months for the data collection to be completed, and the completely-insufficient 12 months of time available to complete my dissertation turned out to be more like five or six months. A laughable period of time to complete a dissertation, I assure you.

Really, I cannot tell you how stressful it was. I cannot tell you how frightened I was. As the time grew shorter and shorter, each night I typed faster and faster, longer and longer. One night, along about midnight, I hit the "N" key on my typewriter, and it snapped off. It flew right out of the machine and landed in my lap. Reacting as though I was a character in a horror movie who just had a bloody, severed head dropped into my lap, I let out a blood-curdling scream and jumped to my feet. I had, for all practical purposes, run my typewriter into the ground. I had actually managed to produce metal fatigue in the mechanism, and now I had no "N" on the damn thing.

This was bad. Very bad. If I didn't have a typewriter, I couldn't finish the document, and as I recall by that time I felt I could not afford even a single night of delay. Panic set in. I paced around my bedroom, hyperventilating, my mind racing, frantically trying to focus. After regaining some—at least superficially—logical thinking abilities, I hatched a fairly desperate plan. I initially thought about continuing to type and then going back and filling in the "N"'s by hand, but I decided that would take close enough to forever as to be impractical. But one of my good friends was an intern who had to take a leave of absence and was away at the time. Well, I had keys to their apartment to water their plants, and I thought—hey, *they* might have a typewriter, and they might have left it in their apartment.

So at midnight, in the 30 degrees below zero Minnesota winter, through ice and snow, I drove to my friend's apartment, praying to every deity whose name I knew that they did, in fact, have a typewriter, and that they had, in fact, left it in their apartment, and that I could, in fact, find it—which I was determined to do even if it required a Joe Walsh-like chain-saw attack on the walls and floor of the place.

I am still not sure which, but one of the deities must have taken pity on me, because my friend did have a typewriter, and I did find it. Jealously clutching it to my chest like a long-lost child, I drove back to my apartment and resumed typing on my friend's typewriter.

The clock continued to tick. Out of desperation I began sending Merlin drafts by—what at the time was a relatively new invention— overnight express mail, (even though, trust me, on my intern salary I could little afford it) and then calling him the next day to see what he thought. I distinctly remember one evening when I called Merlin to see what he thought of the day's submission and being panic-stricken to the point of feeling physically ill to hear him pause, stutter, and say that he had not received the package. I don't remember the specific reasons for this, I think it may have been a Friday so his not receiving it meant we would lose *three whole days*, but something about that particular submission was so sensitive or so late in the game that were Merlin not to have responded quickly—like within the ensuing 12 hours, I really and truly could have missed my deadline and been unable to graduate. Alas, there was nothing I could do, so I put on a game face (yeah, right) about the whole thing, we got off the phone, and I lay awake that night worrying myself, as they say, sick.

But—oh, me of little faith—I had apparently forgotten something very important: I was not dealing with just anyone. I was dealing with the man who moved not just mountains, but mountain *ranges*, the man who accomplished things decreed by God himself to be impossible, the man who once invited me to his house so he could work with me on my research because he was too sick with the flu to get out of bed to come into the office. I was working with the one, the only—Merlin.

Well, it seems that after getting off the phone and feeling genuinely upset by the severity of my not-too-subtle panic attack, in the middle of the night Merlin plopped himself in his car, drove to the psychology department, and searched the place to find the package. And he did. It had accidentally been put into another faculty member's mailbox.

God *love* that man.

Speaking of that wayward package, one other thing I wanted to mention: given everything required to gather my data, analyze it, and write up the final draft, can you imagine my terror at the possibility that one of my drafts might get misplaced, lost in the mail, or otherwise disappear? It was a thought too horrifying to consider, and I was haunted by the possibility of anything from an apartment-house fire (which darn near happened because one night my apartment building filled with smoke and the fire department was called, and they discovered that the little old man standing in his doorway watching with puzzled interest as the firemen ran up and down the hall looking for the source was actually responsible, as behind him something on his stove was merrily burning away with five foot flames licking the ceiling) to a burglary, to anything that would result in its loss. As a result, I made three copies of everything (Remember the "big deal" I said free access to the hospital copiers was? I probably photocopied three or four thousand pages before all was said and done.). I kept one copy in my office at the hospital, one copy in my refrigerator at home (an old author's trick to fireproof a manuscript—refrigerators are reasonably good fire-proof boxes) and one in my car. I figured the chance of my hospital office being burglarized, my apartment burning down, and my car being stolen all on the same day was reasonably slim. But I confess that I felt better still when yet a fourth copy was in the mail on its way to Merlin.

Paranoid? Me?

END GAME

We made it. Merlin and I made it. We managed to exchange sufficient drafts sufficient times through sufficient post offices to arrive
at a copy of the document that we considered to be sufficiently wor-
thy of being called final. It ended up being about 165 pages long,
which is medium-length for a dissertation. Given all the trouble it
was, you'd have thought it would be longer than War and Peace.

Once the content of the manuscript was finalized, my next-to-
last task was to get the thing typed into the right format. Universities
are extraordinarily picky about the layout of a dissertation, as it is to
be bound and placed in the university library as well as sent to The
Library of Congress. So everything had to be exact—the margins had
to be a specific width, the top and bottom of the pages had to be a
specified distance, even the page numbers had to be located in exactly the right place. I remember commenting wryly at the time that
my entire Ph.D. rested on whether my page numbers were in the
right place. It was not much of an exaggeration.

In the current era of small, powerful, inexpensive computers and
printers, laying out the pages of a dissertation would be a breeze—an
evening of work at most. But remember, mine was written in the era
prior to the advent of word processors, so at that time getting something typed as precisely as required for a dissertation was a very big
deal. And while my typing skills were serviceable—somewhat more
fast than accurate—I had neither the time nor the energy nor the
skill to type the document into its final shape. I needed the services
of a professional. So with a little investigation I found, which was not
all that uncommon in those days, a typing service to type my final
copy. I was still running a bit short on time (what else is new), but
they promised they could get it finished in the required time frame,

so I dropped off the manuscript at their office and happily closed the door behind me, feeling at last some degree of relief.

Which was short-lived. In no time at all I discovered that I had one final, unexpected, and potentially serious problem in getting my dissertation finished: my typing service was crazy. *Completely* crazy. I'm talking real, genuine, psychiatric, diagnosable, clinical craziness. As in psychotic. As in "out of touch with reality."

As they worked on the manuscript, our interactions took on a bizarre and surreal quality. Sometimes they would call me with questions about some part of the manuscript and it would be almost impossible for me to identify what it was they wanted to know. Other times it was not even clear they were referring to *my* manuscript. Occasionally their questions would be so strange and disconnected— like asking where in town I was calling from—that I would find myself paralyzed on the phone, unable to reply.

It was really, really weird. I remember a variety of spooky conversations, sometimes talking to them from my apartment, other times at my office, even once from a pay phone downtown. All of the contacts were quite strange, quite confusing, quite illogical, and deeply unnerving. But the problem was that I was pretty much stuck. I could not pull my manuscript away from them and start over with someone else. It was *way* too late for that. And since I had made them swear on a stack of Bibles that they would get it done on time, I took lots of deep breaths and hoped that, as crazy as they might be, perhaps they were at least capable of keeping their word.

They were. By hook or by crook, due to my diligence or in spite of it, through all the jumbled and incoherent conversations, somehow my lunatic typing service managed to do what they said they would do and got the document finished—correctly, and on time. The day they finished, I picked it up and headed out to a printer to have it copied for my committee (at the time printers were the only ones to have high-end photocopy machines—no Kinko's in those days). I had them make me nine copies of the manuscript, which was horrendously expensive. But I needed six for the members of my committee, one for the extra committee member to be assigned by the university, one for storage in my office at the hospital, one for storage in my car, and the original went back into cold storage in my refrigerator.

Then, in the truly final act of completing my dissertation, I packed up the copies for my committee members, trundled off to the post office, and put them in the mail. They were due to arrive, I noted with dry irony, on the exact last day that would allow me to hold my dissertation defense before Merlin went MIA. Possibly a world record for cutting it close, I had finished with—literally—not a single day to spare.

Now that I have finished describing the whole process, let me again note that you must realize the description does not, and cannot, adequately convey the unrelenting pins-and-needles, electrified anxiety that permeated my life for all those months—the chronic, panicky fear that I would not get the thing done on time and would render for naught all of my terrible intensity of effort. I knew then and I know now, some twenty-plus years later, that I never, ever, want to go through anything even remotely resembling that again. Never. It is not hyperbole to say that it was a horrible experience.

Even so, I had pulled it off. The damn thing was finished.

I still vividly remember the day I put the copies into the mail. I did it during my lunch break at the hospital. That evening I came home from the hospital, sat down on my couch, and realized that there was nothing I "had" to do. My seemingly endless enslavement was over, and before me stretched something that I had long ago lost touch with, something that I never even thought about anymore— free time. I realized that I could do anything I felt like doing, that I was even free to choose to do something that I actually *enjoyed* doing if I wanted to. I remember feeling light and happy as I considered what on earth I would like to do with this new experience called a "free evening" that lay before me.

My happiness was brief. Almost immediately I found myself descending from my light and happy state into a deep, dark spiral of psychological and emotional chaos. Why? Because now that I didn't have anything that I *had* to do, I needed to decide what I *wanted* to do. Well, it had been so long since *that* had been the basis of my decision of what to do that it seemed strange and foreign and I didn't know how to do it. It wasn't that I didn't have things that I wanted to do—to the contrary, I was overwhelmed with thoughts of "Oh, *that* would be fun." It was that I had no way to decide *which* thing to actually do. Absent a "should,"or a "have to," or an "all hell will break loose if you don't" attached to any option, I was clueless as to how to decide which course of action to actually pick. Put simply, my ability to identify the strength of something called "what I *want* to do" had essentially vanished, leaving me standing in a tidal wave of endless possibilities with no way of stopping the torrent by saying "Ah ha! This! *This* is what I want to do!" For all practical purposes I was rendered entirely unable to choose what I *wanted*.

So there I sat, on my couch, with my mind spinning out of control, reviewing over and over an endless list of things I would like to do and that I wanted to do and that I could do, all the while sinking deeper and deeper into a state of complete and utter, hopeless paralysis. I simply could not decide. Nor could I stop the flood. All of the options sounded good, all of the options seemed appealing. But with no "should," no "have-to," no external demand on any option, I was out of luck. I couldn't pick. So I sat, and I sat, and I sat, reviewing my options over, and over, and over, like a computer caught in an endless loop, running a circular program designed never to quit and never to change. I sat there, paralyzed, for probably two hours.

I know full well how crazy this sounds. Trust me, it felt every bit as crazy as it sounds. I even feel slightly crazy in the retelling. But it is the honest truth.

Doesn't graduate school sound like *fun*?

The rest of internship was largely unremarkable. Except, of course, for my car cracking its engine block in mid-January, providing me with the distinct pleasure of walking a dozen blocks to the bus stop every morning for nearly two months during the minus 30 degree Minnesota winter—and having the dealership where it was repaired steal the built-in radio and tape player. And having one of my best friends suffer a psychotic break. And having a girlfriend show herself to be floridly borderline personality disordered. And having my landlady, after somehow finding out that I was in clinical psychology, appear at my door one evening falling-down drunk, demanding admittance to my apartment, proclaiming that she needed to talk to me because "she was not a well woman," and returning to her apartment only after I blocked her entrance to mine by refusing to remove my arm from across the doorway—whereupon she engaged in a screaming fight with her husband about me, highlighted by her shrieking "I don't care! He scares me!" (They lived in the apartment next door, so I got to hear the whole thing.) Oh yeah, and having the tenant on the *other* side of me turn out to be some kind of psychopath who not only kept getting hassled by the police, but who spent a not insubstantial amount of his time in the wee hours of the morning screaming about it on the phone while throwing what sounded like large and/or hard and/or breakable objects around his apartment.

But other than that the rest of internship was largely unremarkable. It even had some guilty pleasures—like Professor Munchie's Hot Fudge Milkshakes.

There was this funky little eaterie tucked away in a neighborhood close to mine with the cozy name "Professor Munchie's." Well, they made this thing called a "hot fudge milkshake" that was not only exactly what it sounds like, but was ten-fold better. Furthermore, they were not only delicious, they were *huge*. Many Saturday evenings I would meet up with the intern who was my best friend and confidant during that year and we would head off to "The Professor's" to indulge in a couple of the delectable delights.

We would sit ourselves down, order, try not to drown in our drool as we waited, and after they were delivered spend the next half hour making giddy goo-goo eyes at each other over the gigantic glasses as we spooned out and sucked down the thick, creamy chocolate concoction laced through-and-through with sticky, gooey, dripping rivers of hot fudge. Had I not been actively working myself to death trying to do both internship and dissertation, I'd have ended up looking like Meat Loaf at his prime. And I would not have cared one bit.

I also managed to clean up sufficiently a time or two to go highbrow and attend the Guthrie Theater. In case you are unfamiliar with it, the Guthrie Theater is a Minneapolis landmark, a world-renown playhouse presenting all manner of eloquent dramas. I went to several plays there, and they were uniformly brilliant, powerful, and, in at least one case nearly intolerably heart-wrenching. With the exception of seeing the original London cast of "Les Miserable" in the original theater in London, during the death scene of "Camille" I have never before—nor since—cried that hard for that long in that big a dark room filled with that many strangers. Without feeling embarrassed.

I also found some time to take advantage of the natural beauty of the place. Minneapolis is a beautiful city with stunning parks and lakes, and I lived not far from one of the most famous, called "Lake of the Isles." It is where the opening sequence of the old "Mary Tyler Moore" show—where she threw her hat into the air—was filmed, and where the roller skating sequences in the movie "The Personals" were filmed.

When the weather was good, Lake of the Isles became one gigantic neighborhood block party with hundreds of people walking, running, having picnics, bicycling, playing music, sunning, and playing volleyball. It was a blast. During the warm weather I stuffed my bicycle into my car, drove over, and joined the fray by pedaling myself into some serious sweat and heavy breathing on the bike path surrounding the lake. In the winter I left my bicycle at home and jogged around the lake on the snow-covered jogging path while praying that the unbelievably frigid air would not freeze my windpipe and related structures permanently shut. Of my entire time in graduate school, the hours I spent at Lake of the Isles were probably the most peaceful I ever spent, and I can still feel a pleasant sense of calm when I think about it.

THE FINISH LINE

Come summer, internship headed toward a close. As did my life as a graduate student. By August my sole remaining task was my dissertation defense.

Gulp. As I mentioned before, a dissertation defense meeting is a highly unpredictable animal. It can be domesticated and docile, or it can take on the demeanor of a pack of rabid dogs tearing at the intellectual meat hanging from a candidate's weary intellectual bones. I had seen both kinds—I'd seen some easy defenses where the committee was pleasant and respectful, and I'd seen some awful ones where they cut the student not one tiny bit of slack on any detail about anything and left them shaking with self-doubt. The unpredictability was the primary element that made the whole thing frightening. And you were never safe until everyone actually walked out of the room, because the beast could start out nice and then suddenly turn on you, chomp on precious body parts, and run off with them.

Isn't that just like graduate school—unnerving to the bitter end.

Just like the proposal meeting, a dissertation defense is an open forum. It must be advertised and the public invited. So, as I did for my proposal, I had flyers printed that summarized the topic of my dissertation and listed the date and time of my defense. This time I mailed them to a fellow student who put them up for me, as I was still in Minnesota and could little afford to fly down just to distribute a bunch of leaflets.

My meeting was set for the last Tuesday in August. This was how close I had cut it—Merlin's last day as a faculty member at my university was that very Friday. I had made it with exactly three days to spare. But even that was not enough to guarantee my graduating, because even if my committee "passed" my dissertation, I still needed to get Merlin's signature on the document before he disappeared into the night. And that was more complicated than just having a successful defense meeting.

You see, just as in the proposal meeting, during the defense your committee can demand alterations or corrections in the final document. Now, unless you have been very, *very* bad in a past life and the gates of hell have opened in preparation to swallow you, the changes demanded tended to be manageable in scope. After all, they approved the study in the first place, so they'd better not have gripes that were *too* extensive. But any changes still had to be incorporated into the document. That meant additions or subtractions of any length would require the document to be retyped—at least from that page on. While I had made it through my proposal unscathed, I had no hope whatever of repeating that miracle at my defense, and I figured I'd have to make *some* changes. Well—do you remember the happy little time I had with my psychiatrically disturbed typing service? If the changes demanded at my defense were at all extensive I was in trouble, because I would have exactly *three days* to get them typed into the document in order to get Merlin's signature before he fled. That meant I had to get someone who could type that much that fast, which was going to be one neat trick.

It was all very important because your committee's signatures were all that really mattered. The document was not formally approved until each and every committee member *literally* signed off on it. There is a page at the front of a dissertation with a space for each committee member's signature. Until that page is completely filled in, you don't graduate. Given that it was already late August and graduation was coming up fast, if I had to ship the document to Merlin's new address to be signed, I would almost certainly miss graduation and not be able to call myself "Ph.D." until after Christmas.

As a side note, the very worst outcomes I heard about in graduate school were cases where the members of a candidate's dissertation committee became so deeply hostile toward one another (never mind the student) that some committee members refused to sign the document if certain other committee members signed it. I never heard how these cases were ultimately resolved, but as far as I'm concerned no court in the land should convict a doctoral candidate who held such asinine committee members at gunpoint until they signed the document.

The potential delay of August to January in getting my degree might sound like making mountains out of molehills after everything I'd been through—unless you consider that I fully planned to be gainfully employed and living a "real" life well before the end of the year. It would make things just that much easier on me if I could tell prospective employers that I already had my Ph.D. rather than having to do a song and dance about how I really *was* finished with my degree, it was just that I couldn't graduate until after the fall semester because I missed the August deadline, etc., etc., etc.

Furthermore, from a psychological standpoint I was desperate to get that diploma into my hot little fist. After expending such a monumental degree of effort under the pressure of so many demands for so long I felt physically and emotionally depleted beyond description. I felt like my recovery couldn't really begin until that part of my life was *over*. So I wanted no loose ends. When I left that place, I wanted to leave cleanly and for good. I wanted to be 100% *finished*, and the only way I could do that was to leave with my Ph.D. in hand. So I was willing to move heaven and earth to get everything done before Merlin slipped from my grasp. Then I could leave with a clear mind and a clean slate and get about the task of regaining my membership card in the human race.

The first thing I had to do was to design my defense meeting.

Now, a defense is a much more formal gathering than is a proposal, and different people designed defense meetings with different atmospheres. They ran the gamut from completely casual to extremely professional. I decided that if the university held the dissertation process to be the pinnacle of formal academic achievement, then by God I was gonna give 'em formal. I decided to make my meeting a full-out high-brow event. While I had held my proposal meeting in a regular classroom in the psychology building, for my defense I reserved "The Trophy Room" at the Student Center. "The Trophy Room" was the most formal room on campus, the one used by university committees when meeting late into the night to make the gravest of decisions. It was called "The Trophy Room" for the very reason you'd expect—its walls were lined with glass-front cabinets behind which stood various trophies won by various university sports teams. In the center sat an elegant, wood conference table with formal chairs all around.

I went even further and arranged to have the meeting catered. I ordered a large cart of coffee, tea, and various irresistible pastries to be delivered in order to feed my committee as they hashed out the final question of whether or not I was, in fact, suitable for the stamp of "Ph.D." (I learned this trick from treating adolescents and schizophrenics—"when in doubt, feed 'em." And since what I was dealing with here was university faculty, the similarities should be obvious.)

And, of course, I had a friend make a special trip to a local donut shop to pick up those goddam chocolate-covered donuts for the committee member who had made it so abundantly clear that they were required if I wanted to avoid coming out of the meeting with serious internal injuries to my career. I even made a point of handing that professor the bag of donuts myself, in person, immediately prior to the meeting, just to make the point. He could not have missed the point.

Lastly, I wore a suit. I know that doesn't sound like much, but remember that this was in the late 1970's and early 1980's, when all manner of formal dress was largely considered repugnant. No one dressed up. Everyone, professional and nonprofessional alike, dressed casually. I never once wore a tie or a sport coat on internship, much less a suit, and I had essentially worn the exact same clothes every day of graduate school—a denim work shirt with rolled-up sleeves, blue jeans, and running shoes. So for me to show up in a suit was a spectacle in and of itself.

Now, as you might figure, most people did not go to all that trouble for their defense meeting. They held it in a classroom and it was a very informal affair. To hell with that. If the university wanted the dissertation to be full of pomp, then I was by damn going to rub their face with circumstance. And Merlin, God bless him, was cheering me on 100% with that sly, half-evil grin that only he could pull off as being a clear sign of support.

The next thing I did was to confer with Merlin to plan our attack. As in my proposal, he would open the meeting and then turn it over to me. I would review the study and the results. This time, though, no standing up. And no blackboard. First off, the Trophy Room didn't have one. Second, my committee members were supposed to have read the document. So they should be able to follow along easily. Of course, the truth is that human beings being what they are, (and remember we're not even talking about human beings here, we're talking about university faculty), it was likely that several had never even cracked open the document and had no earthly idea what my results were. But you didn't want to show up anyone as having shirked their duty and make them feel bad for being discovered as the slime they were and then have them take their humiliation out on you. So by reviewing the study you were covering your butt. Merlin gave me a couple of other pointers about how to answer questions they might ask that required knowledge (specifically in the area of statistics) that were beyond the scope of the study or of my training. We rehearsed.

At that point Merlin said something that I thought was a bit strange, but that I remember to this day. He told me that I could relax and consider the meeting essentially over as soon as a committee member asked me what I was planning to do after graduation. I wondered how he could be so sure this would happen. But I tried to remember who I was dealing with here, so I just tucked it away in my mental "Merlin" file, and off to the meeting we went.

In sharp contrast to my proposal meeting, very few spectators attended my defense. I think there were, maybe, two or three people, one of whom was my girlfriend at the time. So it was a small gathering of my committee, me, and a couple of diehard friends, bless them for attending.

Merlin opened the meeting, handed me the ball, and I ran with it. I reviewed the study and the results. My results were not complicated, and they were striking. It turned out that my "failure" condition had successfully induced a Learned Helplessness effect. My "loss of control" condition had not. That meant I had actually shown the entire Learned Helplessness theory to be wrong, and to be based on a confusion of terms. Where the theory said that "loss of control" produced Learned Helplessness, my study said that was not true. My study said that what made people feel bad was that they failed— irrespective of whether they had control over it.

My study was, in short, bad news for the Learned Helplessness model, and a pretty impressive piece of research, if I do say so myself. I would have published my study and reveled in my role as the spoiler had the Learned Helplessness people not beaten me to the punch with a preemptive strike—by changing their theory. Damn.

After I reviewed my results, my committee began to make comments and to ask questions. For a while it was a breeze. They asked none of the potentially difficult questions that Merlin and I had planned for. Instead, they were conversational in tone and affable in style, commenting on the implications of my results and the design of my study.

Then, after a while, things picked up a bit and they started to mix it up. They started speculating about the implications of my study. And they started to disagree with one-another. That raised my anxiety, given the stories I had heard of refusals to sign documents. At one point two committee members started getting into it with each other about a point in the study. They were disagreeing about what it meant. Nervous, I barged in to try to prevent escalation and bring some understanding and civility to the conversation, and one of the members held his hand up toward me in a "stay out of this" gesture as they continued to spar a bit with each other over a particular point. That went on for a while. So did my nervousness.

Now, remember that there was one committee member present who I did not know and in fact had never met prior to my defense meeting. This was a faculty member from another department who had been assigned by the university to participate in my defense as an outside observer. This was always done, and the general lore was that this was a figurehead committee member. Most times they could not even be bothered to read the study. After all, it was a university "duty" to be assigned to other faculty's committees, so they weren't about to put themselves out for a student who was not "theirs" and for whom they got no credit. I don't even remember what department the man was from.

Surprisingly, though, as the other members of my committee began mixing it up between themselves, this committee member chimed in. He said he had a couple of comments himself. Everyone stopped. His first comment was that a statistical chart on page such-and-such had an error in it. He pointed out that the column that was supposed to list the "Standard Deviation" of a statistical procedure actually listed the "Mean Square" of that statistic. Stunned, Merlin and I flipped to the page. He was absolutely right. I had copied the wrong values into the table, and neither Merlin nor I had caught it. Oops. Merlin nodded in agreement, and said we'd fix it. I don't think I was over-reading to take Merlin's reaction as a touch of embarrassment over missing such an obvious and silly mistake. Me, too.

What unnerved me, though, was that this guy had not only read my document, he had studied it in the kind of great gory detail that none of my other committee members, save Merlin, seemed to have. He appeared to know my document inside and out. What unnerved me even *more* was the fact that he was clearly setting it up to take the floor and pontificate. I didn't know the guy and I didn't know what he was up to. I swallowed hard.

The outside committee member took a deep breath and commented that he knew why my "loss of control" condition had failed to show significant effects. Everyone looked at him.

My "loss of control" induction had been based on telling subjects a "percentage of likelihood that they would be successful in accomplishing the problem-solving task." We made it up, of course, but then the degree of similarity of their success on the task to their *predicted* success was the measure of how much they lost control. If we told them they had a 0% likelihood of failing and they did, in fact, fail, then it was not "out of their control," rather it was expected. According to the original Learned Helplessness theory, that should have been OK and not induced Learned Helplessness even though they failed. But it hadn't worked. The level of "predicted" success had no effect on the subjects.

This faculty member said that the reason it hadn't worked was obvious. He said that students were unlikely to respond to a specific prediction of success for one simple reason: Mr. Spock.

Yeah, that's right—*Mr. Spock.* Pointy-eared Vulcan. "Star Trek." *That* Mr. Spock.

All at once everyone in the room turned to look at this faculty member who suddenly sounded like a complete loon. But he was a dead-serious loon. He wasn't kidding. He continued.

In "Star Trek," he said, Mr. Spock was always saying something like "Captain Kirk, in this situation we have less than a ten percent chance of survival!" But here was the problem—no matter how bad the odds, they *always* made it out alive. So, he said, students were unlikely to believe *any* prediction of an outcome because Captain Kirk always succeeded even when Mr. Spock said that it would be a cold day in statistical hell that they'd survive.

Silence. I didn't know, and I don't think my committee knew, how to take the guy. We didn't know if he was pulling our leg, if he was being literal that we were working with a tainted subject pool, or if he was being metaphorical in trying to say that statements of outcome probability just don't hold much sway in people's expectations.

Whatever. We all just kinda looked at him. He smiled and said that because of that, he could understand why my "loss of control" induction wouldn't work. Then he sat back and for all the world seemed to feel finished and self-satisfied.

I had to hand it to him—he went some place I didn't know how to follow. I had no idea what to say. So it was Merlin to the rescue.

Merlin made a quick comment that straddled the fence between sarcasm and acknowledgment, and asked if there was anything else. The committee members looked at each other. Then the member to my immediate left turned to me and said, which I swear I am not making up: "So, Greg—what are your plans after graduation?"

Holy guacamole—how on earth did Merlin know? He had never met with my committee about my defense, so it couldn't have been a plan specific to my meeting. I carved another notch in my mental totem pole called "Amazing Feats of Merlin," and said I was going to move away and get a job. He nodded, we talked about this and that for a few minutes, and then Merlin dismissed me—and my spectators—from the room. The game was almost over.

The process is this: the candidate and spectators are sent from the room, and in private the committee talks among itself and votes on whether to accept the dissertation. You can imagine all the stuff that goes through your head while you're waiting outside the room. While the truth is that your committee is probably discussing the schedule for their upcoming tennis round-robin, you're outside the room worried sick over the "and" on page 56 that someone said should be a "but."

The tradition is this: When the committee is finished talking and voting, your chair, and only your chair, comes out of the room and closes the door behind him or her. He or she then walks up to the candidate, and if the news is good holds out his or her hand and says "Congratulations, Doctor," and shakes your hand. It is intended to be a moment of great grandeur, although you are not supposed to actually faint.

In about fifteen minutes, Merlin appeared. He walked up to me with a kind of bemused expression on his face. He stood and looked at me, and then around at my friends. He didn't say anything and I started to feel a little bit worried and even a little disappointed that he might not do the traditional greeting with me, which I wanted with all my heart for him to do. Then he nodded, smiled, said "Well done, all the way around," and held out his hand. "Congratulations, Doctor," he said, grinning. We shook hands. We hugged. I got covered with goose bumps. My girlfriend hugged me. My friends congratulated me and Merlin smiled, chatted for a minute and then disappeared back into the Trophy Room. Then my committee emerged, shook my hand, and set about signing my signature page—even without the corrections being made. They said they "trusted me" to get them made. Wow.

I did have to make a few alterations in the manuscript. I had to get that statistics table fixed, for one thing. But none of the changes required the page numbers to be redone, so I was able to use my own typewriter to redo the sections that needed correction. Within the next two days I was able to get it finished. I sent the document off to the university printer to be bound, and that was it. The university ordered two copies of the bound document for themselves, and I ordered two additional copies—one for me, and one for my parents who, through their long-suffering ordeal of enduring their son joining the enemy and becoming a psychologist, ended up being good sports about the whole thing and had given me substantial financial support through much of graduate school.

In fact, you know, I have to give some specific credit where credit is due. During my time in graduate school my father came to an internal resolution that allowed him to actually experience pride in my career choice. Somehow, in some way, he decided that while *psychiatrists* were all crazy, *psychologists* were OK. I have no idea how he got there or if he was even aware of using internal psychological machinations to get me back into the big house, but the pleasant effect was that he would introduce me to a friend or colleague and say, with genuine pride, "Greg's going to be a psychologist!"

My mother, I have to admit, never did quite get there. I love her and she loves me, but we don't talk about what I do.

After I got my dissertation corrections completed, I filled out the forms required for me to graduate, turned them into the registrar's office, and walked out the door with every single thing completed to be awarded my Ph.D.

My diploma came in the mail about a month later.

You know, it would be tempting to say, and you might even expect me to say, that after everything I went through it was sort of ho-hum, or maybe even a letdown, to get that diploma. But remember that I'd had my "Post-Ph.D. Depression" much earlier—I had been done with it for over a year. So I can say, in all honesty, that when I opened that folder and there, right before my eyes, lay a parchment with the words "(My University) has conferred upon—Gregory William Lester—the degree of Doctor of Philosophy," it was one of the most thrilling moments of my life. It seems silly to say that all of my years of striving and working and going to the kinds of extremes that I would not have believed I could live through had I not done so, produced a piece of paper that made it all worthwhile, but it did. That was the single most beautiful piece of paper I have ever seen. And I have stared at it, lovingly, for over twenty years now. It still hangs in the place of honor, at the top of my wall of certificates. My two state psychology licenses, my Phi Beta Kappa certificate, my memberships in national and state psychological associations, my undergraduate diploma and my internship certificate all hang beneath it, yielding to it its rightful place of honor.

Oh, and I didn't attend the formal graduation ceremony at my university at the end of that academic year. My father had died in the interim, and without his being able to attend my graduation, the ceremony lost its meaning for me. Missing the ceremony meant nothing to me. Missing my dad did.

PART IV: INTERMITTENT REINFORCEMENT

THE REAL WORLD: PART I

Have you ever had this experience—you're really sick with a cold or the flu, and on the day you finally feel better, you discover feeling "normal" feels wonderful? That was me entering The Real World. After the nuclear-holocaust level of stress I'd experienced in graduate school, The Real World—where all I had to worry about were things like jobs, money, and terrorists wielding radiological dirty bombs—felt like heaven.

In September, when internship ended, I handed over my belongings to a shady moving company, grabbed my diploma, dropped myself into my car, and drove across the country to my new city of residence. Luckily for me, at that time this particular city was experiencing a period of unprecedented economic expansion, and jobs of every description in virtually every field were plentiful—including clinical psychology. Looking back, I am still struck with my good fortune to have entered my field at the time I did. Mental health was booming in every way, and insurance companies were basically adding unlimited mental health benefits to policies faster than the policies could be written, so obscene amounts of money were pouring into the field. It was a heady time. I drove into town, moved in with a friend from graduate school who was just starting his internship, and started looking for a job.

Now, under even the best of circumstances, looking for work is never a thrilling activity, but all things considered it wasn't so bad. After all, I'd been up to my neck in the River Styx for the past four years, so about the only thing that would have truly unnerved me would have been being interviewed for a job by a herd of giant, blowgun-wielding roaches.

I had already subscribed to some local psychology newsletters that posted job listings, and I began scanning the newspaper and calling some contacts as well. To be honest I'm not very good at making calls about jobs and at times I was uncomfortable having to do it, but like I said—compared with the past four years, it was OK. And it produced enough nibbles to keep me going. All told I spent just over three months looking for a job, and in that time I talked to right around 35 different practitioners, agencies, associations, and state services (I still keep the list as a souvenir of my stick-to-it-ness). I even snagged a few job offers. But none seemed a good fit for my interests, so I kept looking. On one interview the woman considering me for the job even hit on me, which was pleasant—more pleasant than the job she ultimately offered me. I never did call her back.

Since the job market was hot, I decided I'd try to hold out for something that seemed a good fit for my interests and abilities. Fortunately, while I was looking I was able to support myself by doing some free-lance evaluation work for several local practitioners who were accustomed to taking advantage of "eager new talent" in town to get some good work done at a good price. I found out later that some of these guys had checkered reputations and in some sectors were considered to be the psychology equivalent of pimps hanging around the bus station looking to pick up the psychological version of naive runaways in order to exploit them. But I never felt that way at all, and I was never abused by any of them. Most treated me very well, related to me like a competent colleague, and paid me more than fairly. In fact, for me at the time, I was earning a great deal of money for working only a few hours a week. And goodness knows I was making them a fortune. So despite the sometimes unnerving rumors questioning the moral fiber of a couple of the groups, as far as I'm concerned the arrangements worked well for everyone and I have no bad feelings about anyone from that time.

In December I had an interview with the director of a social service agency connected to the Catholic Church. He was a priest who had just graduated with a Masters in Social Work from a very good program in order to return and take the helm of this particular agency.

Now, admittedly my relationship with organized religion in general—and Catholicism specifically—has always felt to me something akin to trying to find the least painful position in which to lie on a bed of nails, but I was willing to talk to anyone about a job, even someone religious. As it turned out, any possible theological differences I had with the man, or his church, were clearly a non-issue with him. He was warm and personable, and I liked him immediately. Better yet, he seemed to genuinely like me. In that first meeting we had a really nice time together and I remember it fondly to this day.

But while his liking me was all well and good, it was pretty much icing without the cake, because he didn't have any job openings to offer me. The place had a turnover rate on the order of 0% a year, because people liked working there—*a lot*—so about the only way staff ever left was on their back, feet first. So he offered little realistic hope of an opening appearing during this lifetime. It turned out that he had agreed to talk to me only because he had liked me on the phone and was impressed by my resumé. But bless that man for being willing to see me even though he couldn't hire me.

In January one of the groups of practitioners I was doing evaluations for offered me a full-time job. That was good. The terms they offered me were terrible. That was bad. Acting as though I was too stupid to notice how cheaply I would be selling my soul, they made it clear that their offer involved little salary, no benefits, and a maximum of two weeks of vacation per year—that I could start taking only after six months on the job. And every time we talked they offered me a successively smaller office, to the point where I feared that by the time I took the position I'd be working from a closet. I thought their making me such a poor offer was either pretty insulting or pretty gutsy given that the job market was good and I would actually be making less money per hour as their employee than I had been as a free-lancer. I mentioned that to them and it didn't seem to matter, as they just looked at me blankly. I told them I'd think about it, and left their office feeling sufficiently sickened by their offer that on the way home I considered gagging up a sizeable furball.

The problem was that I did need a full-time job. So despite its disgusting nature I was tempted to take their offer while I looked for something a bit less unpleasant. I decided to mull it over.

The very next day changed everything. I got a call from the secretary of the priest I had liked so much. She said that he wanted to talk to me again. Intrigued, I said of course I'd come talk to him again, and set an appointment to meet with him. Upon sitting down in his office he informed me that he had liked me so much and had been so impressed by both me and my resumé that he had gone to his board and demanded that a new staff position be created at the agency—

just for me. He said they'd never had a psychologist on staff before—the staff was mostly social workers and case managers—but he had convinced the board that a psychologist would be a strong asset to the place and a selling point to their funding agency. They bought it, approved the position, and he had called me in to offer me a job.

Wow. And this time it was not just a full-time job offer, it was a *good* full-time job offer. The salary wasn't great, but it was more than the practitioners had offered me combined with terrific benefits and an entire month off per year that I could start taking any time I wanted. Further, because I would be the only psychologist at the agency, I could basically design my own position. In fact, I would *have* to design my own position because they'd never had anyone like me on staff and didn't really know what to do with me. Technically, I would be a member of the Family Counseling Department, but it would be up to me to decide how I wanted to organize my schedule and what, exactly, I wanted to do.

Are you getting all this? What I *wanted* to do? He told me I could do what I *wanted* to do? I mean, however contentious my relationship to formal religion, this man was the answer to my prayers. I couldn't believe it. I wanted to kiss him.

I didn't. But I did shake his hand. And I accepted on the spot. And I left his office walking on air. After the grueling and insane years of graduate school, I now not only had a full-time job, I had one where I could do anything I wanted. It was like starting my own practice, but not having to worry about bringing in business. All I had to do was to sit around all day and "do psychology."

Are you still getting all this? That day, nearly six years prior, when I had my flash of insight and decided that I wanted to "do psychology?" Well, it was here. It was finally, really here. I was going to "do psychology." All day long. Awesome.

I started work two weeks later, and found that the reality of the place was every bit as good a fit for me as I had hoped. The atmosphere could not have been more perfect for someone just emerging from the Macy's Thanksgiving Day Parade of Pain called graduate school. In fact, compared with graduate school the place was so laid-back that I worried the entire staff was suffering from a pervasive depressive disorder. They weren't—it had just been so long since I'd seen human beings who were *not* under so much stress that they were spewing brain matter out their nose that I didn't know how to take it. In truth it was just a very relaxed place and the demand level was very, very low. It was a nonprofit agency, after all, so money wasn't even an issue. We were all there to serve clients, and that was it. As I got to know the staff I made friends and got to like and respect most every one of them. The place was warm, homey, and like a big family. It was perfect for me. Absolutely perfect.

There were about seven of us in the Family Counseling Department. Most had Masters of Social Work degrees and were strong and competent practitioners. And the department ran with an eerie similarity to our graduate school clinic. We were each on "intake" duty on a regular schedule, and on those days we took the appointments that were scheduled and then decided whether to keep the case, refer it out, or bring it to a staff meeting to get someone else to take it. It was completely up to us. Better still, we had a ninety minute weekly staff meeting where all the counselors met to present cases or to train in new clinical material. We even had an outside psychiatrist who volunteered his time to meet with us and do training for us. In addition, we had one afternoon a month where the whole agency met with yet *another* psychiatric consultant for even more training and case consultation.

I could not have designed a job that was more perfect for me. I commanded immediate respect for being the only Ph.D. in the place, there was no one looking over my shoulder or questioning me, I had no particular case-load that I was required to keep, and all day every day all I had to do was to *see patients*. And get *paid* for it. I was ecstatic. I also always wore a suit to work, which everyone thought was hilarious because everyone else dressed informally.

So I started seeing patients. I took on every case I could get my hands on. I saw couples, families, adults, and children. I started therapy groups. I was energized and excited, and my patients seemed pleased to have gotten me as their counselor. I quickly built up a good-sized caseload, started developing a reputation as a hot property, and grew to love my job more and more. "Doing psychology" was everything I had hoped for. The job gave me satisfaction, pleasure, and the joy of knowing I was helping people.

It also gave me something that I had not anticipated—it gave me time to think. Once I started living in The Real World, not only were my evenings my own, but even at work, between patients, I had substantial quiet time during which I took to drinking China black tea and gazing out my office window at the beautiful gardens that lay just outside. In those first few months I spent many hours with my office door closed, just sitting quietly, drinking my tea, and experiencing the soothing calm and quiet of Real Life. I don't think in my entire life I have ever been that content to just sit quietly for hour after hour. It was wonderful, and like the silence of going home after teaching attention-deficient kindergartners all day, I *needed* it. It also gradually cleared my head and my thoughts gained greater and greater clarity.

Now, the danger of having time to think is that you can start to think about things you've been spending a whole lot of time and energy avoiding thinking about. Which is exactly what happened to me. During graduate school I had paid very little attention to my emotional state, as my goal was just to get through and get out no matter what. So if I felt awful, or terrified, or overwhelmed, it was just too damn bad—I pushed it aside because I had to keep going if I wanted to make it through. But now, for the first time in five years, I began to think about how I was feeling—to examine it, to define it. For the first time in goodness knows how long I actually began to pay attention to whether I was happy, or sad, or excited, or what. And as I examined it, I came to the growing, unpleasant, and progressively unavoidable conclusion that although I loved my job and found living in The Real World quite wonderful, the prominent emotion I was feeling every day was something along the lines of "grinding unhappiness." Not exactly misery, mind you, but certainly a closer kin of it than of happiness. And it all had to do with the one leftover element from graduate school that I had not yet handled: my personal life.

My personal life was a train wreck. No, it was worse than that—it was a toxic waste site. As I noted earlier, during graduate school I had become involved in a string of chaotic, conflictual, and volatile relationships that were physically and emotionally exhausting. In truth they fit quite nicely in the context of graduate school. The place was one gigantic drama-machine, so having relationships that were filled with conflict, upset, over-intensity, and shifting emotions seemed quite natural, even appropriate after a fashion—an insane fashion, perhaps, but a fashion. Well, just before I left graduate school I'd done it again, and I had become involved in yet another of my little dances with the devil. The problem was that I had not left it where it belonged—in the craziness of graduate school. Nope. Along with my books and my bicycle I had packed the whole thing up and brought it right along with me into The Real World.

Which was creating a horror of the first order. The drama and intensity of the relationship fit *not at all* in my new, calm life in The Real World. Like something that has managed to claw its way out of hell and into reality, it was showing itself to be crazy, destructive, and wildly out of place. In fact, it was the sole issue of upset and problem in the context of my newfound sense of peace and comfort. I loved my job, I loved my colleagues, I loved my apartment, I loved my free time, and I loved being a psychologist. But the relationship was a disaster. It was making me miserable.

The whole thing was genuinely terrible. My girlfriend was living on the west coast at the time, and every day she would call me multiple times at all hours of the day and night. It got to where even my receptionist, whose only contact with her was to put her calls through to me or take a message if I was with a patient, started dreading her calls. When I would ask if I had any messages, my receptionist would start out by mumbling "Well, *she* called. Again." To my embarrassment, I later found out that along about this time my personal life became a significant source of gossip around the agency. Thanks to my receptionist's big mouth.

Further, most of the time when she called, my girlfriend would be in some escalated state of emotional distress. She would alternate between spewing out intolerable feelings of neediness and loneliness with the clear, implied demand that I wave my magic wand and banish the gremlins, (I decided that this was an unfortunate and unintended consequence of having adopted the role of Super Student in graduate school—other people came to feel about me like I felt about Merlin and assumed that I could do, or make happen, essentially *anything*. So she was quite convinced that I could save her from her upset.) and raging that I was being totally insufficient to meet her needs and what a filthy, slimy, dirty rat I was. She would often hang up in a huff—after we had been on the phone for two hours.

Then she would *immediately* call back and apologize for being all over the map emotionally and being so mean to me and would promise to be good. The next day it would begin anew.

I was spending hours and hours on the phone trying to find some measure of emotional equilibrium in the face of this bubbling fountain of relationship pathology, and it was making me sick both emotionally and physically. Worse yet, during one of my episodes of judgment so poor that when viewed objectively bore a frightening resemblance to a transient psychotic episode, some time prior to my leaving graduate school she and I had talked—seriously—about getting married. And those were, in fact, the plans. We were going to get married. If I survived that long.

But as awful as the phone calls were, her visits, infrequent though they may have been, were even worse. We'd end up in terrible fights and with her not speaking to me for the rest of the day. I felt as though I could do nothing right in any way at any time. During one visit she got so mad that she screamed "Well, just forget the whole thing!" and demanded that I drive her to the airport so she could leave me right then and right there. To her surprise I wearily agreed— at which point she found reason after reason to put it off.

During that same trip we returned to my house after a fight and with her in her usual state of mute rage. As we entered, my roommate naively chirped "Hey—when exactly are you guys going to get married?" to which my girlfriend barked "Never," and without missing a beat my roommate quipped sardonically "Bad day?" Funny man.

Now I need to digress for a moment.

In my enthusiasm for all things psychological, once I was working full-time I had joined every psychological association known to Man. One of those was the local psychological association of the city in which I now lived. I didn't know anyone in it, of course, but I started going to the meetings to try to meet some of my now-colleagues. And at the holiday season I went to the annual Christmas party, which was hosted by a local psychologist who lived in a very posh house in a very posh part of town.

I also knew that there were two practicing psychologists in town, a husband and wife, who were mid-level honchos in the Transactional Analysis world. They had written a couple of books—quite good books, I might add—and I knew their work. I had been wanting to meet them to ask if there was any TA training going on in town that I could get involved with. But I had been too chicken to just up and call them out of the blue. I mean, they were *somebody*—I was not. They were supposed to be at the Christmas party, so a lot of the reason I went was in hope of meeting them.

I went to the party and looked for them. They weren't there. They finally did arrive, and I recognized them from their books. I was nervous about introducing myself because they were more-or-less celebrities, and I feared that pushing my face into theirs would ensure my place as either a bother or an annoyance. But by screwing up my courage and trying to act like a good party guest rather than the timid church mouse I felt like, toward the end of the party I finally got up my nerve, walked up to them, and introduced myself. I said that I knew of their work, thought highly of it, and wanted to know if they or anyone else in town was doing training in TA, as I'd been a member of the organization for some years, loved TA, and was interested in learning more.

Well, I'll tell you—I have no idea how they answered that question, because as soon as the wife of the couple, Rita, (I'm using a real name this time) turned around and said "hello" to me, the content of the conversation vanished. The manner in which she greeted me was so stunningly inviting, so completely warm and accepting, so deeply and genuinely friendly, that it very nearly knocked the wind out of me. It gave me a feeling that I had never had before. It was like she was not just saying hello to me, she was greeting my *soul*. It took my breath away, and I don't remember much that we talked about except for them saying they were really the only TA people in town and they had some groups going, but nothing formal in the way of training. I also remember that our conversation was short because they were trying to leave in time to make another engagement (the result of my waiting until the last minute to introduce myself). So I said it had been nice to meet them and that I wouldn't keep them because I knew they needed to get going. They said goodbye to me with the same warmth with which they had greeted me. They left.

I am very clear how goofy this is going to sound, so just bear with me. I knew, somewhere deep in my bones, in the first moment, in the very first moment, by the way Rita greeted me, that she was the right person to be my therapist. I didn't think it—I *knew* it. I could sense that she had something that I needed. There was something that woman had that I needed *desperately*. I didn't know what it was, but I knew it was there. I remember thinking very clearly to myself "*I want Rita to be my therapist.*"

Oh, and I hadn't even thought about seeing a therapist, mind you. It wasn't like I was looking. But something about her was so right—so completely right, that it triggered off all those thoughts.

OK, back to the topic.

Combine my reaction to Rita with my growing awareness that my personal life was behaving like something in need of an ankle monitor, and it's not hard to see where I ended up. The very next Monday morning, at work, I decided that I was going to call Rita to see if she was willing to see me as a patient. The problem was that I was so nervous I couldn't get up the guts to call her. I mean, she had been wonderful to me in our short conversation and all, but she was still *somebody*. I still was not.

I basically spent that whole day trying to screw up my nerve. I never made it. But the next morning I took a deep breath and dialed her telephone number. She answered the phone herself. Stuttering, I mentioned that I had been the new psychologist who had introduced himself to her and her husband at the party that past weekend, that I was looking for a therapist and wanted to know if she saw patients and, if she did, whether I could have an appointment to see her.

Her response on the phone gave me the exact same feeling of warmth and acceptance I had experienced at the party, and she replied reassuringly that yes, she did see patients, and that in fact many of her patients were therapists. (I would later learn that she had seen as patients damn near half the therapists in town. Some years later after, we started working together, I pretty much ended up seeing the other half.) I wanted to jump through the phone into her lap. She asked when I would like to come in. I commented that I was flexible and would be happy to come in whenever she could fit me in. We settled on a time later that week. She said that she worked out of her home and she gave me directions and instructions. Then she asked if I needed information on fees. I said I guessed so, and she told me how much she charged. I thanked her and we hung up.

What struck me after I got off the phone was that her question about fees had surprised me because to that point I had not even thought about the cost of seeing her. This was a notable oversight because, you see, even though I was making a salary I was not, shall we say, highly paid. This was a non-profit social service agency connected with a church that I was working for, remember, so money was not plentiful. In truth, I was well aware that I had no business paying private practice psychotherapy fees. But that told me just how strong my drive was to see her really was, as it was way out of character for me to ignore financial ramifications. But somehow after meeting her I had decided that, if I could, I was going to see her, and that was that. Money was not an issue.

Way out of character.

On the appointed day I drove to Rita's house, parked in front, walked up, and, as instructed, rang the doorbell. Rita, dressed elegantly and professionally, answered the door, greeted me, invited me in, and shook my hand. She said that she remembered me from the party. She said that she worked on her sun porch, to follow her through her living room. We walked into a glassed-in room at the back of her quite beautiful home. She invited me to sit in one of the two large, white rattan chairs in the room. She closed the doors to the room, sat down in the other chair, gently put her feet up on the ottoman in front of her chair, looked up, smiled at me, and asked what had brought me in.

I immediately noticed two things. First, the sun porch where she saw appointments was beautiful. It was very soothing. It had glass on two sides and faced her back yard which was green and flowering and gorgeous. Second, Rita had a striking, calming, and attentive serenity about her that made me feel immediately at home and safe to say anything I needed to say. The feeling I had on first meeting her was still there, if not more so.

I took a minute to compose my thoughts, and said that I had called her "because I was having trouble in a relationship and wanted to get some guidance about it." I detailed for her the relationship I was in, my personal history, my girlfriend's history, my present circumstances, and her present circumstances. I talked for probably fifteen minutes or so, telling her everything I could think of about the situation, whereupon I felt I had said the important stuff, and paused.

At that, Rita carefully and dramatically cleared her throat. She looked down for a moment, looked back up, smiled, and then she proceeded to pick up and throw, into my face, a very large, and very cold, glass of psychological water.

"Well, Greg," she said. "The first thing I want to do is compliment you for coming in now, before you made the relationship legal. After you do that things get a lot more sticky."

She paused for emphasis.

"You know," she continued. " I've been around a long time. I know I didn't have this much gray hair when I started." She chuckled to herself and ran a hand through her salt-and-pepper hair.

"And what that's enabled me to do is to see how relationships look on the front end and then how they turn out down the road. I've pretty much seen it all—the good, the bad, and the ugly. And one thing I've seen and one thing that I know for sure is that the kind of problems you're reporting are the kind of problems that do not get better."

Pause, again, for more emphasis.

"Now, if you two had been married for fifteen years, and you had a couple of kids and a whole life established on the relationship, well, it just might be worth your while to try to learn to live without something. But you—you're young, you're just getting started, and there's no good reason in the world to willingly get yourself into a difficult situation like that."

Another pause for yet more emphasis.

"And if you two are not going to get married, then I really see no reason for you to keep seeing each other."

I could almost hear the bones in my neck snap. Of all the things I expected, of all the possibilities I was thinking about, "getting out" was the only one I had never actually considered. Really. In fact, I had seen a therapist for some sessions during internship, when the relationship had first started to depressurize, and he had looked at my girlfriend and me and said "I sure hope this works out. You make a handsome couple." (Alas, he was a fruitcake.) And here was a therapist who, within the first twenty minutes of talking with me, was telling me to get the hell out of the relationship because it was a bone-dry, done-deal, dead-end. Or, as I said some years later to a colleague who knew Rita very well: "She looked at me and said, in that kind and gentle way that only Rita can pull off, 'What the *fuck* are you doing?'" My colleague thought that was about the funniest thing he'd ever heard.

I, on the other hand, needed smelling salts. I just sat there, stunned, looking at Rita for a little while. She smiled, took a sip of tea, and looked back at me, clearly in no hurry and not uncomfortable with my silence. Then, after a few minutes of absorbing her sudden, and— at least for me—completely unexpected pronouncement, a truly amazing thing happened. I felt an emotion that I had long-ago forgotten existed much less imagined that I was capable of feeling: relief. I felt a sudden and profound sense of relief. Dramatic, palpable relief. It was as though my physician had just said "The tests were wrong—you don't have that terminal illness after all. You're not going to die next week, you're going to be just fine." I nearly burst out of my body.

But it was new, I didn't trust it, and I felt scared. I remember saying "Really? You mean it would be OK to get out of the relationship?" Rita laughed. I must have sounded about five years old.

"Listen, Greg," she said. "I want you to remember something. If you *have* to get married, *it—is—a—bad—deal.*"

"Wow," I replied. I thought about it for a few more minutes. Rita drank some more tea.

"Well, that brings up some questions," I said, hesitatingly. "It kinda scares me. How do I tell her? I mean, this is going to be a big deal."

"Yeah," she replied. "It probably is. So be sure to call her before five o'clock, so she can get hold of her shrink."

"What happens if she kills herself?"

"Well, you've got no control whatever over that. If she decides to do that, it's her decision. It's not really your business. *You* aren't her therapist."

"What if I discover that I've made a terrible mistake?" Rita laughed again.

"Look, you and she will remember each other, and if down the road you think it might work out and she's grown up some and you're both interested, you can try again."

I asked more questions. To each Rita responded with a caring, compassionate, and completely rational answer. She didn't dismiss even one concern I expressed, no matter how silly it might have been. She had an answer for everything, and her answers all pointed to the same thing: I didn't have to be making myself miserable by staying in this nuclear-powered threshing machine I was calling a relationship. Rita's answers made complete, absolute, and total sense. I could find no flaws in her judgment or her conclusion.

Finally, after I could think of no more questions and she'd responded to every objection I could conjure up, I realized the simple truth: Rita was right. She was absolutely, completely right. I did have to end this relationship because the SOB was taking me down.

And I had to end it *now*.

I still remember the feeling, sitting in her chair, in that sunny room, looking at Rita, fantasizing about being out of the relationship. I remember how it washed over me. Right there, in Rita's sun porch, I remember the feeling—of being reborn. I felt the weight of the world lift from my shoulders. I felt light. I felt excited. I felt energized. I felt like "me" again.

I felt *happy*.

And then I realized what had been missing from my life and that I had felt coming from Rita the moment I met her—she *cared*. She cared about how I felt. Here she hardly even knew me, but she was on the side of my well-being. She really and truly cared whether or not I was happy. She was saying that it was perfectly OK for me to want to be happy, that there was no rule and no reason that required me to be miserable. She really and truly *wanted* me to be happy.

And the awful truth was that my girlfriend didn't. Whatever was driving her, whatever was the psychological bee that was refusing to leave her emotional bonnet, it made the question of my happiness not just irrelevant, but an outright annoyance. If I was unhappy, well that was too damn bad and just another glaring indication of my incompetence as a human being. It certainly didn't have anything to do with *her* or with the relationship so I should just shut up about it already.

Now I could see that the whole thing was poison and why I'd needed Rita so badly. Rita was the antidote. Somehow, in some way, Rita was the right person, in the right place, at the right time, telling me the right things to counteract the toxins I was so willingly ingesting. (Now let's see—I started out life by feeling miserable in a crazy family where all the craziness was denied—so just how do you suppose I'd ended up feeling miserable in a crazy relationship where all the craziness was denied? Go figure.) Rita had just what I needed in order to undo the damage, to bring me back to life, to give me the permission I needed in a way that I could tolerate hearing—that it really was OK to want to be happy.

Rita, to this day I have never adequately thanked you for what you did for me. I still don't know how to do it. I mean, how do you thank someone for saving your life? For returning to you something so precious that you lost so long ago? I'm not sure there is a way. But rest assured that in my view you needn't have done all the gazillion wonderful things you have done for all the people you have helped for all these years for your life to have been entirely worthwhile. What you gave me, the life you breathed back into me, was a gift so large and so profound that had you done nothing else of value, God would surely have looked down on you and smiled, fully satisfied with his creation. You saved me on that day as surely as if you'd pulled me from a burning building. I don't know *what* I'd have done without you.

I knew what I had to do. Our time finished, I thanked Rita, made sure it was OK if I came back for some more advice if I stumbled or got stuck, got a big, wonderful hug from her, and set out to cut from my life the last vestige of graduate school's craziness.

And I'll tell you the truth—it wasn't easy. Actually, it was gruesome. Pretty much a bloodbath. When I told my girlfriend that I wanted out, she went, as you have probably already predicted, berserk. She said that I was crazy, that Rita was crazy, that I couldn't possibly be serious. I insisted that I was. She insisted that I wasn't.

It took me three, separate, multi-hour conversations to even convince her that I was serious, much less to get across the message that it was really over, no matter what she thought or said or did. Over and over I told her that it wasn't just that we weren't going to get married any time soon, it was that we were done, finished, kaput. She raged and argued and raged and argued. She said it was me, all me, that I was crazy, that Rita was crazy, that we were all crazy. I said she had told me that already, that it wasn't true, and that it didn't matter anyway, because we were done. She screamed and cried, and then pleaded and bargained. I said it was not a negotiation.

It took two more sessions with Rita and a final conversation with my girlfriend that occurred very late one night and that seemed to go on forever, to get it done. And I never could have made it through had another person not shown up in my life as another direct gift from the cosmos put into exactly the spot I needed at the exact moment I needed.

So—I came from a crazy family, right? Well, through the fog of insanity and bad feelings in this crazy relationship with my girlfriend, just when I was fighting for my life, one of my family members appeared on the scene as being not just sane, but as someone willing to pull along side me and become my lifeboat in the middle of the perfect emotional storm. My sister.

Since becoming adults, this particular sister and I had always gotten along pretty well, and I had shared with her my revelation with Rita about the nature of the relationship I was in. She said that she had suspected as much, but that she didn't want to intrude by telling me she thought I had attached myself to a seriously loose wingnut. She asked what she could do to help. I said that I was really scared to have the final conversation with my girlfriend and that I was worried about my ability to stick to my guns in the face of the onslaught of resistance, upset, and pleas for negotiation that I was expecting. Without batting an eye, she said "I am there. Consider me your coach. I will see you though this. We'll get this done, you and I."

So I called my girlfriend that night, with my sister sitting in the room beside me. Whenever my girlfriend would spew out an objection, an accusation, or a desperate plea, I would repeat it as though I was thinking it over—but I was really allowing my sister to hear it. My sister would then, from what became increasingly evident was her clear, sane, and caring point of view, would either whisper to me a response or write down a comment and shove it in front of my face. And I would say it to my girlfriend.

It went on for fucking *hours*. My girlfriend left the phone several times to go throw up—or so she said—and then came back to argue some more. Throughout, my sister never once wavered, grew weary, complained, criticized me, or showed impatience with my seemingly (at least to me) interminable weakness and vulnerability. She stayed glued to my side, coaching, encouraging, clarifying, and bringing sanity to the insane. Finally, at about 3 AM, the conversation wound down. I declared the conversation finished, our relationship over, and I got off the phone. My girlfriend had relented. It was done.

That conversation was a *very* big deal. It was a turning point that reverberates through my life to this very day. First, it got me out of a horrible relationship that would have been the death of me. Second, it cemented the single most secure and long-lasting relationship of my life—my relationship with my sister. I had not known that she cared about me that much. I hadn't known that anyone *could* care about me that much. And from that point forward, she and I have been darn near inseparable. One of my more cynical relatives once made a demeaning comment about our relationship by derisively calling us "joined at the hip."

They should be so lucky.

So in case you have not experienced it, let me tell you that having a close relationship with an adult sibling is one life's greatest joys as far as I'm concerned, and I don't know what I'd do without it. Rita may have saved me, but it was my sister's strength that saw me through what was surely my darkest hour. In fact, some years later, when a physician managed to convince me (inaccurately, inappropriately, and cruelly, as it turned out) that my wife Pam—the only other person on the planet I feel as deeply about—was about to undergo a lengthy, horrible, and excruciating death, (Oh, and by the way—to the son-of-a-bitch who did that to me—and you know who you are, yes you do—I *promise* that the cosmos does not forget or forgive such cruelty and will see to it that someday you pay, and pay dearly for being so unforgivably sadistic) my sister did it for me again, fielding phone call after phone call of my desperate wails and inconsolable hysteria. And, once again, she never for a moment wavered. She just stood there, in the face of the God-awful, agonizing and humiliating storm of my terrible and desperate hours, holding onto me for dear life. And she saved me *again*. Have no doubt—I would willingly die for that woman.

I did have one final contact with my girlfriend. For reasons tangential to the current discussion (OK—for reasons I don't want to discuss), I decided that I owed her a last face-to-face. So I flew to the west coast, and we said goodbye. It was another big scene. At the end I gathered up the belongings of mine that she still had, and she drove me to the airport. After an extremely awkward goodbye, I flew home and she drove home.

My sister picked me up at the airport. As I was getting into the car, she laughed and said "Given that you have all your worldly possessions with you, can I safely assume it's done?" I laughed and nodded that yes, it was done. Smiling, she started the car and drove me home.

THE REAL WORLD: PART II

With my Graduate School Era now completely behind me, my mood changed. For the next six months I lived in a state of pervasive euphoria. I have never experienced anything like it before or since. I woke up every morning happy to be alive. I went to work smiling and whistling. I loved everyone and everything. Had I not known better I'd have thought I was bipolar and in the grips of some long-term manic episode, or someone had surreptitiously installed a cranial morphine pump. Everything and everyone felt good. I made another appointment to see Rita simply because I wanted to crow—to someone who cared—about how incredibly, ecstatically happy I finally was. I told her I didn't know my brain *had* this many endorphins. Rita, of course, was thrilled, and cheered me on with a great, hearty gusto, playfully smacking a gold star square on the middle of my forehead as I was leaving. I moved the star to the inside of my tie and wore it, happily, all day at work.

My behavioral response to my enduring good mood was to put on my psychological Nikes and run completely wild. I started dating three and four women at a time. I took on more patients and assembled another therapy group. I called Merlin and together we cooked up a three-year psychotherapy outcome study that we would run both at his university and at my agency. A group of us from different departments at the agency started going country-western dancing every Wednesday night and getting snockered on half-priced beers as we two-stepped and Cotton-Eyed-Joed with anything that could walk erect. My regular Thursday morning case of red-eye was the topic of much finger-wagging, gossiping, and ribbing around the agency. Everyone I knew had a sister, or a cousin, or a friend that they thought would be *perfect* for me and wanted to set me up with. Women were literally showing up at my apartment at all hours of the day and night. (This could be problematic. One night I was on the phone with a woman I was dating when another woman I was *also* dating decided to "drop by." *That* was some fancy footwork.) Half the female staff at the agency hit on me. My receptionist started making goo-goo eyes at me and rubbing my leg under the table when a group of us would go out to lunch.

I was high, I was happy, and I was binging. On everything. All the time. My years of emotional and physical deprivation had finally caught up with me, and the gloves were off. I was out to have everything. Everyone I met was a potential friend or dating partner. Every available professional activity was a new opportunity. Every art opening or social event was something I wanted to attend. Anything on a plate, I'd eat. Anything in a bottle, I'd drink.

It is hilarious to see pictures of me from that time because I am literally almost unrecognizable. I have always been thin, and the stress and deprivation of graduate school had accentuated it to a frightening degree. In fact, during much of graduate school I ate only one meal a day and I seemed to be sick almost constantly. (I once quipped to a friend that during graduate school I was sick so often I'd concluded that my immune system wasn't compromised, but that I *had* no immune system.) So I came out of that place looking like The Ghost of Christmas Past.

Then, like the survivor of The Great Depression who stuffs their mattress with hundred-dollar bills, the metaphorical and literal deprivation of those years turned me into a warp-drive binging machine, and for the first and only time in my life, I got fat. Really. Not just chubby, I'm talking *fat*. Seemingly overnight I managed to pack a truly astonishing amount of weight onto my relatively small frame. The result was that I morphed into something that in photographs from that era bears a remarkable resemblance to the Pillsbury Dough boy. You should see the pictures—my stomach hangs over my belt, I'm round, I'm bouncy, I have these cute little baby-faced cherub cheeks. I'm adorable.

And I'm *fat*. The ironic thing was that I'd never had any experience with my weight fluctuating more than a pound or two through nearly my entire adult life, (except for getting thinner during graduate school) so I had no point of reference for gaining weight. When my pants started to no longer fit around me, I didn't know what to make of it. I had no way to understand it, so I just figured they were old, or maybe they'd shrunk or something (I know you don't believe me, but it's true—I had no idea I was gaining weight. I didn't even know how to *think* in those terms.) so I just shrugged and went out and bought pants that fit. But make no mistake—I became one farm-raised, grain-fed, big-ass porker. Oink, I say. Oink.

The truth was that I didn't know, and the truth was that I didn't care. I was having *way* too good a time. And my life-is-a-party demeanor wasn't subtle, either, it was right in everyone's face. For example, I always showed up at agency social functions. And I always showed up with a woman. An attractive woman. A *different* attractive woman. Every time. It was kind of fun to watch other staff members' reactions and to hear the whispers. Sometimes I'd run into someone from the agency at an outside social function, and there I'd be again—with yet *another* woman. And this was a church-affiliated place, remember, so they'd pretty much never seen anything like me. To my surprise—and wry delight—before long I had developed a full-blown, bonafide *reputation*. I recall a staff member once shaking her head and saying (during lunch, and in front of several other staff members) that she'd *love* to know how I handled Valentine's day given how -er—*active* my social life was. Oh, how I laughed myself silly with self-satisfied glee over that one. I'd occasionally see Rita for a session or two to tell her what a good time I was having, and she thought the whole thing was a gas. She wryly suggested that I casually drop matchbooks from various upscale restaurants around the agency.

However, my clinical supervisor at the time, a psychologist in practice in the local community, was not so thrilled at either my endless flurry of activity *or* my colorful reputation. She pointed out that my overinvolvement with everyone and everything was starting to smack of a behavior pattern that I'd claimed to have left behind in my recent past—graduate school—and that had previously resulted in my getting dangerously run down and completely strung out. She made several gentle suggestions that perhaps I should slow down a bit, lest I start to re-experience the kind of depletion I had felt in graduate school. I ignored her. So she turned up the volume and insisted that I listen to her cautions and hit the brakes on *something* in order to try to keep myself *healthy*. I laughed. She finally got really, *really* mad and demanded that I sit down for a formal, revival-tent, come-to-Jesus, you-can-walk-without-that-chair meeting.

Look, she growled—I was doing it again. I was exhausting myself. And even though this time I was having fun rather than suffering, the pattern of excess was the same and was going to turn out the same. I needed to slow the hell down or I was headed for disaster. I was just doing too much of too many things in too many ways—I was seeing patients, I was running groups, I was doing research, I was writing articles, I was going out nearly every night, and I was starting a private practice on the side. I needed to do something about it because it was *just too much*. She gave me two choices—either take a vacation "from everything" or go into therapy. I told her that if those were the choices, I'd take a vacation.

Hey—I was fat, not stupid.

In the course of my social activities I'd met a travel agent that I liked, so I went to see her. I told her what was going on and that I was on orders to take a vacation "from everything," and what did she suggest. Her eyes lit up and she said "I have *just* the thing for *you!*" She pulled out and tossed into my lap a brochure from Club Med. "You," she said, "are going *there,*" and she proceeded to regale me with a litany of earthly Club Med delights that turned my legs to jelly and made me salivate so profusely that Pavlov's dog would have been green with envy. Nearly ripping off my clothes in a frantic effort to find my checkbook, I asked how soon she could transport me to this paradise. She laughed and said just as soon as I could pry my excessive little self away from my excessive little activities. I wrote a check and dashed out of the place making a mental list of the cancellations I would be making on the way home.

But—she said, as I was running out the door—one last and one very important thing: I was not, under any circumstances, to list "doctor" on any of my Club Med forms, and I was to tell no one—*no one*—what I did for a living. Her exact words were "If you do, you'll end up setting up shop."

No problema, I said over my shoulder, mum's the word, and by the time I got to my car I knew exactly what I would do. Remember my undergraduate degree? Well, I was finally going to get to use it. Since I'd really studied film, I figured I could pull off a credible act as a "film teacher." I laughed to myself that maybe it wasn't all for naught that I got that stupid film degree, because it was gonna make for a great cover story at Club Med.

Exactly two weeks later, "*Mister* Gregory W. Lester, Assistant Professor of Film at a local university," (See? Your mother was right. It *is* good to have something to fall back on.) was sipping a beer on a plane headed to Club Med.

Now, this was in the heyday of Club Med, and at that time the places were a complete social and physical free-for-all. There were no rules, they specifically *said* there were no rules, and they overtly instructed you to *act like* there were no rules. So everyone did. I spent the first half of the week with a woman I met on the bus from the airport to the club, and the second half of the week with a woman I met at dinner one night. And I took part in everything there was to do at the place—I snorkeled, I surfed, I painted, I went to shows, I danced, (the disco *opened* at midnight) I drank, and I ate. I didn't sleep for the first 36 hours I was there.

Thinking back on it, I don't supposed my supervisor really intended for me to take a vacation where my behavior would be every bit as excessive as it was in normal life. She probably had something like "relaxation" in mind. Silly her. My solution was simple—I never told her.

I had a great time until, halfway through my week, I got sick—not uncommon given that the club was in Mexico and despite importing most of the food it was very easy to eat something that had stuff in it you weren't accustomed to or some kind of wiggly little 24-hour intestine-biter. I came down with the usual suspects—cramps, nausea, and diarrhea. But I decided that I had not come all this way just to wimp out, so despite the goblins playing rugby in my lower tract, I got myself up and went out and took the windsurfing lesson I'd signed up for. And there I was—cramping to beat the band, occasionally doubling over from the pain, standing on a surf board, learning how to hoist that damn sail. I was proud of myself. And I had a completely fabulous time.

Of course, I had a completely fabulous time as "*Mister* Gregory W. Lester, Assistant Professor of Film at a small liberal arts university." And my lie only caused trouble twice—well, three times if you count minor sadism. Once was during a trivia contest when the first five questions were about movies. (By the fourth question I was getting paranoid.) As soon as a film question would be asked, everyone I'd met turned toward me (of course) with an expectant look of "Well, *you* know this one, right?" And you know, I got lucky and did know a couple of them. But the others I didn't, and that seemed odd to several people. I laughed it off and said I hadn't taught the course that covered that part of the business for a couple of years, so I was rusty. That worked.

The second time was at dinner one night at a table with about seven other people when some topic came up that concerned relationships or some such thing. Before I'd even realized it, I'd spent a good five minutes pontificating on the research about such things and how the issue was seen from a clinical perspective. I looked up to see everyone at the table staring at me with wide eyes, food dripping from their open mouths. Suddenly realizing what I was doing, I frantically backpedaled and mumbled something lame like "Uh, well, see, reading about this stuff is, uh, kind of a hobby of mine," and promptly changed the subject. A near-miss.

The minor sadism involved something I did with my lie—or more accurately the truth—at the end of the week. On the very last day I told the woman I had been spending time with that I was a psychologist and that I'd been lying about it all week. I know, I know, I know. I shouldn't have. I know, I know, I know. I'm a creep. I got the idea from David Viscott, who tells the story in his book of one of his colleagues doing the same thing on a cruise. I just wanted to see if I got the same reaction.

I did. She pretty much freaked out. There were five minutes of "No, it can't be's," ten minutes of "Oh, my God's," and a half hour of "Tell me what you think about…"

You know, all things considered, she really took it pretty well. Look—I liked her, and I'd never have done it if I didn't think she'd ultimately get a kick out of it. We parted on good terms and talked on the phone a few times after we left, so no lasting damage done.

THE REAL WORLD: PART III

I returned to work refreshed, if not rested, from my "Do it now, regret it later" Club Med vacation, and went at it again. By this time I was well settled into the agency and was not starting many new activities, so my pace really did begin to slow down, much to the relief of my supervisor. At least she stopped yelling at me so much. I was seeing individual therapy appointments, two therapy groups, the couples participating in Merlin's and my couples' therapy research project, and I was consulting with other staff members and agency departments. And I was writing a couple of journal articles.

One of the reasons I had moved to the town where I'd moved was that a friend of mine and I decided that we could set up shop together. He was in a similar field, had lived in this particular city for a long time, and had a contact in the local community who, he said, had lots of business, didn't really want much business, and would be more than happy to feed us referrals. Cool. So at about the same time I took the psychology boards and became licensed to practice independently, he and I rented a small suite of offices to start our practice. It was pretty exciting, even if I didn't really have the money to be doing such things and was in a little over my head. No matter, he assured me, we'd get plenty of referrals, so damn those torpedoes and full speed ahead. OK—I figured if I could grow a large enough part-time private practice, my finances would improve and maybe I could even get a little bit ahead.

But after seven or eight months, the San Andreas fault running through my judgment became apparent yet again as I discovered that things in my practice were not going well, or, more precisely, were not going—period. Somehow the referrals from my friend's contacts were not materializing and my practice was not growing. I was puzzled. But worse than its confusion quotient, the lack of referrals meant that I was not making enough money in my private office to pay for my private office. So I was supporting both myself *and* my portion of the office suite on little more than my nonprofit social service agency salary. Can you say "negative cash flow?"

That was bad enough, but it was compounded by my realization that my future had become murky at best. I had counted on a growing practice to guide me for the future, and now that it was nowhere to be found, I couldn't see where I was headed. And one thing I had figured out for sure was that my future did not lie as a full-time staff member at my agency.

After a couple of years of working there it became painstakingly clear that I did not fit into my agency as a long-term staff member. In more ways than I can list (such as my wearing a suit every day) I stood out as different from the rest of the staff. Apparently this was obvious, too, because my patients were saying to me things like, "Hey, I've been wanting to ask you—and please don't take this wrong—but what are *you* doing *here?"*

The truth was that my agency may have been a well-oiled machine with a staff that did very good work, but it was a little nonprofit social service agency where most of the staff had settled in as a career and were more than happy to draw their modest salary, do the same thing day after day, and count the years, months, and days until they could collect their pension and retire. They were not particularly, to put it bluntly, ambitious.

Which is *so* not me. You have probably already figured out that one of the things I have never been blessed with is a shortage of ambition. And at my agency there was no place for ambition—it was just not on the menu. People had looked at me funny when I'd started therapy groups, much less a "research project," and they'd nearly had a stroke when they learned I was spending time writing journal articles. The place was not designed to grow or expand, it was designed to hum along *as is.* So someone like me who was wanting to create all kinds of new things was totally out of place. As a result, despite my initiating all these projects, there was essentially no place for me to advance in the agency, and there were no expanded career opportunities available. So after working there for about two years I started thinking about leaving.

When the rumblings of my discontent seeped into the agency gossip sieve, it began stirring up all kinds of strangeness. People started behaving exceptionally deferentially toward me. Lots of smiles. Lots of sudden interest in how I was doing. One day, out of the blue, someone from the administration showed up in my office, sat down, and unceremoniously offered me the Supervisor position in the Family Counseling Department. Knowing a hostile takeover attempt when I see one, I asked if they had told my current supervisor that they wanted to replace her. No, they hadn't. I asked if they had been talking with her about being unhappy with her leadership. No, they hadn't. I asked if they had told her they wanted to restructure the department (as they said they wanted me to). No, they hadn't. So I told them to get the hell out of my office and go talk with her about all these matters first. If she agreed to step aside for someone else, then they could come back and talk to me—but to keep my name out of it until such time, or I would turn them down flat. Even though I wasn't very nice about it, they agreed that what I was saying made sense, that it was the right thing to do, and wasn't it oh, so very wonderful, that I had so much integrity. And they never did it.

As time went on I began seriously losing my enthusiasm for "just" working in the same way for the same place with nothing appealing on the horizon that I could look forward to as career advancement, not to mention opportunities that might help my pitiful finances. While I'd gotten quite good raises by the standards of the agency, they were not so good by the standard of trying to improve my standard of living—and to support a private office that was most definitely not supporting itself. I'd just about maxed out the agency salary structure and was clearly making more than almost everyone else on staff, but most of my friends in the field were making at least 50% more money than I, so the whole thing became downright depressing.

So I started looking for a new job. Now I had both experience and a license to practice psychology, so my marketplace value had increased significantly since my first job search. I interviewed with some hospitals and a medical school, and I got job offers from several. But none seemed quite right, and while I would have loved to have taken the job on the medical school faculty, the fly swimming backstroke through the ointment was that they forbade their staff from maintaining a private practice on the side. So I would have no opportunity for supplemental income and would have to dispose of my current private patients, which I was *not* disposed to do. So I turned them down—and was shocked by how furious they were. They were incensed that I had said no. They even tracked me down, on vacation—at my mother's house—to call me up and grill me about having turned them down. Then they sent me a personal follow-up letter saying how thrilled and delighted they were to have hired this other psychologist for the job, and oh, how perfect she was for it. Geez. I hadn't meant for them to take it personally—the job just didn't fit the way I wanted my career to go.

But then, nothing seemed to. I grew discouraged, disappointed, and distressed. I spent a lot of time during that period taking long walks, trying to sort through what I should do, and to get some vision for the future. I wasn't sure what I should do, but I was feeling worse and my financial condition continued to deteriorate.

And then came the turning point. One evening I was in our private offices when I heard my friend in the next office making an appointment with a new patient. Curious, when he finished the call I stuck my head around the door and asked him where he was getting the referrals. He said he was getting them from his contact. Shocked, I noted that I was not getting referrals from his contact and asked why he was getting them when I wasn't. I'll never forget his reply as long as I live, as it remains one of the most arrogant, demeaning, and just plain mean comments I've ever been on the receiving end of from another human being—and one who claimed to be my friend, at that. With a smug, superior, self-righteous smirk, he cooed "Because he's my *buddy.*"

It was like a match to dynamite. That reply told me everything I needed to know. I'd done it again. I'd fucking done it again. I had gotten myself into a relationship where everything was "fine"—except that I was getting screwed and no one was admitting it. Once again I had grabbed the short end of the stick, I had backed up to read the sign that said "Severe Tire Damage." But this time I'd *really* done it—I had built my entire future on a false promise. And I was out in the cold.

At that moment I knew—I'd bitten on the oldest scam there is, the bait-and-switch. The reason I was struggling financially was because the "contact" was feeding my friend referrals, not me, and my friend was taking the referrals for himself—*all* for himself. The truth, as I later discovered, was that the contact had no *intention* of sending referrals to me. They *never* had any intention of sending referrals to me. They could not have cared less about me, and in fact when I confronted them about the situation told me that they *resented* me and resented my friend's attempt to wedge me into the picture. So before I'd even arrived, and without my even knowing it, I had been voted off the island.

The hard truth that I had somehow managed to avoid facing was that my friend had invited me to move to town and set up shop with him because he *liked* me, not because he intended to share the spoils with me. So while I was slowly freezing to death financially, he was happy as a clam doing fun things with his friend—me—while getting multiple referrals from his contact and building a budding little practice for himself.

I had gotten myself screwed. *Again.*

I realized all this in a flash, and my reaction was to go completely feral. Enraged beyond words, I launched into a tirade of such profane, fearsome proportion that it surpassed even my own estimate of the amount of venom I was capable of spewing. Like an eruption of molten lava, the floodgates flew open, out it poured, and it just didn't stop. I carried on for several hours that night, and I continued into the next day. My friend, bless his pointy little duplicitous head, was smart enough to avoid trying to defend himself, make excuses for his inexcusable behavior, or to flee while I was in rage mode, because *then* I would have had his head—and eaten it in front of him. I can still see the hollow look in his eyes that showed a mix of guilt over having been caught and terror at the ear-splitting onslaught of rage he had brought down on his head.

Oh yeah, and the next day I called up the contact and had it out with *them*, as well. (For all their claims of "resenting" my presence since the very beginning, to my face they had always maintained that the whole thing was quite fine with them, and they were in on the deal 100%. So they had out-and-out lied to me from the very beginning—as I told them, in no uncertain terms. Multiple times.)

But the whole thing did serve to get my head screwed on very straight, very fast. I saw that I had done it again. I had gotten myself into a crazy relationship that was custom-tailored to ensure my suffering. I had managed to dig myself yet another hole, and this time it was financial as well as emotional. All of my confusion, distress, and desperation had turned to rage, and it may very well be the most angry I have ever been in my adult life. And I decided to use it to save *myself* this time.

In an attempt to "psychologist heal thyself," I immediately prescribed myself a hefty dose of reality. I concluded that it was high time I stopped all this relationship craziness and started taking responsibility for myself and for my future. I decided I'd better stop expecting these relationships to provide for me, and I'd better start providing for myself. So I sat down with myself, and together we hatched a plan.

First, I ended my relationship with both my friend and his contact. Cold turkey. It was clearly a dead-end street for me and, quite honestly, I felt that I had been sold a bill of goods, (willingly, I admit) and I wanted to ensure no perpetuation of the fraud. So as of that day I quit speaking to them. Harsh, I admit, but I wanted no more illusions. And remember, I was *really* mad.

Second, I decided that I'd skip all the struggle and just do the one thing I thought I could not do—I would up and quit the agency and jump, feet-first, into full-time private practice to see if I could make a go of it on my own. It was the only place where I could envision a future with expanding professional and financial opportunities, so I figured I'd give it a shot. But to do so I needed some financing, because I didn't have any financial cushion or savings. Not a good situation, and I needed to figure out what to do about it.

So I talked to the only person I really trusted—my sister—about my situation and what I ought to do, and she suggested that we talk to a family member about a loan. Now, I'm not wild about debt, much less to family members, but I needed to do something and I needed to do it now, so I took her advice. And despite some haughty comments about "figuring as much" when I said that I had belatedly discovered that I was getting screwed by my friend and his contact, the family member I approached did lend me some seed money. I didn't need much—psychologists don't need much expensive equipment or anything—but I needed what I needed, so we drew up an agreement and I got the loan, for which I was then, and remain now, profoundly grateful.

I gave a month's notice to my agency and began informing my patients that I would be leaving. I said that what they decided to do was completely up to them—I was happy to make sure they got set up with another counselor at the agency, or they could come with me to my private practice and I'd charge them the same sliding-scale fee they were paying at the agency. I was flattered that every single patient asked to come with me.

PART V:
CONTINUOUS
REINFORCEMENT

PRIVATE PRACTICE

I started full-time private practice on Monday, April 2nd. I had wanted to start on April first because I thought beginning on April Fools' Day was a perfect symbol for my undertaking. But that particular year it fell on a Sunday, so the second was as close as I could get.

Surprising no one but myself, I started private practice the same way I seemed to do everything: all-out. On my first day I had twelve appointments. On the second day I had ten. For the entire first week I saw a double-digit number of appointments every day.

And I liked it immediately. I was my own boss, I set my own schedule, and I worked in my own office with my name on the door. I was completely responsible for myself and for my patients. Concerns that I was a closet control freak aside, I seemed to be well suited for private practice.

And it for me. After that first week it just got busier. As past patients called the agency looking for me and learned that I had set up shop, they called me for appointments. My patients told friends and family members about seeing me, and they came, too. Priests and ministers who knew me through the agency sent families from their congregations to see me. Couples who had heard of my marital research with Merlin came. My patients who were parents began bringing me their children.

It never let up. For the next ten years I experienced nothing even close to a slowdown. Traditionally, most professions consider summer to be the slow time, even nicknaming it the "summer slump"—kids are out of school, families are on vacation, and people don't see their therapists. I never had one. My summers were every bit as busy as any other time.

Nevertheless, before jumping into private practice I had obsessively read every book I could find on how to set up a successful private practice. In my zeal to leave no stone unturned in my attempt to stay afloat working for myself, I had bought, and read, everything. And the one phrase that seemed to be the mantra from the "How to avoid starving to death when you're in private practice" crowd was "market yourself, market yourself, market yourself." (One writer's motto was "Marketing or Morbidity.") Authors had ten billion suggestions about how to market yourself and your practice. Newsletters, they said—send out newsletters. Oh—and talks, they said—do talks. Don't forget professional associations, they said—join professional associations. Beating a rhythmic drum and pounding it into your head, they exhorted one and all to get your name out there, get your face out there, make contacts, beat the bushes, market yourself 'til you're so blue in the face you look like a Smurf.

And I tried, I really tried. I took their advice and cooked up marketing scheme after marketing scheme. I wrote newsletters, I gathered lists of groups I could give talks to. The problem was that I was so darn busy from the day I started practice that I was never able to implement any of them. Every time I thought I was about to hit a slowdown I'd wade into my closet, dust off one of my marketing plans, update it, take a deep breath, and prepare to implement it. But before I could even get to the phone to pick it up, wham—I'd get fifteen new referrals the very next week, and be up to my ears in patients. Back into my closet would go the marketing plan.

Within two years I had multiplied my income by a factor of six and was consistently seeing between fifty and sixty appointments per week. When the lease expired on the office suite I'd rented with my friend—to whom I was still not speaking—I unceremoniously and silently moved out and took over the top floor of an old house as my office suite. My sister decorated it—beautifully, I might add—and I moved in. All by myself.

And the patients just kept coming. New ones, returning ones, families and couples, they never seemed to stop. At one point I was averaging three new referrals *per day*.

But maybe the best thing about private practice was that it gave me the freedom to initiate and create. As a result, I became involved in a tremendous number of activities. For starters, I had left my agency with a very nice consulting contract in hand where I was paid nearly a quarter of the salary I had been making for performing three hours of consultation per week. I also continued running some therapy groups for them. And because through the agency I had worked with other church-affiliated agencies, I was asked to evaluate candidates for religious life, which I did for the next ten years. Following that I was asked to teach a couple of courses a year at a local seminary, which I also did for about ten years.

A colleague of mine from the agency had returned to get a Masters degree and approached me about doing her internship with me. That was fun. When she was done with that I hired her as an assistant to work with me in groups and on evaluations and to help me create research projects. (Performing research in private practice is essentially unheard-of. When I would tell people about my research projects, they would ask, "Who's funding it?" When I would reply, "I am," they would just kind of stare at me.)

One of our most successful projects involved creating, funding, completing, and publishing the first controlled study demonstrating that physicians' interpersonal behavior is more of a risk factor for being sued for malpractice than is a bad medical outcome. It was published in a medical journal that covers five states and was abstracted in *The Journal of the American Medical Association*. We got requests for reprints of the article from as far away as Poland. Around the same time Merlin and I went to Germany to present our couples research which had also been published in a prominent journal. Then I was asked to consult with the Department of Justice about the sudden influx into our area of unaccompanied, undocumented juveniles from Central America. I was asked to give talks to conferences and organizations. I wrote articles that were published in everything from magazines for cancer survivors to *The Skeptical Inquirer* (I am especially fond of the title of that article: "Why Bad Beliefs Don't Die." Cute, no?) I wrote a book that has gone into its sixth printing and about which I was interviewed by everything from radio shows to executive newsletters.

Make no mistake—from my very first day of practice I worked *hard*. And I enjoyed it immensely. I ran a thriving little shop, and everyone—both my patients and myself—seemed to be pleased. Life was good.

It also helped that my personal life had settled down at around the same time I started private practice. Some time before the big blowup with my friend, I had gone to a party with another friend and managed to coerce myself into approaching the most attractive woman in the place, striking up a conversation, and getting her phone number. By the time I went into private practice she and I had been dating for a few months—we got married some years later—and we were now seeing each other exclusively. So everything went swimmingly. Once, that is, she got over the impression that I was gay.

That's right—my future wife thought I was gay. What a great "How you met your spouse" cocktail-party story that still makes. Here's what happened:

A friend and I went to this party, and when we got there he made a bee-line for this particular woman, plopping himself beside her so he could pet this cat she was holding. The woman looked up at me, saw what she thought was jealousy in my eyes, and said to herself "Uh oh, I'm making this guy's gay lover jealous." Her reasoning that we were gay came from the fact that we had come to the party together, we were both wearing similar jewelry, and we were clearly not your run-of-the-mill "macho" males, (I think "touchie-feely" was her exact term.) given that—unbeknown to her—we were both psychologists. In addition, unbeknown to me, there were a lot of gay people attending the party. So she added it all up in her head, came to the not-unreasonable conclusion that we were gay, and became worried that I was jealous of her talking to my partner.

She was half right—I was jealous. But I was jealous of my friend having beaten me to the most attractive woman at the party. So the jealousy she correctly saw in my eyes was of *him*, not her. Fortunately, after a while he got sidetracked onto something else, I moved in, and she and I hit it off. (After we'd been dating a while she fessed up about her first impression of me. I asked when she first thought I might actually be straight, and she said, "Well, asking for my phone number seemed a reasonable tipoff." Thank you very much.) We even have a picture of us together from that party. There we are, smiling for the camera—her, me, and my friend's noggin resting on my shoulder like some evil second head. Can't imagine why she thought we were gay.

A nice side-effect of a thriving private practice was that it improved my financial condition exponentially. My money problems straightened out fairly quickly and I started getting ahead. A couple of years into practice I was sufficiently flush that Pam successfully persuaded me to actually *spend* some of my hard-earned money—which I had been jealously hoarding like a survivor of the great depression—and to buy the Mercedes I'd had my covetous eye on. I still remember how the salesman dropped his pen (literally) when in response to his question, "How are you going to pay for the car" I said, "I'm going to write a check." Thanks to Pam's encouragement and support, for the next thirteen years I drove that car, happy every single day that I had it. And that I had her.

So from the start it was all good. Well, with one exception—even with a thriving practice, money, and a stable personal life, I still had one major—or, more precisely—"large" problem to deal with: my weight.

The grand finale in the sordid story of my deprivation-compensating, binge-induced bovine girth came during a trip to a psychology convention that I attended with Pam and another couple. It was a big trip and a big deal, as it involved going to another country and a city where none of us had been before. And to us, at that time, that meant one thing—the opportunity to indulge in exotic taste delights that we could not only enjoy while there, but could also bring home courtesy of bulging hips and expanded waistlines.

So off we went to this psychology meeting, and it was "All Systems Eat." Judging from our frantic food-seeking behavior you'd have thought we were starving refugees from some third world country who hadn't had a bite in weeks. We stepped off the plane, and like gophers on a golf course we put our heads down and chewed our way forward. When meal-time would arrive we would pile headlong into the nearest taxi, demand to be taken to food—any food—good food—right now—hurry up—why is this taking so long—and careen through the streets, bruising our faces as we smashed them into the windows every time an interesting bistro crossed our field of view. Inducing permanent trauma and damaging the auditory neurological system of our drivers, without warning we would suddenly scream, "STOP! STOP THE TAXI!" any time we saw a restaurant that we all thought looked good. We would tumble out of the cab and lay siege to the place like Santa Ana on the Alamo. Allowing nothing and no one to get in our way, we would belly up and demand to be served huge quantities of everything. Incredibly irritated at any delay in the delivery of said food, we made a genuine spectacle of ourselves as we snarfed down everything and demanded more. *Waiters* commented on the quantity of food we were capable of consuming. (At the end of one particularly excessive meal at a very classy Chinese restaurant, a waiter—himself a bit of a character, obviously—rubbed his hand on the stomach of the man of the other couple, shook his head, and shouted with mock shock: "Goddam!" I am *in no way* making this up.) Insatiable and voracious, any gorged lion unlucky enough to have witnessed our display would have crawled into the shadows, suicidal with envy. We ate our way from one corner of the city to the other and back.

And when I got home, I was *disgusted*. I couldn't stand myself. I took a long, hard look at the flab around my waist and the gluttony in my soul, and I came to a decision: it was time to slim the fatted calf.

I became a man on a mission. First, I joined a health club that was exactly eight minutes from my office, and I began swimming, lifting weights, and attending aerobics classes most every day. Second, I read every book on health and nutrition I could get my fat little fingers around. High protein, low protein, vegetarian, grapefruit, you name the diet and I read the book on it. Finally settling on the Pritikin program due to what I felt at the time (and still feel, in many ways) was the overwhelming amount of scientific evidence supporting their philosophy of eating, I completely changed my diet—overnight. One day I was eating triple cheeseburgers, large fries, and half a cheese-cake for lunch, and the next day I was ordering steamed broccoli, unbuttered whole-wheat rolls, and skipping dessert altogether. I began to eat plain oatmeal for breakfast and skinless chicken breasts with steamed vegetables for dinner.

It was an astonishing and dramatic change—even for me—and, true to form, everyone who knew me thought I had lost my mind. This was before the era of popular understanding that diet has any-thing much to do with health or disease, mind you, so any "health" minded diet, much less one considered in some sectors to be as ex-treme as the Pritikin program, was considered fringy—and at times downright embarrassing. To wit: a typical conversation with a waiter during that time:

Me: "And I'd like a baked potato. Plain."
Waiter: "Excellent. 'Baked potato. Butter only.'"
Me: "No, no butter. Plain."
Waiter: Pause. Frown. Tone of disbelief: "You mean—*dry?*"
Me: "Yes. Dry."

Waiter: Pause. Stare. Sigh. Tone dripping with disgust, revulsion, and contempt: "'Baked potato. *Dry.*'"

A colleague of mine, a woman who struggled with her weight, told me that I had become to eating what a recovered alcoholic was to a beer bash. But then, you must understand that she was also a person who stashed back issues of *Bon Apetit* magazine under her bed in guilty piles that she read late at night as a kind of surreptitious, titillating gustatory pornography. So bear that in mind.

I felt sorry for Pam. Although we had been a couple for some time, she had not really been exposed to the dramatic nature of my sudden internal shifts, so she found my overnight change profoundly baffling and incomprehensibly extreme. Wearily commenting to a colleague of mine at a party about her confusion over the intensity of my sudden fanaticism about "eating healthily," he responded in a reassuring tone, "That sometimes people have to go to an extreme to get started on something. Don't worry, he'll moderate."

Clearly *he* didn't know me that well. "Moderate" is one of the last terms that fits me. In fact, by the time all was said and done, not only had I *not* moderated, but nearly everyone I knew started eating more and more like me. Which I took as a personal moral triumph.

Oh, and one other thing. To celebrate my newfound health regimen, I had a sort of a "going away" party to my old eating by throwing a huge party—a huge *dessert* party. Inviting everyone I knew, even my mother in Florida, I sent out invitations to an all-out, no-holds-barred sweets-fest. On the wry invitations I noted that insulin would be available—and probably needed—and that a scale would be placed outside the front door and each participant was required to weigh in upon arriving and to weigh out upon leaving. If anyone had gained less than three pounds they were required to return to the dessert bar and load up further. A very good time was had by all, and the next day I started on my new program.

In an amazingly short period of time my extra weight was gone. In fact, I lost ten more pounds than I had expected, and I ended up weighing exactly what I had weighed in high school—which resulted in an *enormous* tailor bill.

And I continued in private practice. Another positive turn was that Rita and I started working together. Now, it is admittedly a fairly unusual thing that someone who has served as your therapist can become a coworker, but my therapy was short and successful, and

Rita and I liked and respected each other. She was also seeing more patients than she could handle, so she started sending her overflow to me. Then we started running adolescent therapy groups together. We even developed a training on our method of group therapy, called "How to Be an Adolescent Outpatient Group Therapist and Live to Tell About It." The last time we presented the training it was attended by nearly 300 professionals. People were even lined up in the hall outside the meeting room to listen to us and watch our videotapes of our teenage groups.

Ultimately, I rented the bottom half of a building that Rita owned to use as my office, and she used the upper half. I rented out my extra rooms to other practitioners and ended up with a nice little rental income in addition to my patient fees. For a good ten years Rita and I shared the building, referrals, and consultations, and had what may very well be the most satisfying and successful professional relationship I've ever heard of. We did good work, we had fun, and we helped each other.

All in all, it turned out exceptionally well. And after fourteen years in practice, my experience started being tapped by various training organizations who wanted me to develop trainings in topic areas that I had specialized in and become skilled in. So I started doing that as well, which also became very busy. Within four years well over 50,000 mental health professionals had attended my trainings.

In sum, my professional life could not have turned out better, and I continue to maintain a small practice and to do trainings for mental health professionals. It would be very hard to ask for a better life.

FOLLOWUP

I have a couple of follow-ups to some of the events I've related in the book. First, about my graduate program:

A short time before I graduated, and after Merlin had announced he was leaving, my graduate program did something that I still find incomprehensible: they offered me Merlin's faculty position.

Now, I did not exactly have a *bad* relationship with my graduate program, but it was not the easiest or most peaceful of relationships, either. I thought they were crazy—and I had the poor sense to tell them so on occasion, and while they thought I was smart and capable, they also thought I was a fairly frequent pain in the neck—which they told me on occasion. So to actually invite me to *stay* there, where they'd have to continue to put up with me, was beyond my comprehension. Further, I could not imagine they had failed to notice that as a group we graduate students were profoundly traumatized by our experience at the place and would have to have been overtly suicidal to want to stay there—sort of like an abused child clinging to their abuser.

So when they made the offer, complete with a salary quote and everything, I did my darndest not to shriek "Are you *insane!*" and managed to politely decline, saying that I had planned to go into practice and I still wanted to try doing that before I did anything else. In response, they were gracious—or perhaps relieved, which I would hardly resent them for feeling.

After Merlin left, his position appeared to become somewhat of a revolving door, with a succession of psychologists taking on his position. I met a couple of them, and some I liked and from at least one I wanted to flee while I still had my soul.

Second—about the friend to whom I quit speaking:

About two years after my split with him, he called me. He said that he was not satisfied with the state of our relationship and that he wanted to talk. Impressed by both his courage in calling and his apparent desire to have a relationship with me, I met with him. It was still fairly contentious, at least on my part, but we did start hashing out what had happened and how we'd ended up in this mess. For his part, he acknowledged the untenable position I'd been put in and his contribution to it, which was helpful. We met again and kept talking. Over time it got less contentious and a new relationship grew between us and since then we've been friends—of a sort—again. We've even gone on some trips together and to some conferences and the like.

I say we became friends "of a sort" because the whole thing caused what appears to me to be permanent damage to our relationship, and it's never really been the same—at least for me. But it was really good of him to call and to want to try again, and I am pleased that we did repair the relationship as well as it could be repaired. I am glad for the degree of friendship that we do have, even if it is sad that some things cannot be completely fixed, and I've never really trusted him the same way again.

Third—about the woman with whom I'd been in a relationship when I first saw Rita:

She also called me, out of the blue, some *twenty* years later. I was on the west coast presenting a training in the city where she was still living, and somehow she heard about it. Upon arriving at my hotel I discovered a voice mail message from her saying she'd heard I was in town and asking if I'd be interested in getting together to "catch up." Hey—I may not be the brightest crayon in the box, but I know an ulterior motive when I see one, and I knew that "catching up" wasn't even close to being an appropriate phrase given who and what we were and had been. Clearly, she wanted to try to bring some closure to the past. My initial response was to hyperventilate. And to immediately call Pam and my sister for advice.

I called my long-ago ex-girlfriend and we had a very pleasant phone conversation. She agreed to come to the hotel where I was doing my training so we could talk during the lunch break. She appeared in the back of the room as I was sending my hundred or so participants to lunch. As they were leaving I walked up to her and was shocked to have her hug me immediately. We went to my hotel room to talk. In the elevator she said I looked exactly the same, just with more gray hair. I told her that I hated her because she not only looked the same, but her hair wasn't even gray.

No sooner had we sat down to talk than she began to sob. She said that, to her, our breakup seemed much more recent than the twenty-some years it had actually been, and that for all these years she had suffered with terrible guilt and remorse over the horrible way she had treated me. She said that I had given her countless personal gifts, had taught her things about love and about life that she still valued, and that she had never been able to thank me for all that or to say how sorry she was for the abuse she had heaped on me. She said that, from the bottom of her heart, she wanted to apologize for what she had done to me, and to thank me for having the courage to end the relationship because she was unable to do it.

So, listen—I've both been through and I've seen an awful lot in my life through graduate school and as a psychologist, and it takes a *lot* to render me speechless. But that did. I was moved. I was *profoundly* moved. I was moved not only by her courage in calling me, by her honesty about her past behavior, and by her desire that I know I'd been a positive force in her life, but by the depth of her pain. Looking into her face I could see that she *still* hurt over the whole thing. It was *right there.*

I wanted to cry, too—not because I hurt, but because I had no idea how much she had hurt for all these years. And I wanted to take it away. I wanted to tell her that it was OK, that *I* was OK, that for me the whole thing was in the past—*way* in the past—the past of another time, another place, another *life.* I wanted her to know that I had stopped hurting over it long ago, that my life had turned out great, and that I had stopped being angry with her decades before, and that she didn't need to worry or to hurt over me because I had long ago forgiven her. As far as I was concerned the whole thing occurred because we were such very young people trying so desperately to cope with stresses that were far beyond those appropriate to our age. We were doing the very best we knew how under the circumstances. I wanted her to know that she was fine, that she was a good person, and that I *knew* she was a good person.

So that's what I told her. We talked for a long time. (I was late returning to my training.) We talked about the paths our lives had taken, about her work and her husband and her beautiful children.

We talked about me and my work, about Pam, about our precious Maine Coon cat, and our wonderful life nestled close to our beloved mountains. Finally we were both able to laugh. So we went back downstairs, I apologized to my participants for being late, I signed a couple of my books as a present for her, and walked her to her car.

As she was leaving I looked into her face and saw that she looked—reborn. She said she felt so much better she didn't even know how to say it. I thought back to that day in Rita's office and to that feeling, that lightness, that moment of rebirth, and I told her she didn't need to tell me, that I completely understood. She gave me a big hug, and off she went.

NOTES FROM A PSYCHOLOGIST, COMPLETE WITH SOME "FREE" ADVICE

I am aware that throughout this book I have not gone into much depth about the actual "work" of being a psychologist. I haven't presented many case examples nor pontificated to any significant degree about what I do all day in my work of "doing psychology." It is not because this is unimportant—to the contrary, it is what I've devoted my life to. I just wanted to focus the majority of this particular book on the story of what it took for me to get to be able to do what I do. Nevertheless, I know that some discussion of the "work of psychology" is due, so I won't leave you without offering some insights. It's what we psychologists do.

First off, let's get to some questions that people like me get asked, over and over. Question Number One: "Before we talk about the 'work' of psychologists, tell us—is it true? *Are* all shrinks crazy?"

Answer: Of course not—at least no more than any other profession.

The perception that "all shrinks are crazy" does not stem from more mental health professionals being off-center than practitioners of other professions. It's that we *expect* mental health professionals—because they are mental health professionals—to be *more* sane than the general population. It's like priests and the whole sexual misbehavior thing: there's no particular evidence that more priests sexually misbehave than do other groups, but we *expect* priests to be above all that, so when it does happen we are more horrified by it. Same thing with psychologists and others in my field—we expect that, because we are experts in human functioning, we should have applied the knowledge to ourselves and resolved our own issues. But it just isn't necessarily so, any more than being a medical professional inherently produces good personal health habits. I mean, how many medical professionals do you know who smoke—or are overweight? Or are sedentary?

The truth is that becoming a mental health professional is no different from entering any profession—getting in is mostly a function of being sufficiently good at school to be able to successfully complete an advanced degree. And a license to practice a mental health profession is just another academic hurdle—another exam—so it doesn't address one's psychological intactness, either. As a result, you find the whole range of mental health in my profession. We run from the crazy to the enlightened, and the level-headed to the goofy—just like physicians, lawyers, salespeople, and bus drivers.

For example, while I regaled you with the story of how insightful and effective Rita was and how much she helped me, I didn't spend much time reviewing how I'd seen at least two other psychologists during graduate school, and how neither of them had a clue. I saw one after a breakup with a girlfriend when I thought I was reacting inappropriately and wanted to get to the bottom of whatever issue it had stirred up. That psychologist basically told me I didn't know what I was talking about, that I shouldn't mess with things or look too closely, that I was probably OK, and that he didn't think we should try to figure it out. I saw him for one session, and clearly he wasn't helpful. (Oh, and by the way—I *was* reacting inappropriately. I got that fixed some years later by seeing another psychologist who knew what he was doing.)

The other psychologist I did mention briefly—he was the one I saw during internship when my relationship with my girlfriend was hitting the skids. Not only did he fail to help me, or my partner, but an intern friend of mine also saw him, and he ultimately had a psychotic break. While I don't blame the psychologist for my friend's breakdown, I never heard anything about my friend's work with the psychologist that led me to think that he helped much, either.

Now, if you consult a mental health professional, it is better, all things being equal, to see one who is banging on all their mental cylinders. But I know some people who have received some pretty good help from some professionals I consider to be pretty darn weird. So while life would certainly seem more fair if only people with their heads screwed on straight could become mental health professionals or could help people, it just isn't so. In fact, several of the founders of major schools of psychotherapy were, and are, themselves pretty strange ducks. And they came up with some pretty powerful stuff.

Question Number Two: "Why do people see mental health professionals?"

Answer: Two main reasons: they feel bad, or they're having trouble in a relationship. Or both. For most of us, how our relationships go is most of what determines our happiness. So when they go bad, we suffer. That brings a lot of people in to see people like us.

But it isn't always that cut-and-dried. Many times people feel bad and they have some guesses as to why, but they aren't sure. Or they have tried everything they can think of and nothing has helped. So they come to see us.

Question Number Three: "Do mental health professionals help people?"

Answer: Absolutely. Just like anything else, we don't *always* help *everyone* with *everything*, but in general the studies on the work we do show that consulting one of us can be very helpful to many people. So while what we do is not a panacea, it's not useless, either.

Question Number Four: "What's the difference between a psychiatrist, a psychologist, a social worker, and a counselor?"

Answer: A psychiatrist is someone who goes to medical school and takes exactly the same courses as every other physician, from cardiologists to pathologists. Then, after finishing medical school and obtaining an M.D., they complete an internship and three years of "residency" in psychiatry. It is during this residency that they are trained in psychiatry. Residency is "on the job training," and they work in hospitals, clinics, and other settings learning about mental health, psychiatric disorders, psychotherapy and medication. In short, a psychiatrist is an M.D. who "specializes" in psychiatry.

A psychologist is someone who goes to graduate school to get a Ph.D. (Or Psy.D.) in psychology. They study all aspects of psychology, including personality, psychopathology, behavior, neuroanatomy, and the like. The program can take anywhere from four to twelve years, with the average probably being about six years. As part of that training, and before they are awarded their Ph.D., they complete a one-year internship. Just like a residency, internship is "on-the-job training" and is done in an hospital or clinic or other setting. Then, after receiving their Ph.D., they do an additional one or two years of supervised training in order to be licensed to practice psychology.

A social worker is someone who goes to graduate school to get a Masters of Social Work degree, generally a two-year process. As part of their program they have an "on-the-job-training" called "placement" which lasts from three to six months. Generally, to be licensed to practice independently, "M.S.W.'s" need five years of experience after finishing their degree.

A "counselor" is a title unconnected with any one particular profession. Basically it is someone who has permission to use that title, and it varies from state-to-state as to what credentials are required in order to use that title.

That's the formal stuff. Here are the meaningful differences:

First, a psychiatrist is the only one of us who can prescribe medication. The other professions may know a great deal about medications, but they cannot write prescription. For example, while I know more about many of the medications than do most M.D.'s, because I cannot prescribe them myself I have several psychiatric consultants to whom I send my patients if I think an evaluation for medication is warranted. They consult with my patient and prescribe for them, if they conclude that it is, in fact, appropriate to do so.

This is beginning to change, and will probably continue to change, as psychologists are starting to be authorized to write prescriptions. We already do so in a program in the Department of Defense, and laws have been passed allowing psychologists to prescribe in New Mexico and Louisiana. But for now, basically, psychiatrists are the only ones who write prescriptions for medications. Other M.D.'s can write prescriptions for psychoactive medication as well, but psychiatrists are the specialists in the area.

Second, psychologists are basically the only professionals who give psychological tests. We give the intelligence tests, personality tests, inkblot tests, (yes, the inkblot test is real) and the like. So we do a lot of the "evaluations" of patients. In fact, the whole field of clinical psychology was largely begun after World War II by the VA Medical system in response to needing more psychiatric "diagnosticians" for their patient population. So my profession started life as a diagnostic specialty and expanded from there.

Third, social workers are essentially the only professionals who make arrangements and plans for social services, such as setting up home health care for a shut-in, or contacting nursing homes about placements for the elderly. They do other work as well, but "place-ment" work is often specific to their work.

Other than those particular elements, we can all do pretty much what each other does. We can all do psychotherapy. We can all do consultations. One of the jokes in the mental health business is that the difference between a psychiatrist and a psychologist is that to learn to talk to patients a psychiatrist studies gallbladders and a psy-chologist studies rats. Hardy har.

Question Number Five: "If I wanted to see a mental health pro-fessional, which profession should I choose?"

Answer: It all depends. First, besides the differences I have listed above, within psychiatry, psychology, social work, and counseling, professionals differ from each other every bit as much as they differ from those in the other professions. For example, I probably work in ways that are more similar to many psychiatrists than to some of my colleagues in psychology.

If you're going to see one of us, I believe the first thing you need to look for is someone who is "traditionally" trained—that is, they come from an M.D., a clinical psychology Ph.D., or an M.S.W. social work program. I am aware that this is a bias of mine and that others may disagree. Certainly there are mental health professionals who have trained nontraditionally and who are excellent practitioners. But it is my feeling that—all things being equal—you are safest choosing someone who has their M.D., Ph.D., or M.S.W., and is licensed to practice their respective profession. Then you know what you're get-ting, at least as far as their formal training goes, and you're dealing with someone with enough smarts to at least have made it through a reputable graduate program. If it's OK with you to choose someone whose profession is outside of the "mainstream" it's OK with me, but my advice is to make sure you know what you're getting.

Second, I really do think you should try to find someone who has their head screwed on straight. Regrettably, this is a *much* harder task than is checking the nature of their licensure and academic creden-tials. There are five levels of knowledge that you can rely on regarding this, with each successive layer providing more credible information.

The first level is what I call someone's "general reputation." When their name comes up, does it tend to be in a positive way? Do they practice with other professionals who are known entities and are of high quality? Have they been around for a while? Do they belong to professional associations? If you mention their name to a professional who is a friend of yours, does your friend smile and say positive things, or do they run screaming from the room?

The second level is what I call "specific reputation." This means that someone you know and trust has heard something specific about the individual. They've heard that they're good, or they're bad, or that they're very professional, or that they're a quack, or something of the sort.

The third level is what I call "specific knowledge." This means you know someone who knows them personally. Maybe they know them professionally, or as a friend, or maybe they are their patient. But whatever the context, this person has been in a room with them, talked to them, and experienced how they are. If the person doing the reporting is trustworthy, this is a pretty good piece of information.

The fourth level is what I call "personal knowledge." This means that you know them. Maybe you've met them at a social function (as I did Rita) or you've attended a talk or training they've given (as I did with the therapist I saw some years later) or you've met them at a professional function, or have played golf with them. One psychiatrist I have worked with, for example, is an instructor at the martial arts school where I practice. After being in class with him for several years and having him coach me from my white belt to my third degree black belt in two martial arts, I know him really, really well. So I know first-hand that he is a high-level, trustworthy and kind person who knows his stuff—even though I've never seen him in his professional office.

The final level is how you feel when you actually see them as a patient. You ought to feel comfortable with them, they ought to be nice to you—at least generally—and you ought to feel like you "connect" with them. After all, you're going to be talking with them about what are likely to be some very sensitive matters, so you ought to feel like they're handling you caringly and thoughtfully. Also, the feedback they give you—and they should damn well give you feedback in the very first session or in the second at the latest—should make sense to you. You may not like what they have to say, but it should make sense to you. If you walk out of the first or second session without feedback, some new understanding, or *something* of benefit from talking with someone who is supposed to know what they're doing, think twice about going back. There may be good reason why they can't give you feedback that quickly, but if there is, they should be clear about that, and you should consider it to be a good reason, too.

I'll tell you how I work and you can use it to gauge what you want to have happen when you consult a mental health professional. When someone calls me for an appointment, I make the appointment myself. I do not use a secretary. I either answer the phone myself or I return a message left on my voice mail. It's certainly not wrong for professionals to use secretaries, but I not infrequently see as patients people who have high profiles and for whom any kind of additional exposure—even to a secretary—is a very delicate matter, so to get around all that I just make sure that I am the only person who knows who they are. On that phone call we talk about the times they can be seen and the appointments I have available. We decide on a time to meet and I give them very specific directions to my office (which is not in a traditional office building—yet more anonymity insurance) and reconfirm the date and time. Then I ask if they would like information about fees, and, if they would, I tell them what I charge. If they have any questions about me, or about my credentials or my specialities, I answer their questions succinctly, directly, openly, and honestly. If they, or I, have questions about my appropriateness for seeing them, I offer to give them several names of professionals who I know and trust. And if they take the names and decide to see someone else, I always tell them that if it does not work out for them to see those people, to feel free to call me back as I will ensure that they get set up with someone they feel comfortable with. Many professionals do not go to this length, so don't write someone off if they don't do this, but it's how I work and you can decide for yourself what you need.

Finally, on that first phone call I *never* ask what it is they are coming to see me about. I do this for two reasons. First, I have gone to see mental health professionals myself, and I have been very clear—even being a psychologist myself—that the *last* thing I want to do is to spill my guts on the phone to someone I've never met. Second, I don't know where my potential patient *is* when they're calling me. They might be in a cubicle at work where other people can overhear them. They might be at home, but maybe coming to see me is a sensitive issue with family members, so they don't want to be telling me that they're thinking of leaving their spouse and at the very moment they unload that juicy tidbit their spouse bounds into the room.

If they spontaneously start telling me why they're coming, I'll listen politely. But I won't ask for elaboration or investigate further as I will when I see them face-to-face. And if they ask me if I want to know why they're coming in, I'll tell them directly that I generally feel it's best to wait until we can talk about it together in depth during the session and won't get interrupted by the need to end the phone call, but if they feel that they would like to give me a quick summary I would be happy to listen.

Again, the way I work is not sacrosanct, but at least it will give you a reference point. Then you can make your own decisions about what you want in a professional.

Now—a few instructions. If you're going to consult a mental health professional, use some common sense. First, be early for your first appointment. You don't have to be terribly early—about ten minutes is enough. Some professionals have you fill out some paperwork, so you'll need a few minutes. Others, like me, don't use preliminary paperwork, but by being early you get to do two valuable things: One, you get to demonstrate that you are responsible about keeping your appointment. Look, mental health professionals are people, too, and they react like you'd expect people to react—they are pleased with patients who show up on time. And you want this person to respect you and to take you seriously. By keeping your word about your appointment time you are helping yourself to get good care. I'll be honest with you—when I was evaluating candidates to religious orders, if they showed up even five minutes late for their appointment, it made a difference. They knew what was riding on my report—their future—because if I rejected them they didn't get in. So if they couldn't manage to get right something as important, and simple, as their appointment time, it cast doubt on lots more than their ability to tell time.

Two, being on time gives you the chance to see how the professional operates. Now, in some areas of health care it can be darn tricky for a professional to judge time. A dermatologist, for example, cannot closely predict how many minutes they will need to see each patient. If it's a sunburn, the appointment might only last a few minutes. But if it's a malignant melanoma that needs to be excised and biopsied, they might be looking at half an hour. As a result, even though I'm every bit as annoyed as you are at having to wait in doctors' offices, the truth is they are not trying to waste your time, their timing is just unpredictable.

That is *not* the case with mental health professionals. We talk to people all day every day, and we set our appointments by "clock" time rather than "goal" time. So unless it is a *very* unusual circumstance where they have to run over, the mental health professional you see should run pretty darn well on schedule. And if for some reason they are running late, either they or their secretary or assistant should come out, inform you that they are running late, apologize, and tell you how much longer they should be. If I am running more than three or four minutes behind, I excuse myself from my current appointment, walk out to my reception room, greet my next appointment, apologize for running late, and tell them how long I'll be.

And if the professional you are seeing does run late, under no circumstance should they short you on your appointment time. Their time is what you're paying for, so you should get all of it. If *you're* the one who's late, though, it's a whole different story. Then they only owe you the "balance" of the session—no matter *why* you're late. So for goodness sake *be on time.*

If something comes up and you can't make it to your session, call the professional and tell them. Professionals vary in their policy on missed sessions. Some charge if you don't call to cancel at least 24 hours before your appointment (my personal trainer even has this rule—and she enforces it). I'm a bit more lenient. If someone cancels late or even stands me up for a first session, I may give them a pass—while filing it away in my head as a possible pattern in their life that needs attention—and I may even make another appointment with them if they call to say they would like to and that they missed the first one for an understandable reason. With my ongoing patients I tend to be even more lenient, charging for missed sessions only if I feel that missing is part of a pattern that we need to break up. The only exception to this was when I saw patients in group therapy. Then I charged a flat per-month rate, no matter how many of the weekly sessions they showed up for.

The truth is that I may not be a good example of these things because people who see me tend to be prompt, punctual, and responsible about their appointments—partly, perhaps, because I am so obviously rigorous about doing so myself. If I were dealing with a patient population that did not tend to be this way, I might very well alter my policy, I don't know.

Question Number Six: "What is a mental health professional thinking about when I'm talking to them?"

Answer: They're thinking about what's wrong with you, at least initially. Later they'll be thinking about how to fix what's wrong with you. Let me tell you what I mean.

When you're first talking to a mental health professional, there are two potential areas of "malfunction" they're wondering about. The first is whether there is something wrong with *you*. I know this can be hard to hear, but it really is true that if you come to one of us you might find out there is "something wrong with you." So be prepared. There really are malfunctions inside people—maybe including you—that can screw up their lives, make them feel bad, and end up with them sitting in my office. We divide these malfunctions into half a dozen general areas:

One type of malfunction is when someone's thinking is out of line with reality to a significant degree. Perhaps they see things other people don't see, or hear things other people don't hear. Or maybe they have some "wild" or "delusional" ideas that they act on and that causes trouble, like that the CIA is after them or the FBI has tapped their phone. These disorders are called "psychotic" disorders or "major psychiatric disorders," and can cause serious problems in someone's ability to live a productive and satisfying life.

A second type of malfunction is when someone feels "down" more severely or more often than the normal "down day" we all have from time to time. In this type of malfunction someone's psychic energy has run low, and they can feel "bad" in a variety of ways. They may have trouble sleeping, they may be unable to eat or they may overeat, they may feel guilty, or irritable, or like doing nothing, or even like dying. Their "down" moods may be broken by times of excessive and hyperactive levels of energy—but the down mood always returns. These are called "mood disorders," because the prominent feature is a disruption in a "normal" mood, which means feeling "fine" or "OK" unless there is a situational reason to feel otherwise. Our names for these conditions are "major depressive episodes" and "dysthymia."

A third type of malfunction is when someone keeps doing something that causes them trouble but they don't stop. Maybe they're drinking too much, or doing drugs, or overeating, or reading pornography instead of doing what they should be doing. These are called "addictive disorders" because the prominent feature is that someone is "addicted to" (that is, can't quit even though it is causing trouble in their life) a substance or an activity.

A fourth type of malfunction is when someone feels nervous or scared or panicky without reason or more often than is appropriate given the circumstances of their life. (If you're a combat soldier, for example, and feel scared when the bullets fly, that's not something wrong with you—it's appropriate, given the circumstances.) Called "anxiety disorders" with such names as "generalized anxiety disorder," "social phobia, "social anxiety disorder," "panic disorder," "obsessive compulsive disorder," or "post traumatic stress disorder," the prominent feature is an excess of fear or nervousness or jumpiness.

A fifth type of malfunction is when someone has trouble with their ability to "attend" to things. Maybe they half-finish everything, don't seem able to do things they "need" to do or are "supposed to do" rather than things they "want" to do. Called such things as "attention deficit disorder," these are conditions where people can't maintain their attention to the things that are needed in order for their lives to work right.

The sixth type of malfunction is when someone has an ingrained pattern of experiencing or behaving that causes trouble for themselves and others, but they can't see it and may even blame others or deny that they are doing anything "wrong." Maybe someone is arrogant and demeaning, or maybe they can't seem to make a decision without endless advice and reassurance. Or maybe they don't seem to have a conscience or a sense of remorse. Called "personality disorders," these conditions go by such names as narcissistic personality disorder, antisocial personality disorder, (which used to be called "psychopath") and borderline personality disorder.

It is highly unlikely that you, or someone else with any of these conditions, can accurately identify it on their own, any more than you can tell the difference between a really bad cold and the flu. What you usually know is that you *feel bad*, or that things keep *going wrong.* You may have guesses as to why this is happening, but because you are not trained in the cause-and-effect of the human psyche, (as well as trying to use your own eyeballs to see what's *behind* your

297

own eyeballs) your layman's conclusion is quite likely to be wrong. That's the reason that many times people's troubles don't clear up despite all their efforts and attempts to fix things—they can't see what's "really" causing the problems, so they aren't able to address the actual problem.

For example, people are often surprised when I tell them that they're depressed. Most people confuse depression with "sadness," so if someone is not sad and crying, they don't think of themselves as "depressed." But depression, which is low psychic energy, can show up in any number of ways, including being irritable or argumentative. Once we successfully treat the depression, the irritability and argumentativeness clears up. It often looks like magic. It's not.

Remember that these are general categories that I've summarized in "layman's" language. They are hardly exact or exhaustive. The Diagnostic and Statistical Manual of the American Psychiatric Association is the standard manual for diagnosis of mental health conditions, and it runs several hundred pages. So, clearly my short description is neither comprehensive nor rigorous and do not for a minute try to use it as a diagnostic tool. I just want to give you an idea of the terms that we mental health professionals think in when you're talking to us.

The second possible malfunction we're thinking about is that there is something wrong with your *life*. Maybe you're out of work. Maybe you and your spouse aren't getting along, or your spouse has left you. Maybe you or one of your family members has been diagnosed with a serious illness. Maybe your teenager is showing serious behavior problems. Maybe your parent, or boss, or sibling is a very difficult person to deal with, and you have to have a lot of contact with them. These malfunctions tend to go under such names as "situational stress" or "marriage problem" or "family problem" or some such thing.

You have probably already realized that something being wrong with *you* and something being wrong with your *life* are not mutually exclusive. They overlap. If there is something wrong with you, it will likely cause trouble in your life. And if there is something wrong in your life, it can make you go haywire. The late Neil Jacobson's work on marriage problems, for example, indicated that depression in women and problems in their marriage are often so intertwined that if *both* malfunctions are not treated, things don't improve.

But, nevertheless, something being wrong with you and something being wrong with your life *are* separate categories, and we mental health professionals will be trying to figure out, as we talk to you, how much of each is present. Maybe we can see that your thinking is skewed. Or maybe we can see that you've been the victim of very bad luck that has gotten you into a very bad situation that could have happened to anyone. Or maybe there is an interaction between something you bring to the party and elements outside of your control that are problematic unto themselves.

And I'll let you in on a secret that keeps us mental health professionals in business—very little that goes wrong in someone's life, especially over the long-term and when it's repetitive, is either accidental or unrelated in some way to something that is specific to them. That's good news and bad news. The bad news is that if you have a problem that won't go away you have likely been doing something of which you are unaware that has been participating in the problem. The good news is that you can affect the problem by seeing what you're doing unwittingly and then changing it. So even if it seems like the thing that is wrong in your life was delivered in a cosmic accident—well, maybe it really wasn't. That's why talking to a mental health professional can help situations that don't even seem like they are "your fault." One thing that we can be very full of is surprises.

Question Number Seven: "What do you think about drugs?"

Answer: If by "drugs" you mean psychiatric medications, on the whole I think they can be quite wonderful things. If they can help something that's wrong with you, you may end up very glad you're taking them. And remember—this is being said by someone who does not prescribe, so it's not like I have a bias toward drugs based on any kind of self-interest.

We also know a lot more about the causes of some psychiatric conditions than we used to, and the truth is that many conditions have a significant biological component. If you can treat the biological element, the other parts are often much easier to deal with.

It is nevertheless important to understand that everything in life is a trade-off, and psychiatric drugs are no exception. All of them, even the most benign, have side-effects, sometimes significant ones. So to take a psychiatric medication you *must* be evaluated by someone who knows a lot about the drugs and understands their good and bad points. And, generally speaking, in this day and age that means a psychiatrist.

For example, the antidepressant drugs can work wonders on some depressive disorders. There is a class of antidepressant medications called "tricyclics" because their molecular structure contains three molecules. They can be very effective at battling some really serious depressions. But they can also have antihistamine-like side effects (dry mouth, insomnia) along with sometimes inducing a serious tendency to gain weight. They can also be highly lethal in an overdose. So someone who feels suicidal or who is irresponsible about taking them might get themselves into trouble.

There is a second class of antidepressants called "MAOI's" This stands for "monoamine oxidase inhibitors." They can also work well for some serious depressions, but the drugs can interact with a variety of foods to produce a life-threatening reaction. This is commonly called "the cheese effect," because the first food found to interact badly with the MAOI's was certain aged cheeses. Weird, huh? So if you were to take these drugs you'd be given a list of foods that are verboten, and while you're on those drugs *you'd damn well better avoid those foods.*

Then there are the "bicyclic" antidepressants, so called because their molecular structure contains two molecules. Also called "SSRI's," which means "selective serotonin reuptake inhibitors," they appear to increase the level of serotonin in the brain much more specifically than do the tricyclics or MAOI's. As a result they tend to have fewer serious side effects, but they can still have some, such as loss of sex drive or ability to achieve orgasm, some weight gain, and possible sleep interruption. Sometimes they also don't work as well as other classes of drugs do on very serious depressions.

Finally, there are some "atypical" antidepressants that don't seem to work like any of the others. They affect various brain chemicals in various ways and also have advantages and disadvantages.

And those are just some general comments on a very few of the antidepressants. We haven't even started talking about stimulants and norepinephrine uptake inhibitors for attentional problems, or traditional and atypical neuroleptics for major psychiatric disorders, or anxiolytic medications for anxiety disorders. Covering the pros and cons of these would consume a book. Several books, in fact.

The bottom line is this—for some mental health conditions drugs can be really, really good—as long as you are evaluated by someone who knows their stuff. Along these lines, one of the current trends about which I have an axe to grind is that many, if not most, of the prescriptions written for psychoactive medications (especially anti-depressants) are now written by non-psychiatric M.D.'s such as internists or family practitioners. Admittedly, I have met some family practice physicians who have boned up on psychoactive medications and who do a fine job of evaluating for drug type, specific brand, side-effects and dosage. But I have seen far more who don't know the intricacies of the drugs and who make prescription errors that either render the drug ineffective or potentially troublesome. Believe it or not, many of the errors involve prescribing too low a dose, with the result that the person is taking a good drug but feeling no better. So they think the drug doesn't work when in truth they have not yet had an appropriate trial of the drug.

I was consulted by a man who was clearly and seriously depressed. I asked what medications he was taking and he named a very good, very powerful antidepressant. I asked what dose he was taking. He named a dose that was less than *one-third* the standard therapeutic dose for that particular medication. To have felt *any* effect he would have needed to essentially triple his dose. And he was consulting me specifically because "antidepressants hadn't worked for him." Well, his prescription had been written by his internist. I sent him to a psychiatrist.

The bottom line is that I strongly urge you, if you are taking a psychoactive medication or think one might help you, to consult a *psychiatrist* who knows his or her medications. I know that people can recoil from the idea of seeing a "psychiatrist," but get over it already—a little embarrassment is nothing compared with being poorly prescribed medications that can have profound effects and sometimes concerning side-effects, or missing out on something that could make your life tons better.

Probably about half of my patients are on some kind of medication, and the reason is very simple—it helps them. Sometimes a lot. That's why some of them tend to stay on the medications, sometimes for a very long time. And let me tell you—if a medication works for you, you're likely to stop caring about "having to take drugs" or "something being wrong with you." You are much more likely to say "Why the hell didn't I do this years ago?" Or, as one of my patients who was prescribed an appropriate SSRI, said: "If I need this medication to feel like *this*, to hell with it—I'll stay on it forever! And I'm going to call my brother to tell him that he's got what I've got, and he needs this medication, too!" Another patient said "This is the way I've always wanted to feel, and thought I *should* feel."

Question Eight: "If you like medications so much, what do you think of psychotherapy? And by the way—what's the difference between 'psychotherapy' and 'counseling'?"

Answer: I like psychotherapy every bit as much as I like medications, if not more. After all, it's what I do. But, just like with medications, it should be applied only when someone has been evaluated for it and is a good candidate for it. Someone needs to have a good likelihood of being helped by it and a low likelihood of being distressed by its side-effects (yes, psychotherapy can have side-effects, too).

At this point in time, "psychotherapy" and "counseling" have come to pretty much mean the same thing. "Counseling" originally meant "giving advice," such as "career counseling" where someone gives you tests and says "you probably should do such-and-such as a career." "Psychotherapy," on the other hand, was originally designed to change how you function and feel so you work better psychologically. Over time both terms have expanded and are now used pretty much interchangeably. One of the finest psychotherapists I have ever known had a degree in "Counseling" Psychology. So you can't tell what you're getting by the particular term being used.

Psychotherapy works very simply—it enables you to see things about yourself or your life that you can't currently see and that is affecting how you feel, what you do, and what happens to you. Once you can see what has been making the things happen that have been happening, you can get your hands around it and do something to improve how you feel, what you do, or what happens to you.

You may have heard that there is a wide variety of "types" of psychotherapy, or "theories" of psychotherapy. You're quite right, there is. When I was in graduate school some enterprising researcher tried to count the number of theories of psychotherapy out there and came up with something around 125. Pretty amazing, no?

Fortunately, you don't have to worry about that. All you have to worry about is whether the mental health professional you consult makes sense and is helpful to you. The theory they use, the structure by which they organize their mental understanding of you in order to figure things out and be of help, is irrelevant except to the extent that what comes out of their mouth is good. So I wouldn't worry about it. Let them worry about it.

Let me return to the topic of drugs for a minute. Sometimes the value of a helpful psychoactive medication is that it enables you to be able to focus on and do good work about improving yourself and your life. So medications and psychotherapy are not mutually exclusive—not by a long shot. Often, even if medication does work for you, there will be things in your life that you want to work on. That's where psychotherapy—and people like me—come in.

Question Nine: :"How do you know if psychotherapy is helping?"

Answer: You either feel better or the problems you're concerned with get better, or both.

Question Ten: "How long should that take?"

Answer: That's a bit like asking how long a baseball game takes—there is no set time, because everyone's different and every circumstance varies. There is no general rule.

Question Eleven: "Are you glad you're a psychologist?"

Answer: Absolutely. Not only do I think it's fun, but it's rewarding to help people and an honor to be invited into people's lives to work with them. As far as I'm concerned, it's the best thing I could have done with my life.

Question Eleven: "What advice would you have for someone wanting to go into the field?

Answer: First, get a "traditional" degree (sound familiar?). Second, unless you're going to do research, don't bother with a Ph.D. Third, unless you want to prescribe drugs, don't bother with an M.D. An M.S.W. is a great degree—perhaps the best degree—if you want to see patients and you don't care about teaching, prescribing, or doing research. It may take a bit longer to be licensed to practice independently, but if what you want to do is see patients and nothing else, I think it's the shortest route from where you are to seeing patients. And I know many M.S.W.'s who are outstanding clinicians.

Fourth, understand the finances of the whole thing. As you are undoubtedly aware, our system of health care costs and payments is a God-awful mess. But don't get down on the U.S. system, because other countries' systems are just as bad, if not worse, in their own ways. But be aware that the area of health care most squeezed by the payment mess is mental health. Financially, we in mental health are kind of the bastard step-child of health care. We work differently from everything else, and no one knows quite what to do with us. Further, because mental health is so labor-intensive, our field is expensive and a good place for payers to cut.

So if you do go into this field, the chances you will make a lot of money are slim and none. You can make a living and support yourself, but if you're looking to get paid like a Rockefeller, you're barking up the wrong tree. Go into business instead. Be a stock broker. Be Martha Stewart (without the stock-selling shenanigans, of course).

Question Twelve: "Do you still see patients?"

Answer: I do. I no longer maintain a full-time practice as I did for many years, where I saw fifty or sixty appointments per week. Now I have a select group of patients that I see, and I spend the rest of my time traveling and presenting training for mental health professionals on how to do the things that I've learned how to do, like treat personality disorders. These days I'm on the road doing training for professionals about a hundred and fifty days a year. And I love it.

AFTERWORD

After being involved in psychology and mental health for the past twenty-five or so years and seeing the lives of—literally—thousands of people, I have come to a few philosophical conclusions that I'd like to leave you with.

First, understand that life for human beings is inherently messy. No one "gets it all" with no downside. No one avoids trouble, and *everyone* has demons with which they must contend. Whether these qualify as "normal" or "abnormal" is a function of their frequency, duration, and intensity. If you have some "down" days, welcome to the human race. If you can't force yourself out of bed for days at a time for no apparent reason, you have the signs of a clinical condition. But the fantasy that someone, somewhere, has the perfect life that you can and should have "if you just do everything right" is fantasy—*complete* fantasy. Life is *always* a trade-off. The best you will ever get is a trade-off that works well for you. So get real—everyone is struggling. Everyone is out there trying to do the best they can.

Second, no one really knows what they're doing. Really. Just like you, we're all flying by the seat of our pants and making it up as we go along—yes, even the gurus who seem so sure of themselves and who seem so enlightened. Trust me, late at night when they're tired and alone, they have just as many doubts and fears as you do. I'm not saying that we psychologists don't know some valuable things about life—we do—it's just that no amount of "knowing" is ever enough to make you *feel like* you really know what you're doing. Everything still ends up being some version of a "best guess."

But that's not really so bad, because if you ask advice from someone all you really need for it to be of value is for their best guess be a little bit more informed than yours. Or as we say in teaching: "To

305

sound like you know what you're talking about, all you have to do is be a half-page ahead of your students."

My point is this: don't feel bad because you think other people have it all handled in life and you don't, because no one does. Psychological experts get divorced. Spiritual gurus die of alcoholism. Writers who seem to understand it all commit suicide. As Calvin's father said in an episode of the most psychologically astute comic strip ever written, "Calvin and Hobbes": "I wouldn't have been in such a big hurry to grow up if I'd known it was all ad-libbed."

Third, there is no magic. I wish there *were* miracle cures for the things that distress us in life. I wish that there really were "energy fields" or "spirit guides" or some such thing that could be rearranged, or contacted, or summoned up to clear up our worries, upsets, and struggles. There aren't. Instead, there is just plain, old-fashioned persistence, work, and step-by-step improvement. As the song says so well: "There is no distance far enough away to let you be tomorrow what you weren't yesterday."

I'm also not saying that you can't change things—often you can. What I'm saying is that it's usually *hard* to change things. The only real enemy is your notion that it ought to be easy. Once you give up that silly idea, it's not so bad.

Finally, I think the Buddhists are right about this much: They have a proverb that says "All paths are the same. All you need is a path with heart."

Look, the most reliable experience of joy available in this life comes from finding something—anything—that you can devote yourself to, that you can lose yourself into, that you are committed to, that you can identify with. When "your heart is in" something, you have access to the state of greatest happiness and satisfaction available to a human being. For many of us the easiest way to find this state is to be of service to others, but it could just as easily be through devotion to art, or music, or even business. I get annoyed when people assume business is a soul-less endeavor. I know people for whom business is a calling every bit as profound as joining a monastery. It brings them, and others, as much joy. Sometimes more. Losing yourself into something above and beyond yourself is the very definition of "love," and that's the best it gets for us human beings.

Which is why I feel so fortunate. In the face of all the inhumane craziness of graduate school, the struggle and pain of working with human beings on some of the most difficult and fearsome of issues, the inadequacy of any solution to make everything OK in life, and dealing with my own issues while attending to those in the lives of my patients, I love what being a psychologist has allowed me to do. I love what being a psychologist has allowed me to become.

So, for me, I am *very* clear that I found the right thing. Whether or not it's "healthy," (doing mental health work can be hard on the lives of practitioners) and whether or not in a hundred years we find that what psychologists do is of truly lasting benefit, I found the path that, for me, has heart. It is a path I love. If I could go back, would I change some things? Of course. But change the path of being a psychologist? Not on your life. What could be more fun than participating in this divine comedy called human life, up close and personal, in the company of family, friends, and patients that I love and respect?

As far as I'm concerned, I've got the best seat in the house.

Give the Gift of

Shrunken Heads

to Your Friends and Colleagues

CHECK YOUR LEADING BOOKSTORE OR ORDER HERE

❏ **YES**, I want _____ copies of *Shrunken Heads* at $24.95 each, plus $3.00 shipping per book (TX residents please add 6.25% sales tax per book). Canadian orders must be accompanied by a postal money order in U.S. funds. Allow 30 days for delivery.

My check or money order for $_____ is enclosed.

Please charge my: ❏ Visa   ❏ MasterCard
                              ❏ Discover   ❏ American Express

Name _____

Organization _____

Address _____

City/State/Zip _____

Phone_____ E-mail _____

Card # _____

Exp. Date_____ Signature _____

Please make your check payable and return to:

Bookworks Distributing
15110 Benfer Road
Houston, TX 77069

Fax your credit card order to: 281-895-8668